SCIENCE POLICY: A BEHAVIOURAL APPROACH

Science Policy: A Behavioural Approach

CORNELIUS A. HAZEU
The Netherlands Organization of Scientific Research

Avebury

Aldershot · Brookfield USA · Hong Kong · Singapore · Sydney

Published by
Avebury
Gower Publishing Company Limited
Gower House
Croft Road
Aldershot
Hants GU11 3HR
England

Gower Publishing Company
Old Post Road
Brookfield
Vermont 05036
USA

ISBN 1 85628 057 8

Printed and Bound in Great Britain by
Athenaeum Press Ltd., Newcastle upon Tyne.

Contents

Foreword

The philosophy of management at arm's length is progressively gaining ground in policy for scientific research. In this perspective the form of management adopted by the government is based in particular on output. Research organizations and institutes are forced to widen their perspectives and make decisions concerning the application and distribution of their resources between the production factors.

The results booked by TNO (Netherlands Organization for Applied Scientific Research) show that such a management philosophy does indeed yield results. Example is better than precept: more and more research organizations and institutes are turning to developing their own strategic orientations in dialogue with the government and drawing up plans for implementation.

The Netherlands Government became aware of the significance of management at arm's length at an early stage. Relevant recommendations were taken to heart and used for the development of business management instruments so that institutes would be able to take into account the (long-term) orientations they will need to develop.

Dr. Hazeu's dissertation is of special significance because of his theoretical and conceptual in-depth approach to the problems concerning the (financial) relationships between government and the research system. With a view to the increasing level of internationalization it was decided to publish his dissertation in an English-language version.

I warmly recommend this book for economists, those working in the field of public administration and policy-makers. It is a publication which I hope will contribute towards similar developments in other countries and thus, also in an international context, can contribute towards increasing the effectiveness and efficiency of scientific research.

Director General for Science Policy,
Ministry of Education and Science, the Netherlands

Dr. E. van Spiegel

PART I
THEORY

1 Introduction

A reciprocity between institutions and behaviour for analyzing and explaining the functioning of the research system

1.0 Summary

The object of this study is the system of scientific research, in particular that of universities, which is generally government-funded. This system is looked at from an economist's point of view as a value-conversion system. It is governed by an organization structure; a structure which consists of a number of levels of actors that fulfil specific tasks and responsibilities, from assisting on the shop-floor of research organizations to the development of a national science policy at the very top of the system. These actors each have discretionary competences and, within certain boundaries, each can aspire to his own aims. This implies that the objectives of the research system are multiform by nature: differing at the various levels and not unambiguous to a particular actor. In other words, aggregation into a single set of objectives without assessment is out of the question. This complication is solved by provisionally postulating three criterial assessment opinions as to the functions required of the system.

This study deals with the question of the optimal institutionalization of the research system and is based on the hypothesis that the behaviour of actors is influenced by the way in which an existing order is institutionalized. Strategic variables in that influence are the choice of levels in a stratified decision-making structure and the allocation of tasks and responsibilities at each level within that structure.

With regard to the behavioural aspect, the main point is to find incentives (carrots and sticks) and preconditions which lead to a maximization of the various actors' goals in such a way that desirable behaviour is promoted and undesirable behaviour opposed. In doing this we assume that the behaviour of the actors in the research system is rational. This gives us a link with economics as the explicative theory. We have made particular use of the theory of public choice, an economic sub-theory which provides an insight into the underlying motives and rationale of the behaviour of actors in collectivities.

Chapters 1 to 3 set out the theoretical framework. In the practical part (Chapters 4 to 6) this framework is tested by means of three case studies. Finally, a number of conclusions are deduced from the confrontation between theory and empiricism in Chapter 7.

1.1 The relevance of the subject: development and problems of policy

Within the space of only a few decades the Dutch university system has undergone radical change. The elite university, which had been able to maintain its position without any great changes for centuries, is now a thing of the past. Such universities have been replaced by huge, democratized institutions; democratized both externally and internally. The external democratization can be regarded as the motor of the process of university transformation. Since the sixties there has been an enormous increase in the number of students from various social backgrounds and the motto in the welfare state, characterized by wide spread affluence and relatively egalitarian relations, is "Higher education for many".

The internal democratization of universities took a less smooth course. The turning point in this process was the promulgation of the University Administration Reform Act (WUB) in 1970 after a period of student agitation. This act makes provision for an administrative system of councils (university council, faculty council, department) comprising not only scientific members of staff but also non-scientific staff and students. In other words, the Act signified the dismantling of the traditional professoriate university.

Characteristic of any system of higher education is the promotion of knowledge. This fundamental quality is accompanied by other characteristics of higher education systems which have not changed fundamentally since the first universities came into being (Van Vught, 1987, p. 20 ff.). The accent on promoting knowledge implies a principle of organization in which scientific disciplines are central (so-called *professional organization*). Scientific disciplines are the lines along which the organizational integration of higher education takes place.

Another feature of higher education systems is the relatively less hierarchical, strongly fragmented structure of their organization. An organization based on scientific disciplines result almost automatically in a structure of specialist cells which are only linked together to a low extent. From as far back as the Middle Ages there has been a high level of *autonomy* in the basic units of universities (whether that be a faculty, a school, or a chair).

A third characteristic of systems of higher education which is connected with the promotion of knowledge is the somewhat *diffuse decision-structure*. In an organization where highly knowledge-intensive production processes are involved there is a need to decentralize the power of decision. If such an organization is also characterized by a high degree of fragmentation, the power of decision is also spread over a large number of units. This implies that an institute of higher education tends to lean towards a federal system in which disciplinary units operate as small sovereign states.

Finally, the *meritocratic* relationships of authority are a fundamental feature of the organization of the scientific research system. Here, at least in part, the guild culture is alive and kicking (Van Vught, 1987, p. 21). The guild culture denotes a special system of values and norms with regard to the relationships of authority within social systems. In a guild culture there is a combination of personal authority and collegiate management. The superiors exercise personal authority over their subordinates and, as a group, they manage a larger organization made up of individual cells on a basis of fellowship.

The system of university education and research shows a number of universal traits. These have been described above. Yet the institutional structure of these systems differs from country to country depending on the politicocultural values which determine the relationships within a society. If we take a closer look at these various institutional blueprints we see that a differentiation can be made between perhaps three approximate administrative concepts: i.e. East European, West European and North American. The East European higher education systems are characterized by central planning. The higher education systems of Canada and the United States lean towards the other extreme. The West European systems are profiled as a reasonably heterogeneous group having characteristics of the two other variants. These three different blueprints are interwoven with a given society's deep-rooted preference as to how issues are tackled. The problems of the university system analyzed in this study are thus partly universal by nature, partly West European and partly typically Dutch.

One of the characteristics of the Dutch university system is that it is based traditionally on the Humboldt school of thought. Wilhelm von Humboldt (Germany, 1767-1835) was a supporter of the 'Bildung' concept: focused on education and the development of talents. Von Humboldt took this concept and moulded it into the principles of 'Lehrfeiheit' and 'Lernfreiheit' for lecturers and students respectively. This ideological basis implied that the university should be a sanctuary for the study of science, free from all outside influence. In Von Humboldt's vision, the goal of a university was to advance and develop knowledge through research. The result of this concept is the indissoluble connection between education and research being accepted as a matter of course. This basic principle was also carried over into the organizational and funding structure of Dutch universities. Scientific staff are generally appointed to teach and carry out research. In the history of Dutch universities we have seen very few separate schools come into existence in which education programmes were organized, nor have any institutes been created for the purpose of research alone. Until recently the basis for government funding of universities was the number of students. The university research task was not financed as an independent category but as an additional sum to the teaching budget.

The rapid increase in the number of students in the sixties and seventies created the capacity for research. This increase is shown in the table below.

year	university students
1965	64,000
1970	103,000
1975	120,000
1980	151,000
1985	165,000
1988	175,000

Source: Central Statistical Office, the Netherlands

It will be clear that this enormous increase in scale alone lays a claim on the management capacity of universities. Managerial positions (vice-chancellor, dean, head of department, etc.,) are generally taken by professors. Professional skills in the field of teaching and research are the main criteria for appointment to the status of professor. Administrative and management skills are 'nebenbei'. Now that so much more importance has been attached to management in universities this is being paid for in the sense that such positions are generally placed in the hands of well-meaning specialists in other fields who emerge as amateur managers for a relatively short period of time.

The inherent management problem facing universities, resulting from the enormous economies of scale, is intensified even further given that society has gradually set other demands on these institutes. Indeed, universities have been given little rest since the sixties. They are no longer insular but have become completely integrated in society. It is expected of universities that they contribute towards solving the problems of society, towards expanding the innovation potential of trade and industry, that they produce graduates with the appropriate qualifications, etc., etc. The capacity to help society and to solve problems is one of the criteria against which the results of the research system will be measured in this study. We shall return to these criteria in section 1.2 where the problem definition is set out.

As a result of the endogenous and exogenous factors described above, friction has grown between societal needs and attitudes (the environment) on the one hand, and on the other hand the university-internal structures in which the production processes of education and research had been shaped. The result was that government became increasingly dissatisfied with the way in which the university system functioned and this dissatisfaction culminated in a growing interference with universities. Two aspects can be discerned if we express this dissatisfaction in economic terms:

1. dissatisfaction with the university production *process*; and
2. dissatisfaction with university (education and research) *products*.

The former concerns the question of *efficiency* (production efficiency, technical efficiency, is it being done right); the latter concerns the question of *effectiveness* (welfare efficiency, economic efficiency, is the right thing being done). Let us explain both aspects.

1. Inefficiency is the case if a better input and/or output of a higher quality could be achieved from a given input. This is a question of efficiency on the *supply side*.

   The decline in economic growth in the seventies and early eighties led – under an increasing demand for funds elsewhere – to cuts in the state budget for universities. Given this financial stringency after a lengthy period of unbridled growth in funding more attention was devoted to pre-conditions such as the duration of courses, the average student stay at university, cost of education per student, etc.

   The changed government budgetary situation also led to the various considerations being made more disciplined and well-founded. In turn, this led to the government becoming more concerned about the allocation of the scarce funds. The way in which universities had handled their autonomy in the past, and how researchers had acted as regards their professional responsibilities, became subject of discussion. Government wished to see more value for its money and requested universities to be more specific in accounting for their expenditure. The quantitative aspect of this is that greater pressure was put on producing (especially research-) outputs. The aspect of quality is illustrated, among other things, in the emphasis being laid on participating in fields of research in international scientific forums (see, for instance, Ministry of Education and Science, 1988a).

2. Contrary to the above, ineffectiveness is not a question of whether the supply is realized efficiently or not, but rather whether the outputs produced adequately meet the *demand side* of the production process. Government's dissatisfaction on this point relates to the responsiveness of universities to the needs of society.

As far as education is concerned, it is often voiced that the qualifications of those who have completed their studies are not in line with the needs of trade and industry. As regards research, it is particularly the increased social complexity that gives rise to the call for universities to make a (more) direct contribution towards solving social issues. Illustrative of this train of thought, in which science is seen as an instrument by which to steer society, is for example, the Policy Document on Behavioural and Social Sciences (Ministry of Education and Science, 1983, p. 17), in which the expectation was formulated that "research in the field of social science (can) increase our insight into those mechanisms which cause certain sections of the community to be in a peripheral position and thus (can) contribute towards breaking down social inequality". Especially the latter exaggerates the role of science which in itself is not always and only solution-oriented but, on the contrary, can also make one aware of problems.

The following policy operations, which were implemented in the university system in the early eighties, should be seen against these backgrounds:

- shortening the duration of study, achieved through introducing the *two-phase structure*;
- the specific design of the (selective) second phase by creating the position of *trainee research assistant* (AIO): a low-salaried member of staff that is given a period of four years in which to complete a thesis. The introduction of trainee research assistants also has organizational consequences: special institutes and networks are set up here and there to provide shelter for such graduation study. These turn out to be the forerunners of a system of research schools announced by the minister in 1990;
- *conditional funding* (VF), set up for the allocation of research financing by the Ministry of Education and Science on the basis of programmes which have been sanctioned by external committees of representatives from various disciplines. This system involves the funding of research separate from the funding of education;
- the *Key Document concerning the policy plans for the academic staff of universities* (Ministry of Education and Science, 1981) which makes provisions for the restructuring of academic staff grading. It is hoped that this restructuring will achieve a certain level of hierarchy in staff grading. The grades of university lecturer and senior university lecturer are introduced. High demands are set on the position of senior lecturer. In turn, this restructuring of the academic staff also leads to lower average expenditure per staff member, which helps create financial latitude for the introduction of trainee research assistants;
- two major economy operations, namely *Taakverdeling en Concentratie* (TVC; 1982) (Distribution and Concentration of Tasks), which over a period of a few years was to achieve a cut-back of 258 million guilders net, and the *Selectieve Krimp en Groei* (SKG; 1986) (Selective Shrinkage and Growth) which, on balance, should lead to a saving of 130 million guilders.

Both the TVC and the SKG are goal-oriented economy operations (apart from modest funds for new initiatives). The other four composite measures are aimed at a higher level of efficiency and effectiveness; this can result in lower expenditure. The introduction of the two-phase structure, the introduction of trainee research assistants and the restructuring of the academic staff is in effect government intervention in the way in which, and by which means of production, universities generate their education and research. These, therefore, are measures intended to promote efficiency. In conditional funding effectiveness also comes into play in addition to efficiency. Efficiency relates especially to the fact that a critical mass is required in respect of the research programmes requiring financing (researchers working in teams should lead to scale benefits). The aspect of effectiveness is to be found in the checking the content of these programmes as to their relevance and importance.

These government initiated operations, the greater part of which were implemented simultaneously, placed enormous pressure on the Dutch university system. With reference to Von Humboldt's twofold principle this mainly affected the 'Lernfreiheit' of students. This can be seen, for example, in the student quotas, the labour market considerations that played a role in the above economy operations (particularly the SKG), the increasing trend towards a modular structure of the curriculum resulting in undergraduates taking programmed courses, the assistant research trainee, plus various secondary measures with the objective of ensuring that the implemented two-phase structure really did lead to a shorter stay at university (this included higher tuition fees and the loss of the right to claim a study grant after more than six years of study). The consolidation of higher education therefore went hand in hand with a shift in accent from 'Lernfreiheit' to professional training (cf. Van Vught, 1987, p. 24). More has remained of the academic freedom – Von Humboldt's Lehrfreiheit –. The conditional funding scheme did not, as some had feared it would, result in government interfering in the choice of topics for research programmes. Also, trade and industry's influence on the ins and outs of universities has grown but, on balance, remained relatively limited to date. Contracted education and research, financed by trade and industry, has increased to some extent but has not yet boomed.

Section 2 of this introductory chapter defines the problem dealt with in this study. This definition of the problem addresses the question of which institutions best fit the research system. To be able to answer this question we must first of all establish what demands we may reasonably set on the research system. Secondly, we must attempt to explain and forecast the behaviour of the actors in that system (their reactions towards institutions and any changes therein).

As far as the goals of the research system are concerned, we have opted to posit three of them. We chose this approach given that the various actors at the different levels in the research system attempt to validate different goals which can not be aggregated without assessment. The angle from which the research system is viewed, as a stratified and multiform system, is discussed in more detail in section 3 (the empirical object).

The theoretical approach to the aspect of behaviour is explained in more detail in section 4. We assume that the behaviour of actors in the research system is rational, giving us a link with economic theory. We then take a deeper look at the theory of public choice as a component of economic theory. In turn, this sub-theory provides an analytical framework which is particularly appropriate for explaining the behaviour of actors in non-market situations.

Finally, the structure and scope of this study is explained in section 5.

1.2 Definition of the problem

This book deals with the question *how the research system should be institutionalized: which organizations (actors) should be involved, and what are the relevant tasks and responsibilities?*

The basic principle is the hypothesis that the way in which a system is institutionalized has an influence on the actors in that system. Strategic variables of that influence are the choice of levels in a stratified decision-making structure and the allocation of tasks and responsibilities at each level. This choice of levels is the result of weighing up the advantages of a more central control – the greater the chance that transactions will be made in conformity with the aims of the central actor – against the disadvantages: the higher the relevant (transaction) costs. An optimal institutionalization can therefore be defined as an (accumulation) of situation(s) at the point where effectiveness (maximization of results) and efficiency (minimization of expenditure) converge, in which the goals of the research system are maximized within the restrictions imposed by economic aspects (scarcity, alternative use and rationality; see also section 1.4.1).

The main theme of this book is therefore the optimal institutionalization of the scientific research system. An *institution* is something that moulds human actions. In other words: institutions condition behaviour. Behaviour is crystallized in (decision-making) processes and the results of these processes can be checked against the goals. Such a check can give rise to the need to revise the institutions. Here lies the potential policy-relevance of this study.

When analyzing the definition of the problem a role is played by the aspects of efficiency and effectiveness. Problems of verification arise in respect of both these aspects. To determine efficiency we must know what the output is (see Chapter 3, section 4 in particular). When establishing effectiveness we are faced with a dual problem. In the first place, the state of affairs of decision-making in the research system entails the formation of goals at different levels and by different actors. In other words: we have a multiform decision-making framework in which several values are valid. This faces us with an aggregation problem ("Whose values count?"). Secondly, the goals of the different levels or actors are seldom unambiguous, explicit and consistent. Goals which are acknowledged in government documents (stated goals) can not, for example, be taken on face value: the 'do-behaviour' does not always coincide with the 'say-behaviour'. We sometimes see hidden goals. Occasionally a motive (the improvement of quality for instance) will be argued as the reason to make cuts, on other occasions it will be the motive to spend more. Sometimes we come across conflicting goals and no indication is given as to the priorities of the different goals.

Given that precise, explicit and consistent goals are not established in advance – and even if they have been, cannot be aggregated without assessment – we will not take the dubious route of checking stated goals but prefer to formulate a number of criteria which, within all reason, can be set for the research system. No normative valuation judgments will be made in respect of these criteria. They are postulated provisionally as criterial valuation judgments in the form of '*if-then-statements*': *if* this and that are the goals, *then* that and the other are the most appropriate instruments (organization patterns, institutions). "*If* you wish to travel from Rotterdam to Amsterdam by train, *then* you can do that via Haarlem, Schiphol or Gouda. Giving such an example of the possibilities on the basis of a so-called 'train timetable' is not in itself a statement as to the preferability of destination, route or mode of transport" (Wolfson, 1988, p. 12).

We regard the following criteria as plausible goals for the research system: (1) scientific significance / the augmentation of knowledge; (2) willingness to help the community / the ability to solve problems; and (3) accountability (i.e. are the actors at the various levels willing to take the responsibility and account for the manner in which they deploy the power of decision to which they have been assigned?).

The results that may be expected of the problem dealt with in this study relate to the optimal institutionalization of the scientific research system. These results are twofold: there is a criterial and a normative component. The criterial component consists of the analysis of a number of recent (proposed) institutional changes such as the termination of the separate ministership for science policy, the introduction of the Higher Education and

Research Plan (HOOP), the transformation of the national science council (the Netherlands Organization for the Advancement of Pure Research (ZWO) became the Netherlands Organization for Scientific Research (NWO)), etc, on the basis of the requirements set out above in respect of the research system. The normative component of the results of this study is the fact that we suggest certain institutional changes, always giving reasons why these could contribute towards the improved functioning of the research system.

A major guide-line used in our analysis is that we do not take the behaviour of actors as a given fact but assume that this behaviour adapts along with institutional changes and the ensuing incentives. For the analysis of this behaviour we use concepts of economic theory, especially the economic theory of public choice – which is explained in more detail in section 1.4.

1.3 Empirical object

The empirical object of this study is concerned with the decision-making processes in the research system as the resultant of the reciprocity between institutions and behaviour. Moreover, we are concerned with decision-making processes at both intra-university level (in one university; several layers) and inter-university level (supra-university level; university collaboration, coordination, allocation of tasks and joint promotion of the common interest), and at supra-university level (relevant government bodies, independent administrative bodies and governmental advisory bodies). The shaping and structuring of the inter-university decision-making level is also dependent upon intra-university structures. Typical for our approach to the research system is that we regard research *activity* (within universities) and science *policy* (at inter-university and supra-university level) as a continuum, whereas most other studies in this area are limited to either the organization of research or science policy.

Decision-making processes are analyzed as the result of an interaction between organizational and behavioural characteristics. By organizational characteristics we mean the design of the institutions which influence the behaviour of the actors. Thus the output of the research system is the result of institutions on the one hand and behaviour (rationale, motives) on the other. Different types of output are delivered at the different levels of the system. The primary processes are to be found at the lower levels (researchers, research groups). This is where research results are achieved; the *primary output* of the system (see section 2.3). At the higher levels we have the various forms of *administrative output*, i.e. the results of decision-making which make primary output possible, or directive recommendations which – via the links in the system to the primary processes – have an influential effect (e.g. they influence the choice of research subjects).

This study centres on the government-funded research system, focusing in particular on the university system. The specific empirical object is the decision-making processes in that system; a system which is seen as one consisting of various layers (levels, echelons) at which extremely diverse decisions are made: from decisions in support of implementation to the articulation of societal norms and values, and the translation thereof in science policy. In practice it is apparent that the various levels are institutionalized to varying degrees. It is also apparent that as the system is subjected to the pressure of tumult in surrounding areas – in this case measures imposed by the government over the past few years, described in section 1 – some levels are strengthened while others are weakened. The measures referred to above had the particular effect of affecting the autonomy of universities; a fact which government has now also acknowledged. This was apparent in the ministerial document 'Higher Education: autonomy and quality' (HOAK; Ministry of Education and Science, 1985), the 'Picture of the future of higher education and scientific research' (Ministry of Education and Science, 1987), the Higher Education and Research Plan (Ministry of Education and Science, 1987a) and the bill on higher education and scientific research (WHW; Ministry of Education and Science, 1988). The philosophy acknowledged by these documents is that government is taking yet another step back in order to give universities the opportunity to regain their autonomy. Should this philosophy be brought into practice (and there is a great deal of scepticism in this respect), then it would mean that ultimately it will not be a question of the trend of a ministry continually gaining power and a continual loss of power for the universities (an opinion held by many) but rather of surges in the management of the research system. The dynamism of the system would in this sense be self-correcting. The HOAK concept of policy and its significance for the research system is one of the cases dealt with in this study (Chapter 5).

One of the main functions of practicing science is closely connected with the ideology of 'Lehrfreiheit' described above: criticism of the system. System critique can emerge from within the scientific system itself or from external sources. Coming from within it can relate especially to the paradigms applied in the practise of science. Criticism of the system from outside is, for example, related to established public attitudes or to government policy. This latter form of critique comes mainly from the social sciences given their empirical object.

A criterion of scholarly character is that others within the profession must be allowed to judge the foundations of the system critique. This judgment is entrusted to the *scientific forum*. Sound fulfilment of that forum function calls for independence and quality. Hence the reason why the lion's share of government-funded research is performed by autonomous organizations in which researchers are given a great deal of professional freedom. Apart from the small amount of research carried out in the research departments of some ministries government itself performs very little research. The implication of the choice for this *arm's length model* is that the government does show a certain respect for the freedom of research organizations to pursue their own policies and for the motivation and creativity of individual researchers. Government therefore restricts, quite voluntarily, its own scope for policy-making: it is prepared to pay; not (willing to) take decisions.

Government's choice for this arm's length model can be explained in a rational decision-making paradigm. The assumption is also made that the government's choice for a certain organization structure is based on the total cost per output unit incidental to that particular form of organization. The costs relate not only to the purely technical production costs of the goods and services in question but also to the *transaction costs* resulting from a specific production organization. Transaction costs are those costs involved in specifying, checking and actuating agreements (transactions) which have to be made between actors in order to realize the desired production. For example, the cost involved in drawing up explicit contracts between suppliers and customers in respect of certain goods and services, and also the cost of administration and management *within* an organization, plus the cost of ensuring that the stipulations of that contract are indeed observed. For the greater part, transaction costs are information costs. Given that the procurement and handling of information about the products and production technology of research would result in prohibitively high transaction costs for the government, it is only rational for it to refrain from central administration as the form of organization for the research system. The production processes that take place at the lower levels, such as universities, are 'black boxes' for government.

The research system is therefore not managed from a central cockpit. Such administrative centralism would be ineffective. On the contrary, as regards the initiation, coordination and execution of research, important tasks and competences are allocated to organizations and boards (institutes of higher education, independent research institutes, NWO, WRR (Scientific Council for Government Policy), RAWB (Advisory Council for Science Policy), sectoral research councils, etc.) outside the immediate sphere of government. This does not imply that the structure of the research system is a centralistic 'rank and file' order in which those at the top of the hierarchical ladder decide and the those at the base act out. Nor is it an anarchy of small autarkic kingdoms in which only academic freedom reigns. The research system is best typified as a divided and stratified decision-making structure. Simon (cf. Simon and Ando, 1961) introduced the term *holarchy* for such systems in order to differentiate from the pure form of rank and file hierarchy.

That situation implies on the one hand that an actor at a higher level can impose restrictions on the behavioural possibilities of actors at a lower level, while on the other hand it also implies that a lower level (as a result of the autonomous powers of decision designated to that level) imposes restrictions on the freedom of action at higher levels.

We refer to this line-up of conditions that influence behaviour as *institutionalization*. The assumed goals (more on this in section 1.4.2) on the one side, and the method of institutionalization on the other, determine the behaviour of actors in public decision-making processes and thus the optimality of a (collective) system (like the research system) as such.

There is absolutely no rigid hierarchy in the research system whatsoever. The higher levels can issue orders to the lower levels but only if those orders are pertinent to the mission (task assignment, job agreements, etc.) of that lower level. This is the normative implication ensuing from the arm's length model. It is also important that all levels have contact with the *environment* relevant to that level and thus ensure a three or four-way link at all times. For example, a faculty not only has an internal administrative link with a governing body at the next higher level, it can also maintain a relations network with organizations in its own environment such as affiliated faculties, allied institutes, colleges of higher vocational education, or organizations which have a regulating function in specific areas (sectoral research councils, planning boards). An NWO foundation not only has to do with the higher NWO bodies but will also maintain contact with the faculties in its discipline, sectoral research councils, evaluation committees, industry, etc.

A top-down approach towards the research system would suffice neither as a description of the empirical reality, nor as a criterial standard. In both respects it neglects the role of the lower echelons in the system which is so very important in professional (bottom-up) organizations. It is for this reason that we have opted for the multi-level system. The heuristic value of this view is to be found in the fact that it sheds light on the causes of a number of bottlenecks and points of friction in pursuing policy. In practice, bottlenecks generally arise because certain levels are inadequately institutionalized (e.g. faculties which are inadequately equipped from an administrative point of view) and thus certain administrative outputs are either not realized at all or not at the appropriate level. In the latter case decisions are made at a level which has little to do with the nature of that decision. If, for instance, certain decisions are made at too great a distance from the level where the activity is to take place it can lead to bureaucratization and the responsibilities of the lower levels being undermined. If, on the other hand, higher levels are inadequately equipped in terms of organization and instruments, far too much is left to the lower levels and therefore strategic (directorial) decisions will fail to be realized.

The question therefore remains to be whether different kinds of decisions (outputs) are made in whatever form, and whether they are made by the most suitable actors (has the power of decision within the system been correctly allocated?).

An organizational design theory is explained in the next chapter. This design is used throughout this study as a conceptual framework for describing the research system as a multi-level system. There are seven levels differentiated in the research system, each with its own specific tasks and responsibilities. There are certain actors at all levels, each producing a different kind of output – decisions and recommendations (to both their lower and higher levels). At the lowest level, for example, we find support personnel whose authority is limited to decisions at shop-floor level. The higher we go up the ladder, the greater the scope of the output: the highest (political) level deals with the articulation of societal norms and values and the translation of these into government policy.

At this point it is important that we stress yet again that in this conceptual framework the stratification of the system is not determined by a structure of hierarchical subordination but by the nature of the administrative outputs (the scope of the decisions) generated at the various levels. Describing the research system as a top-down rank and file order in which a certain common (joint) goal is established at the highest level is, in this concept, out of the question. On the contrary, the research system is a multiform system and the various actors in that system (support personnel, researchers, teaching and research units, faculties, organizations and the bodies wherein they cooperate, governmental advisory bodies and independent administrative bodies in the realm of science, relevant government bodies) all pursue their own specific goals, each taking a certain stand. The goals of the various levels will sometimes be in harmony but many times there will be conflicting interests.

Before going into the cognitive object of this study (see the following section) in this section we have described the research system as an empirical object. We have thus formed a picture for ourselves of the relevant problems. In summary, we may state that this picture is determined by the culture of the research system, the basic principle of which is 'Lehrfreiheit'. *If* the research system cannot therefore be described as a rank and file order with a single set of goals at the top, *then* the following three criteria would appear to offer a plausible framework for verification: (1) scientific significance / the augmentation of knowledge; (2) the ability to solve societal problems; and (3) accountability.

1.4 Cognitive object

In order to describe, explain and predict the behaviour of the different actors, in this study we have used economic theory (section 1.4.1), especially the economic sub-theory concerned with the explanation of the behaviour of actors in collectivities (the economic theory of public choice; section 1.4.2) as the cognitive object. In certain parts eclectic use has been made of other theoretical insights such as the public goods theory and the sociology of science (see chapter 3 in particular).

1.4.1 Rationality assumption as axiom

The central hypothesis of this study is that the *behaviour* of actors is either stimulated or restrained by the way in which the system in which they operate is institutionalized. A subsidiary assumption is that each actor is expected to generally gear his behaviour towards the realization of specific *goals*, whereby the interaction between institutions and behaviour gains a certain degree of predictability and controllability. This brings us to the subject of the *rationality assumption* as the main behavioural hypothesis of economic actions (Wolfson, 1988, pp. 18-22). Rationality implies that actors (1) arrange their preferences consciously, to the best of their knowledge and ability (i.e. on the basis of a more or less explicit intellectual approach), in accordance with what they feel is best, (2) relate those preferences to the limit of the possibilities within their reach as indicated by the budget restrictions (or competences or time limit) applying in their particular case, and (3) to then allow themselves to be guided in their ultimate choice by the pros and cons.

The assumption of rationality must be seen as an *instrumental* concept (cf. Hirschleifer, 1985), an *axiom*. In this sense, although it is of no importance whether such an assumption fully reflects the real situation – this is obviously not the case! – it is important that the real situation can be explained and predicted as well as possible, assisted by such an assumption plus the law of averages.

The organization of the research system can be judged against this background: what behaviour does it provoke; what behaviour does it inhibit?

Given that in this study the working of the research system is seen as a question of *optimality* (what reciprocity between institutions and behaviour leads to the best possible reconciliation of efficiency and effectiveness) we have analyzed the behaviour in this system starting from the discipline of economics. Issues of optimality belong within the realm of economics. The cognitive object of the economics discipline consists of the elements 'scarcity', 'alternative use' and 'rationality' (cf. Wolfson, 1988, p. 13). These elements are also present in the processes of allocation and distribution in the field of scientific research. In other words, scientific research can be regarded as an economic phenomenon.

When explaining economic phenomena (economic subsystems and/or the economic order as the aggregate) economists differentiate between two structuring mechanisms:

- the price and market mechanism;
- the budget mechanism (or public choice mechanism, bureaucratic mechanism or hierarchical mechanism).

The price and market mechanism dominates in the market sector; the budgetary mechanism in the public sector.

Dominance, not monopoly, given that on the one hand we see hierarchical structuring mechanisms in the various market units (a firm or a family for example), and on the other hand in a number of situations government behaves as a market unit.

Both of these structuring mechanisms function in scientific research as an economic subsystem. Nevertheless, the empirical object of this study is limited to university research and by far the greater part of that research is funded by government. In the university system the price and market mechanism is therefore subordinate to the public choice mechanism. This led us to choose the economic theory of public choice from the economists' methodological toolkit as the analytical tool to explain the behaviour of actors in the system.

As stated earlier, the motives of the actors in the research system are not always unambiguous, explicit and consistent. Also, the results of the production processes in scientific research are surrounded by an inherent uncertainty (see also Chapter 3). These factors make the research system the perfect example of a *complex system*. If such a system is moulded on a single disciplinary (sub)theory there is always the risk of irresponsible reduction : relevant phenomena go unnoticed or are simply 'explained away'. Therefore, in order to be able to adequately analyze the links between institutions and behaviour in the research system we adopt a conceptual framework derived from organizational theory as the 'warp'. This framework is apparently suitable for *describing* the research system but to actually *explain* the workings of a system and its internal dynamics we need a behavioural theory to act as the 'weft'. Because we are interested in the conditions required for the system to generate optimal results (the economic aspect), and because in this case we have defined the boundaries of the system in such a way that we are dealing with the government-funded research system, the economic theory of public choice is the most suitable one to be used as the behavioural theory.

Explaining the dynamics of the system is done as follows. A change in the assignment of the power of decision to the actors at the various levels gives rise to changes in behaviour. These can be explained or predicted by deploying the theory of public choice. The effects of these behavioural changes can be expressed in terms of transaction costs and information costs. By using this information we can establish whether, and to what extent, there has been a change towards optimality or whether adjustments are called for (feedback). The optimal institutionalization of the research system can only be thought of in terms of a process of tâtonnement.

1.4.2 Economic theory of public choice

Public choice is a broad concept. It refers not only to decision-making processes in terms of the government (at various levels: state, local authorities, etc.) but also to decision-making in all kinds of organizations and groups which are not statutory or public by nature (a family, a firm, a sport club, etc.). All such groups have mechanisms to achieve joint decisions. Some of these mechanisms are informal; others are embedded in legislation and regulations. The purport of these decisions also differs: they can be common-or-garden decisions, but they can also be decisions about decision procedures (constitutional choice; Buchanan and Tullock, 1962). Despite the structure and scope of decisions the main point is always how (a group of) subjects reach consensus – in other words, reach joint decisions – without endangering the continuity of their group relationship.

The university research system is also regulated by processes of public choice in which decisions are made as to the allocation of scarce, alternative procurable funds. The various actors in the system assert their preferences (rationale, goals, motives) during these processes. The rationale will vary according to the actor's position in the system. However, the rationale of different actors holding the same position within a system (researchers for instance) can cover a wide range of aspects: e.g. inquisitiveness, prestige, recognition, idealism, dedication, earning money (from an invention). These, and other *ultimate motivations* are characterized by the fact that they are not operational. To be able to achieve these ultimate motivations in practice one must have the *power of decision* (on budget or competences) in all cases. Striving for this power of decision can be referred to as the *regulating motivation* (Stevers, 1967): that which can be referred to in operational terms.

The difference implied in these twin concepts can be clarified by example. The regulating motivation of politicians and political parties is generally assumed to be the maximization of votes. The larger the group of voters increases the chance of realising various underlying motives (the ultimate motivation). The ultimate motivation can vary from bringing about a different social order to relaxing the fiscal regime. Ultimate motivations can therefore be both idealistically (altruistically) tinted and characterised by enlightened self-interest (being appointed to the attractive position of mayor, or hitting the headlines as often as possible).

Another example of public choice is that of the bureaucrats (in the sense of: those employed in the public sector), of whom it is generally assumed that they aim for the biggest possible budget (regulating motivation) in order to be able to strive after various underlying goals (Niskanen, 1971) which, once again, can cover a wide range: income, power, prestige, a settled position, but also the urge to serve the public cause, involvement in a sector of policy or serving the minister. Yet whatever the ultimate motivations of actors may be, in an economic approach the validity of one motive is no less than the other. It is not befitting of an economist for him to express his opinion on this; he is only interested in the revealed preferences that come to light as a result of those ultimate motivations.

One of the characteristics of the economic theory of public choice is that numerous parallels are drawn with the (traditional) price and market theory (e.g. Mueller, 1979; Van den Doel, 1979). By analogy with the explanatory model of the behaviour of consumers or entrepreneurs, the 'general interest' (or the 'interest of science' or the 'interest of the university', or any other comparable collective category) is not assumed to be the regulator of the actions of actors in processes of public choice, but the maximization of their own interests. It fits in with the public choice concept to assume that actors in the system of scientific research also strive towards the power of decision with regard to budget, goods, competences. It is quite possible that a very multiform spectrum of potentially ultimate motivations are concealed behind this regulating motivation; from the above collective and potentially altruistic categories to restrictive egoism. What the precise make-up is of these motivations is a psychological question. In this study we are looking into whether the maximization of the power of decision (keeping within certain limits) – as the simplifying proxy for ultimate motivations – offers an adequate framework for explaining the revealed preference of the actors in the research system.

This study comprises an analysis of the (realization of the) outputs of the various levels in the research system, the extent to which those levels have been institutionalized, the interaction between the levels, and the effects of changes in the higher echelons of the system (in this case: government policy). As stated earlier, each level has its own actors that strive after their own goals (they attempt to maximise their own interests). Most typical of the research system is that the various actors have a formal autonomy and/or professional qualifications. This is the reason why their interrelations are extremely low, as in a top-down rank and file order. In such a multi-level system the actors restrict each other's freedom of action, not only of those below but also of those above (Mesarovic and co., 1970).

It is particularly the government, at the top of the system, which voluntarily restrains its own range of power. Assisted by public choice (Elster, 1979 and 1983) we are able to explain that such *self-restraint* need not automatically imply that an actor, in this case the government, acts against its own interests. Self-restraint can be explained in a rational behavioural paradigm: by imposing restraint on future actions and options one impedes one's own future irrational behaviour. Self-restraint is therefore a form of optimization in the long term. "Burning one's boats" is an example of self-restraint at the personal level; constitutional restraint an example at public/political level. In specific situations the constitution seems to be an obstacle standing in the way of government and parliament. Matters could be speeded up and performed more efficiently if the constitution could simply be shifted aside. However, the other side is that a number of crucial matters are established in the constitution, especially the way in which decisions are made with regard to the decision procedures. For example, without the constitution the decision procedures could be brought up for discussion time and again. We can also translate the rationale of (constitutional) self-restraint in terms of expenditure: by establishing a number of fundamental affairs (in the form of constitutional law or statutes, or by deciding that local councils or universities can be given a certain degree of autonomy) it is quite possible to achieve a gigantic saving on transaction costs and information costs.

The theory of public choice has been applied many times in this study in order to explain the behaviour of actors within the research system. One important application is the analysis of how accountability is shaped (accountability of researchers, teaching and research units, faculties, universities). Universities are for the purpose of teaching and research. In recent years a stronger emphasis has been laid on accountability in respect of research-performance. This has already led to various behavioural reactions (this is dealt with more extensively in Chapter 3):

- despite the higher intake of students relatively more time has been devoted to research and less to teaching;
- we now have reports of scientific production; there are still no comparable teaching reports;
- publications are now more often co-produced (giving rise to an increase in the number of individual output);
- researchers pursue a more sophisticated marketing policy by publishing their findings in as many possible articles and journals;
- there is also an increasing trend to publish (more or less) the same article more than once;
- there has been a reduction in empirical research given that this is generally more labour-intensive than theoretical study;
- in order to meet the urgency to have one's work published, new journals and magazines are being introduced and the number of (symposium) compilations published is also on the increase, neither of which are always of immense scientific value.

Also in recent years various systems have been applied to measure and classify the value of different research outputs. This has also resulted in behavioural reactions, depending on the classification system.

From all these behavioural patterns it is apparent that self-interest (prestige, recognition, etc.) is the main driving force. The previously referred to maximization of the power of decision would seem to offer an adequate framework for elucidation. Striving for scientific progress (or a similar category) is inadequate as an explicative factor but nevertheless can be the result of individual motives.

Another application of the public choice theory in this study – worked out in more detail in Chapter 5 – is related to whether or not the level of the research system (at which decisions are made on matters of coordination, cooperation, allocation of tasks, joint promotion of interests, advising government, etc.) functions properly. If it is considered capable of making binding decisions then it is perceivable that an organization such as the VSNU (Association of Universities in the Netherlands) would operate at this supra-university level. The theory illustrates that the fact of having a common interest (a 'group good' in public choice terminology) is still not an adequate condition for the realization of an effective team of actors. Applied at the level in the research system referred to above, the shortcomings of the Academische Raad (Universities Council) has shown that the universities were incapable of realising an effective joint promotion of interests and that this has caused them to adopt a defensive position towards the government. By applying one of the main theories of public choice – Olson's group theory (Olson, 1965) – it can be shown to be quite plausible that the group of actors (in this case thirteen universities) is too large to realize the group good on a voluntary basis from the bottom-up. Due to uncertainty as to whether the others are also willing to share in the cost (in whatever sense) of working together, each organization is continually tempted to withdraw from the group's decision-making process if they feel it goes against the grain (the so-called prisoner's dilemma). This dilemma can only be broken down through the intervention of an actor at a higher level that has the power of decision (in this case the government). Such intervention can assume two different forms: the decisions (output) that could be taken at supra-university level are taken at the political level, or the political level creates an actor at supra-university level and designates that actor with sufficient powers of decision (in other words: that which cannot be achieved at the lower level is initiated at the highest level). The British University Grants Committee (UGC), the predecessor of the University Funding Council (UFC), is an example of the latter option (cf. Pratt, 1987). No such organization exists in the Netherlands. The only time that this option was applied in the Netherlands was during a short period in 1982 when it was instigated for a specific purpose (the realization of major cut-backs): namely the task allocation body set up by the Minister of Education and Science within the framework of the TVC (Distribution and Concentration of Tasks) operation.

1.5 Scope and structure of the study

1.5.1 Scope

This study can be regarded as a study in the field of public sector economics. Basically, research financed by trade and industry and the respective organizational patterns have not been taken into consideration. It is a study which deals with the research system as a subsystem of the public sector, comparable with the educational system, the health care system, the social services system, the police services system, etc.

Another limitation is that this study is restricted to university research, which is about half of the total amount of research funded by government. The other half goes to TNO (the Netherlands Organization for Applied Scientific Research), a number of other large and small research institutes and industry. Nevertheless, extramural (government-funded) research comes into the picture in two ways:

- as an example (of organizational patterns, funding and other administrative mechanisms, methods deployed for evaluating, verification and justification, etc.);
- given that the university research system is not insular but – on the contrary – an open system which maintains contact with its *surroundings*, including extramural research, at all levels. This implies that we also come across those organizations which have the task, amongst others, of tending to the coordination of (the systems of) university and extramural research (especially sectoral research councils, RAWB, WRR).

Also of importance is the fact that universities have a dual mission: research *and* teaching. Generally speaking research and teaching tend to overlap in practice, both in terms of subject content and organization. Although this study is structured from the research perspective, that the subject of university education will crop up now and again is quite unavoidable.

A subsequent delimitation is that this study focuses on Dutch problems and Dutch institutions. Yet the Netherlands is by no means unique. The problem detected is – to a varying extent – partly typically Dutch by nature, partly typical of the West European higher education systems, and also has a universal character in part. Given that this is not an (international) comparative study, foreign cases have not been dealt with systematically. In a number of places we have, however, taken examples from the situation abroad.

As has already been stated, this is a public sector study and as such it focuses on a significant organizational pattern in the public sector (and outside it): the vertical relations between the various levels with actors designated with specific competences. In other words: we are concerned here with the age-old issue of (de)centralization: how much sovereignty (autonomy, self-mastership, self-management) is due to which circle (level, layer, echelon)? It is also apparent that there is a mixture of autonomy and co-management (enforced management by a higher *or a lower* level) on each layer. What is specific about this study is that the (de)centralization approach is not applied to the relation between the state and local governments, but to the relation between seven different layers in the research system (in which the relevant government bodies are regarded as the highest layer). An attempt has however been made to link a number of conclusions to this study which are sufficiently 'general' for them to be applied to the organizational patterns of other subsectors in the public sector.

The conclusions can also be of significance for the organization of research outside the realm of the public sector.

Finally, for the sake of clarity it must be pointed out that this study does not provide the answers to questions such as: how high should the total amount of government funding be for university research, how should that total sum be weighed against other categories of public spending, and how should that sum be distributed among the main categories of scientific research. Such non-scientific questions fall outside the scope of this book. In this study we deal with the issue of at which level in the system of science policy should such questions be dealt with. In this case it is the government, which can obtain advice in this respect from strategic advisory bodies such as the RAWB and the WRR.

1.5.2 Structure

This study is made up of three sections: a theoretical part, an empirical part and a concluding section in which empiricism and theory are coupled together. The theoretical part is covered in Chapters 1, 2 and 3; the empirical part in Chapters 4, 5 and 6. The coupling between empiricism and theory is made in Chapter 7.

The conceptual framework used to describe the research system is explained in Chapter 2. It is a model based on a job-grading system which we have worked out in more detail and made more appropriate for this application. The basic principle is formed by the tasks (functions, missions) which a system must be able to fulfil. Typical of our model is that the relations between various task levels are characterised by different types of relations (both rank and file and non-rank and file relations). The levels differ from each other in that the scope of the tasks increase in ascending order. When applied to the research system we arrive at a model comprising seven levels. The actors of each level are then indicated as identified in the Dutch system.

Why is the research system not completely managed by a top-down approach but consists of several more or less self-governing levels? The answer to this question is connected with the specific characteristics of the system's product and production technology. If a higher level in the system wishes to obtain and use production information for the benefit of control processes, then it will be faced with extremely high transaction costs. This problem is dealt with in Chapter 3 where we look at the primary processes which take place in the research system: how are research results generated, measured and valued? This question is dealt with against the background of the general problems of production processes in the public sector. We also look at a number of specific characteristics of the research production process. These specific characteristics help to determine the behaviour of researchers. This should be taken into account in the description and institutional shaping of research and science policy at meso and macro levels.

Chapter 4 is the first in which the cases are discussed. Here, the most important policy trends over the past twenty-five years in the university system are explained in terms of the model developed in Chapter 2. Special attention is given to the science policy pursued by government. This chapter is therefore concerned with the macro level. In Chapters 5 and 6 two case studies have been chosen which are connected with the various components and the various decentralized levels of the (para)university research system. The analysis also focuses on what happens if tasks and responsibilities are transferred to a lower (or higher) decision-forming level in the system.

The case study discussed in Chapter 5 concerns the ministerial memorandum 'Higher education: autonomy and quality' (1985). In this document the Minister of Education and Science introduced a new policy concept of the relationships between government and the universities. This was coupled with a new planning procedure (The Higher Education and Research Plan). In the HOAK memorandum government takes a step back in order to give the university more scope for policy-making. This policy philosophy has been thought out in terms of the seven-level system. Analysis of the sixth level (of cooperation, coordination, allocation of tasks and joint, binding decision-making by universities) has been given particular attention.

In addition to the physical organizational pattern there is another pattern in the research system: the subject organizational pattern. In the Netherlands this is given form in the so-called indirect funding organization: NWO (ZWO prior to 1988). The organization of the indirect funding system is dealt with as a case study in Chapter 6. After lengthy debate a bill was passed in 1987 for the transformation of ZWO to NWO. The objective of the NWO Act is to achieve a different organizational structure: a new administrative layer was introduced at the intermediate level; the so-called NWO councils. Chapter 6 examines the tasks of and relations between the various layers of the new system of indirect funding from an angle of (de)centralization of the multi-level model.

The conclusions of this study are given in Chapter 7. A number of conclusions are drawn as to the optimal institutionalization of decision-making levels in the research system based on a confrontation between practice and theory.

2 A research system institutionalization model

An organizational concept of seven levels, their tasks and responsibilities

2.0 Summary

The research system can be seen as a multi-level system with a stratified, dispersed decision-making structure. In this study we have made a distinction between seven different levels, each with their own actors (persons, organizations) with their own specific tasks and responsibilities within that system. The higher the level, the greater the reach of the decisions made at that level: from carrying out research projects and programmes to planning, coordinating and allocating tasks, to the development of a coordinating strategy and to the translation of societal norms and values into priority areas for science policy.

2.1 Introduction

Many of the discussions about research policy and science policy are concerned with the question of which actor should do what – and more importantly – what that actor should not do. Does the individual researcher have total academic freedom or do other organizations have a say in the choice of the subject of his research? Should a faculty pursue research policy or leave it to the teaching and research unit? (this also applies to the relation between university and faculties). Should the allocation of tasks and the concentration of research capacity in a certain area be left to the universities, or should this be organised by the Minister or possibly even a different body? Should the VSNU be allowed to make binding decisions or does the autonomy of organizations have top priority?, etc., etc.

Given the large number of actors in the system, each with their own diverse goals, positions and competences, there is no single answer to these questions. However, it is quite clear that to answer them we must first of all know which levels can be differentiated between in terms of a system hierarchy, and the whys and wherefores of these levels; in other words, what are their respective tasks and responsibilities. Presenting the research system as a multi-level system is of both heuristic and practical value. The practical value is tested in the second part of this study; the part dealing with three case studies.

The heuristic value is to be found in the fact that light is shed on the origins of a number of bottlenecks and areas of friction in the implementation of policy. In practice, bottlenecks often emerge because certain levels have been inadequately institutionalized, giving rise to certain outputs either not being realized at all or being realized at the wrong level. In the latter case decisions are made at a level which does not correspond with the nature of that decision. If, for instance, certain decisions are made at too great a distance from the executive level, it can lead to a higher level of bureaucracy and the competences of lower levels being undermined. On the other hand, if higher levels are inadequately equipped in terms of organization and instrumentation, and subsequently far too much is left to lower levels, strategic (directorial) decisions will not be accomplished.

This study sees the research system as a multi-level system, consisting of seven layers (including the government at the highest level), each with its own tasks, competences and tools. The higher we climb in this multi-level system the higher the level of aggregation and the greater the complexity of the relevant type of decision-making.

It is essential for us to stress that the research system is not controlled direct from a single, central cockpit (at the highest level) through directives issued to the lower levels. Government – as the central actor – places public funds at the disposal of the research system and combines that with a number of indirect steering mechanisms such as rules, coordination, planning and consultation. The choice for this decentralized method of managing the research system implies the responsibility for important tasks and competences at the lower levels. The organization of the research system is therefore not a centralistic rank and file system in which the highest level makes the decisions and the lower echelons do the work. Nor is it an anarchy of small autarkic kingdoms in which only academic freedom reigns. On the contrary, the research system is characterized by a divided and stratified decision-making structure. The relations between the levels can therefore be determined through various types of competences. There might be a direct line between certain levels, yet having said that it might be the case that the task of the level one step up the hierarchical ladder, vis-à-vis its subordinate level, is primarily one of coordinating, advising, monitoring, etc. Therefore, when in this study we refer to the research system as a system hierarchy (cf. Simon and Ando, 1961) it must be kept in mind that we do not mean the pure form of rank and file hierarchy. Koestler introduced the term '*holarchy*' in order to distinguish such systems from rank and file hierarchies. A holarchy consists of holons: parts of a whole which also have their own identity. A holarchical structure in itself says very little about the balance of power and authority within that structure. Competences can be dispersed between the component parts in many different ways. In a holarchic conception of a federal state, for example, power is not automatically the prerogative of the national government.

The research system is a mixed order containing elements of hierarchy (the execution of tasks at the orders of higher levels; joint management) and of holarchy (the autonomous execution of a task by one level). The relations between two adjacent levels are thus determined by various types of tasks and competences. It is also important that at all levels contact is maintained with the *environment* relevant to that particular level. In other words there is a three or four-way link at all levels. For example, a faculty not only has an internal administrative relationship with a governing body at the next higher level, but can also independently, or through disciplinary consultation, maintain a relational network with organizations within its own field such as associated faculties, sister institutes, or organizations that act as supervisors in problem areas (sectoral research councils, planning boards).

This chapter contains the following: the multi-level model, on which this study is based, is explained and geared to the Dutch science and research system in section 2. We take a closer look at which people and organizations operate at which levels and what the respective tasks and competences of these are. In section 3 a number of aspects of importance for a sound understanding of the application of the multi-level model in practice are investigated in more depth.

2.2 The multi-level system

To illustrate the formal relationship in an organization use is often made of charts showing 'established' main line managerial relationships and staff hierarchy. Such diagrams can be misleading given that in practice procedures are not always what they should be. With this in mind organization experts have developed the term 'informal organization', reflecting the true relations as they have grown in reality.

One of the reasons why organization charts fail to show the true picture of an organizational system is that they generally take the main lines between the levels of an organization as the starting point: level (person) X can issue directives to level (person) Y 1 to n (inclusive) and can accept directives from level Z. The charts are then filled in further by differentiating between the various staff departments for instance. However, the relations between the various levels of an organization need not be determined primarily by main line managerial relationships but other relationships between the levels can also characterize the links between levels; a coordinating relationship, a supervisory relationship or a monitoring relationship, for example. The basic principle that the relationships in an organization, or an even larger system, can be based on different types of relationships between work-levels was developed and applied by several British organization experts (Jaques; 1976, Rowbottom and Billis, 1977, 1987). These experts worked out five levels, more or less in detail, and identified an additional sixth and seventh level in large systems. This concept of the theoretical organizational structure was chosen as the basic principle because it seems the most appropriate one to define the relationships in *professional organizations*. Characteristic of such organizations or systems is that their outputs are most difficult to describe accurately beforehand (not bicycles or motor-cars but research, health or safety). In such organizations it is the individual effort, attitude and capacity of professionals which is decisive as regards the quality of the output. It is partly because of this that relationships other than main line managerial relationships play such an important role.

Rowbottom and Billis (1977, 1987) developed their hierarchy of work-levels on the basis of empirical studies in trade and industry and several public organizations such as the British system of health care and the social services, ministries and local government. This study expounds their model to make it suitable for the scientific research system. Additionally, there is a significant difference between the approach taken by Rowbottom and Billis and the far wider one in that Rowbottom and Billis are mainly concerned with a hierarchical order of types of work *within a (large) organization* (e.g. with the aim of achieving a job evaluation system), while in this study we are more concerned with differentiating between the tasks and competences *within a system of multiple organizations*. This implies another deviation from the original model: while Rowbottom and Billis are still able to relate all work-levels to people, in the 'scaled-up' model applied in this study the work-levels often have to be related to organizations (or parts of an organization). For the fulfilment of these tasks we therefore speak of *actors*, a term that can be applied to both people and organizations.

In the remainder of this section we shall describe, in an ascending level of abstraction, the tasks and competences of the seven levels. The classification of seven levels must be regarded as an analytical tool; the number is not God-given. These seven levels differ in the type of output they produce (in terms of the transaction costs concept): the kind of *transactions* concluded at the various aggregates). We must not forget that in this context *information* is also dealt with; information which varies to a great extent in level of detail. This implies that not all the information available at shop floor level (on the production technology of research for instance) is passed on via the intermediate levels until it reaches the highest level of science policy or vice versa, that it is not always fecund for lower echelons to converse with the driver when "travelling as passenger". The fact is, and this applies to all levels, that it is irrational to try to obtain full information about the transaction processes that occur at the other levels. Given the characteristics of the production process of scientific research this in itself would entail exorbitantly high information costs. Moreover, the fact that the actors at the various levels can assume opportunistic behaviour must also be taken into account. Opportunism can be described as self-interest seeking with guile. Opportunistic behaviour is, for instance, the provision of selected and distorted information or making promises which one is unable, or does not intend to keep. It is not assumed that all actors behave in this way. It is sufficient that some actors can behave in an opportunistic way and that it is extremely costly to determine who those are. Within Simon's concept of bounded rationality it can therefore be stated that the information costs are only controllable by allowing only the 'tip' of information to pass from one level to the next one up. It can therefore be expedient for a higher level to regard the production processes that take place at lower levels as 'black boxes'.

The multi-level model and cost terminology described above are not only useful means for describing the stratification of the research system, they also serve to explain the dynamics of the system. This dynamics analysis is performed as follows. A change in the allocation of the power of decision to the actors at the various levels brings about a change in behaviour. The effects of these changes can be expressed in terms of transaction costs and information costs. By using this information it is possible to establish whether, and to what extent, these changes are in the direction of optimality or whether there is cause to make adjustments (feedback). The optimal institutionalization of the research system can therefore be thought of in terms of a process of tâtonnement.

The figure opposite shows the seven levels. Also illustrated is how they can be, or are, institutionalized in the academic research system; in other words, which actors correspond with the different tasks and competences.

level	*task*	*actor*
1	duties aimed at prescribed output	support research personnel
2	situational response	researcher
3	systematic provision	research group (teaching and research unit, NWO study group)
4	comprehensive provision	organization unit (faculty, institution, NWO foundation)
5	field coverage	coordinating organization (university, TNO, NWO)
6	conglomerate strategy	national advisory and consultative councils (WRR, KNAW, RAWB, ARHO, sectoral research councils)
7	articulation of societal norms and values and the translation thereof into policies	minister(s), government and parliament

Levels one to three form the micro-structure of the research system: the 'shop-floor'; levels four and five the meso-structure: organizations and their main departments; levels six and seven form the macro-structure of political and non-political bodies responsible for the research system at national level. This multi-level model is worked out below in more detail on the basis of a more finely detailed description of the tasks and competences.

ad 1: duties aimed at prescribed output
Duties performed at this lowest level are aimed at output which can be specified in full beforehand. For example, a predesigned object has to be pieced together, a prescribed service provided, the assignment to collect certain information, the performance of a prescribed test or control procedure. These duties are *executory*; no decisions are required as regards the outputs produced at this level. That is done at a higher level. Should questions arise with regard to the targeted output, or how the task should be executed, a superior can be approached (on level two). Examples of level one duties are: the adjustment of a machine, performing a routine check, making up a prescription by the chemist's assistant, duties performed by the cashier or tea lady. In research organizations non-research (support) staff are the main people at this level.

It must be emphasized that it is the prescribed *output* which is characteristic of level one. It does not imply that all the work is completely planned as well. As a rule there is also a certain degree of discretion attached to the way in which the work is carried out at level one. It may call for special skills, an appropriate attitude or good powers of judgment. With regard to production work one will have to be able to deal, for instance, with materials of varying quality or with varying characteristics; if the work involves providing a service account will have to be taken with the different qualities and characteristics of people. If there is no discretion whatever involved in the work to be performed – i.e. no special skills, attitude, or powers of judgment are called for – then we speak of unskilled work. This is the kind of work which is the first to be considered for automation.

ad 2: situational response
The work carried out at level two is also related to concrete situations or problems which have to be tackled on an individual basis. How this is done depends on the actor's judgment,

who will constantly be required to interpret the questions fired at him. The duties at this level are therefore more difficult to establish beforehand and the solutions to questions or problems (the outputs) depend more on the person performing the work. The execution of tasks on this level usually implies that an *evaluation* is made of the needs and wishes of others. Typical of situational response is answering questions asked by customers, patients, students. It is not therefore simply a matter of executing a task – as is the case on level one. On level two, for example, we come across salesmen, teachers, doctors and social workers. Level two is also the first level where we see jobs which are mainly managerial. One is then responsible for the allocation of tasks to personnel on level one, implying that one is expected to be able to assess their capabilities and wishes.

Individual researchers are also to be found at this level. It is at this second level where the actual creative research work takes place, both during and after consultation with level three on the choice of research subject. The interpretation of questions pertaining to the research is a perfect example of situational response. When performing their work researchers will need to issue instructions to support staff at level one.

ad 3: systematic provision

At this level reactions are not geared towards individual cases (as is the case on levels one and two). Here, systems and procedures (or frameworks) are developed which make it possible to deal with *a series of cases* at all times, indeed those which will emerge in the future as well. This requires the talent of conceptualization. Given the targeted output the staff at this level give thought to the technical and organizational improvements and innovations for the production process, to questions of how to achieve a better combination of production factors, how to increase quality or reduce costs. Typical examples of level three activities are the development and implementation of improved procedures for dealing with customers, patients or students, or the development of improved systems for dealing with orders, queries or complaints. The development of a new curriculum should also take place at this level. Level three is the first level at which the tasks have a policy-making character.

In the research system the most important activity at level three is the development of research programmes for research groups (e.g. teaching and research units). It is at this level that we see research managers (e.g. professors in the university component of the research system) who oversee a complex of duties. They hold prime responsibility for the design and development of research in a specific field. The corresponding management task is related primarily with the execution of research projects (discussing the choice of subject with the researchers at level two; encouraging and supervising them). Research initiatives emerge from the lower level in interaction with level two. Study groups of NWO foundations also operate on this level (see Chapter 6 for the organization of NWO).

ad 4: comprehensive provision

Compared to level three there are quite clear differences in respect of the targeted outputs at level four, and also the environment with which one comes into contact. It is no longer adequate to ensure of systems which produce outputs in response to the needs of customers, patients, students, etc. Level four is not so much concerned with a task but rather a specified set of tasks in a defined area within a given territorial or organizational context. At this level one must be attentive that there are no gaps in that set. Constant attention must be given to the introduction of new products and services and to bringing a halt to the production of those outputs which no longer come up to standard. At this level one is involved in market research in order to trace the potential needs of the target groups (students, science forum, etc.) It also implies that priorities are set and translated into budgets.

The tasks involved at level three must be carried out with the given means of production, the people available, tools and various other means. Cash expenditures can be made within set limits (budgetary items). Conversely, at level four the management is responsible for integral planning and budgetary decision-making. Although there is also a certain amount of freedom to (re) allocate in respect of investment decisions, major decisions are taken at level five.

Level four output consists of the management of larger organizational units, such as a TNO institute or a factory which is a part of a larger concern. At this level the management has a full task with regard to the production process. This management task includes organization development: the (re)arrangement and coordination of groups at level three and the allocation of funds thereto, personnel management (selection and appointments policy, the development of assessment procedures, the promotion of mobility, careers planning).

Level four is also the level at which university faculties and NWO foundations operate. There are several target groups aimed at within a discipline. The research programmes and curricula developed at level three have to be approved at the faculty level. Also, the faculty is where personnel policy and policy on the teaching and research units (how many, which) is pursued. It is also here where decisions are made as to the procurement and allocation of several important substantive facilities which are characterized through their collective use. Institutionalized contacts are also maintained at faculty level with the relevant environment in order to keep in touch with the needs for certain research programmes and curricula.

ad 5: field coverage

This level is concerned with the provision of an extensive set of tasks which are no longer limited by territorial or organizational boundaries. Priorities are set at this level in response to investigations into the needs within a wide area which has *not been defined in advance*. It is at this level where we find the umbrellas of level four's organizational units insofar as they address that lower level. The output of this level includes strategic planning in the medium to long term coming from the existing organization(s). It is the task of the actors at level five to formulate specific goals for, and in consultation with, the actors at level four. The strategic dimension of the management task is also concerned with organization: should units at level four be increased or reduced in number, combined, etc; what cross-links will need to be made? Organizations at level five are distinguishable from those at level four in the sense that they are large enough to look for synergic effects. The specific set of facilities is therefore not established in advance but characterized by a ceaseless strife towards innovation. Not only the technological, but the social, political and financial viability is also taken into consideration.

The management of large industrial concerns, for example, takes place at level five. At this level the actors are not concerned with specific production plans but with long-term strategy; not with the fixing of detailed budgets but with the general financial management, etc.

The Board of Directors of TNO or the executive committee of NWO – as the umbrella organization for disciplinary foundations – also function on this level. Another example is the military defence top (not the political level; that is located on level seven).

At level five we also see the universities, which have wide field coverage in the form of various faculties. In the original sense of the word a university has at its disposal a complete spectrum of faculties. Governing bodies and university councils not only distribute funds to the existing faculties, they are also involved in the planning of new faculties and fields of study. Initiatives can be taken in respect of reasonably sized interdisciplinary studies and curricula. This is established in the development plan of a university.

Given that the consultative body for the associated universities (in this case the VSNU) does not have the authority to make decisions which are binding for the universities it functions at level five and not at level six. This is explained in more detail below.

ad 6: conglomerate strategy

The output of this level consists of giving shape to *directional processes of change* in which the existing organizational structures are no longer the basic principle. The concern here is to develop strategy at (inter)national level. These strategic decisions can relate to the specification of areas which will need to be given priority in the future (in main lines and in global terms), and also to the development of the organizational infrastructure and management tools. Issues of field demarcation are dealt with at this level: what possibilities should be available in the health care system for private initiatives?; is it desirable that the universities of technology and TNO compete against each other in certain fields, or that task boundaries are strictly defined?; what collaborations should be created between institutions for the purpose of setting up a national programme for research into health care for instance?; how should one shape an informatics stimulation plan?, etc.

The level of conglomerate strategy forms part of the macro-level which is above the levels (one to five) that can be used to describe the organizations in which a system's primary processes (the manufacture of bicycles or the production of health care or education and research, etc) take place.

Whereas the tasks of levels one to five can be defined with a high degree of accuracy, it will be quite clear that having reached level six we are faced with task descriptions which are both abstract and complex. In terms of an automation system one speaks at this level of an *interface* function. In terms of the object of this study we are speaking of the interface between research activities in the restricted sense (levels one to five) and the science policy system (level seven). Here too it is more than obvious that the seven-level model is not a rank and file hierarchy but a system hierarchy of tasks in ascending degrees of abstraction which must be fulfilled for the system to function adequately.

The interface function consists of three aspects:

1. the various value systems are *translated* as appropriate: between those of researchers and stakeholders, between those of the suppliers and those creating the demand, the providers of funds and those who receive;
2. a *platform* is created at a high level, on which the representatives of government, interest groups in society and research organizations meet; decisions of strategic significance can emerge at this level;
3. the level functions as a *buffer* between government and the research organizations. If there is no such network of bodies of representatives between government and research centres there is a danger that government will become directly involved with the practise of science, while it is the arm's length model in particular which is beneficial for the healthy development of the research system. Hence the reason why level six is able to fulfil the role of maintaining stability. Its composition guarantees that a wide range of influences from closely connected areas are taken into account and thus protects the research system to some extent from the government.

The level of abstraction and degree of complexity of the tasks at level six imply that the manner of institutionalizing this level of the system is relatively the least crystallized. In practice, various modalities have developed alongside one another. We can distinguish four modalities at level six.

a. The mildest form of institutionalization: a body at level six functions as the *consultative platform* for the organizations at level five in a specific area. One could think in terms of a body within which the trade union federations, or employers' federations hold joint consultation and reach common viewpoints. Another example of a body which, in principle, can be perceived as operating at level six is the VSNU, the platform on which all universities are represented. The VSNU functions as a board which promotes the interests of all universities. It will be quite clear that in this form of institutionalization the relationship between levels five and six is at most one of coordination. If the (autonomous) organizations at level five fail to pass on any responsibilities, the consultative body only functions as the mouthpiece for joint interests. No decisions or statements are made about matters on which agreement can not be reached. In this case the course of decision-making is based on voluntariness and non-commitment (cf. Van den Doel, 1979). All organizations at level five possess a de facto power of veto. We only regard a joint consultative body of organizations at level five as a level six body if it is empowered to make binding decisions. If, on the contrary, the consultative body only acts as an extension for level five, such as the VSNU, then the scope of its tasks reaches no further than level five.

b. The main tasks fulfilled at level six are *advisory tasks*. In this interpretation of level six we can think especially in terms of government's external advisory councils which fulfil a strategic function. The output of level six lies therefore within the realm of advising level seven and responding to levels four and five (entering into dialogue about the goals of the organizations at those levels). Decisions made at level six are based in part on an analysis of other factors which determine the course (e.g. what will happen in industry or abroad). With regard to the specification of research areas the institutions referred to above can advise on the relative importance of certain societal areas of priority for the future (think, for example, of the policy-oriented forecasting of the WRR and the advice given in the past by the RAWB on aspects of growth and shrinkage). With regard to organizational infrastructure, level seven can be advised on the setting up of new organizational units (at level four or five) or the closing down of existing ones. Concerning the development of instruments, advice might be given on an optimal organization and/or funding structure for research.

Such advisory councils with a strategic function tend to be composed of outside experts acting as private individuals. It is this that distinguishes them from the 'interest' councils referred to under point a. Their strategic function is to be found in the fact that they can inspire the government – which by nature tends to fossilize in management instruments (regulations, planning, hierarchy) – to demand predictability of policy.

In this specification of the model the weight attributed to level six organizations is determined by two factors:

– the composition of these councils: to be able to speak with authority it is most essential that such organizations are staffed by the 'top dogs' of the system (cf. for instance the composition of the WRR and the RAWB, in which the quality of their members plays a decisive role, while political colour is of minor importance);

– that in order to bring about dialogue an institutional rule is established which forces the organizations (at level seven and/or five) addressed by level six organizations, to respond to the output of the level six organization. With regard to recommendations put forward by the WRR for instance, it is established by law that government must determine its stand within a period of six months.

c. A step further is taken in the modality in which level six, in addition to a *primary advisory task, can also apply the budgetary instrument as an incentive instrument.*

   In this case, level six can support its decisions by extending financial incentives to the lower levels (in this case levels four and five; not directly to level three; this is not in line with the strategic set of tasks of level six and would affect the positions of the levels between) with a view to the development of certain research programmes. In the Netherlands this option played a part in the debate on whether sectoral research councils should have their own research budget (see Chapter 4).

d. Finally, we can also envisage an interpretation whereby level six fulfils the *important task of budget allocation* (which would then not take place at level seven and/or five).

   This equipping of level six was chosen in the British system in which the power of the purse was bestowed upon the University Grants Committee, which was succeeded by the University Funding Council in 1989 (see Chapter 5). It also implies that binding decisions on the allocation and concentration of tasks, etc., in respect of organizations operating on level five are made at this level. It is obvious that the composition of the level six body must be a sound reflection of the interests of the research system and those of the science policy system. It is also important that level seven is not completely dependent upon level six for its science policy but that it also has at its disposal several channels and financial options to allow it to counterbalance or make adjustments if necessary (this subject is discussed further in Chapter 4 which deals with the case studies on the shaping of national science policy).

In the Netherlands the choice out of all the various modalities for institutionalization was mainly for organizations with consultative and advisory tasks. In the Netherlands there is no major budget allocation body at level six. It is a mix of organizations which operate (or operated) at level six in the world of science: the Universities Council (up to 1986), WRR, KNAW (Royal Netherlands Academy of Arts and Sciences), RAWB, ARHO (Higher Education Advisory Council), sectoral research councils, a number of investigative committees and several other ad hoc committees such as the recent advisory committee on research schools. Also belonging at level six are those organizations which can oversee the whole research system, both the university and non-university component, and make decisions on the cooperation and allocation of tasks between (components of) these two areas. The RAWB in particular is eligible for this role.

The strategic function of level six is very important. By nature the government tends to 'play safe'. Yet in a society which is becoming progressively more complex the degree of uncertainty also grows. This applies à fortiori in the selection of areas for research. All the more important therefore is the function of independent external organizations at level six which, if necessary, provoke and contradict government.

ad 7: articulation of social norms and values and the translation thereof into policy
Level seven is the *political domain*: government, minister(s) and parliament. It is at this level that the norms and values of our society are (re)formulated and translated into policy priorities in various social areas and into institutional frameworks. This policy is then

implemented in administrative actions (laws and other regulations, the apportionment of finances). In the view taken in this study we ascribe the public domain to the multi-level model as regards the aspect of science policy. Science policy at this level is geared towards optimizing the working of the research system, or to the various components of that system. Ideally, the output at level seven consists of forms of *meta-management* (management at arm's length). The economic theory of organization teaches that (research) organizations cannot be governed directly by external management (in this case by the government). As a rule there is too little sophisticated and specific information to be able to do this. Direct management by the government would thus only lead to bureaucratic meddlesomeness at the expense of the decisiveness of the organizations thus managed.

Meta-management implies that the organizations at the meso-level of the research system have the disposal over their own management tools with which to fulfil the tasks and responsibilities allocated to them.

Meta-management is aimed at strengthening the intermediate levels by increasing the relevant management possibilities. This demands a structural interpretation of the allocation of tasks to and between levels six, five and four in order to give substance to the lower levels' responsibilities and tasks. Certain aspects can be illustrated in the progress of technology policy. The way in which society assesses the value of technology policy has changed quite radically over the past decade. Economic growth and technological progress are held (once again) in high esteem. Partly as a result of this, government policy now attaches greater importance to the stimulation of technological innovation in trade and industry. This is expressed in the reinforcement of the Ministry of Economic Affairs (level seven) at the expense of the Ministry of Education and Science (Directorate General for Science Policy), the request for advice from ad hoc boards of representatives at level six (Wagner committee, Dekker committee) and subsequently the initiation and funding of several innovation programmes and collaborations at levels five and four (INSTIR (Innovation Incentives Scheme), IOPs (Innovation-oriented Research Programmes), regional centres).

As far as ministers are concerned the Minister of Science and Education and the Minister of Economic Affairs (with regard to technology policy) are of particular importance in the system of scientific research. During the period 1971 to 1981 a major role was played by the then Minister for Science Policy (see Chapter 4). The Lower House regards the Standing Committee for Science Policy and the Standing Committee for Education and Science as important actors.

2.3 The multi-level system in operation

"He who makes the decisions, pays" is an adage which is left undisputed as regards the administrative-financial relations between various governments. Yet whether it also applies the other way around – "he who pays, makes the decisions" – is very debatable. In a plural society such as that in the Netherlands, where several values and interests can be manifested, it has always been so that the government finances certain matters without any involvement as to their content. This applies in respect of the so-called 'freedom of education'. We can also think in terms of the arts and science. Art is a matter of taste. What is, or is not subsidized, purchased, preserved or reaped, is not determined by the Minister of Cultural Affairs and his civil servants, but is left to the Arts Council, museum directors, etc., (a minister cannot violate this rule without causing a major commotion).

One of the functions of science is criticism of the system (system critique). This requires independence and quality. To guarantee this the lion's share of government-funded research is performed by autonomous organizations within which the researchers have a large degree of academic freedom. Apart from the small amount of research carried out in the research departments of some ministries, government itself performs very little research. The implication of the choice for this arm's length model is that the government does show a certain respect for the freedom of research organizations to pursue their own policies and for the motivation and creativity of individual researchers. The government therefore restricts, quite voluntarily, its own scope for policy-making: it is prepared to pay; not (willing to) take decisions. The rationale of such 'self-restraint' was explained in the previous chapter.

The research system is therefore not controlled from a single, central cockpit. As regards the initiation, coordination and execution of research, important tasks and responsibilities are set aside for organizations and councils outside the immediate sphere of government (universities, independent research institutes, NWO, WRR, KNAW, RAWB, sectoral research councils, etc.). This does not imply that the structure of the research system is a centralistic 'rank and file' order in which those at the top of the hierarchical ladder decide and those at the bottom act out. In terms of the multi-level model explained in the previous section, the relations between the different levels are only determined to a very small extent by typical main line managerial relationships. On the contrary, other types of relationships such as coordinating, advising, supervising and monitoring, are characteristic of the research system.

The multi-level model described in the previous section is conceptual by nature. It is a model that must be tested in practice. We have already done that in terms of classification by categorizing the various levels on the basis of the actors in the Dutch system of scientific research. Yet we obviously do not wish to suffice with a *classifying description* of manifestations of actors that play a role in the research system. 'Classifying' is only the first step, ultimately we must think in terms of 'clarifying': *reaching understanding through analysis* in respect of the causes that lead to actors misunderstanding or being uncertain about the tasks they are expected to fulfil. This is done by criterial analysis, resulting in criterial value judgments. In other words, we do not make any statements as to goals but only evaluate whether an instrument (organization pattern, etc.) is suitable to contribute towards the established or assumed goal. We therefore use the multi-level system to clarify the faults and shortcomings in the structure of an organizational system based on the basic principles explained in section 1.2 and to illustrate how improvements can be made therein (organizational design). Faults and shortcomings, for example, are the lack of an actor at a certain level, or on the contrary, two actors getting in each other's way, or an actor taking on several tasks which belong at different levels, etc. Certain aspect will be illustrated on the basis of case studies in the second part of this study.

If we subject the multi-level model to further investigation one of the first questions to rise is whether the system used implies that all levels must be 'strongly' developed. The answer is both yes and no. No if we mean that each level should have its own formal-hierarchical (main line) competences vis-à-vis the lower levels. It has already been stressed that the relations between the various levels in the multi-level model can differ as to type. Not every level is equipped with formal-hierarchical competences. In some areas the main aspects will be coordination, sounding out, response and stimulation.

The answer is also yes: each level must be 'strong' in that it must be adequately equipped to produce the outputs expected of it. The term 'output' should be seen in a wide context here; it relates to the degree of fulfilment of the specific tasks and functions of a certain level. For example, at levels two and three it refers to the outcomes of primary processes – the products of education and research –, but level six, for instance, yields quite different outputs which are to be found in the managerial sphere: decisions, recommendations, etc., offering the opportunity for consultation and shaping such consultation.

When using the term 'output' in the more restricted sense, denoting the results of the primary processes, we shall use the term *'primary output'*.

A separate chapter (Chapter 3) is devoted to the primary output of the scientific research system and the question of how that research output is generated, measured and valued.

When using the multi-level model it becomes apparent that not all organizational systems investigated reach the highest level. The 'highest expected work level' (Rowbottom and Billis, 1987, p. 57) will differ in each system. The bicycle factory, for example, only reaches level four, possibly level five, if it is the subsidiary of a large concern that manufactures transport equipment. However, there is no national bicycle factory policy (at least not in a country such as the Netherlands), nor do we have an intermediate body that can volunteer strategic views on this.

In this sense, the multi-level model has a universal pretension that, starting from the highest level available, all levels lower than that are also present, whether the system reaches to level four or level seven.

One of the aspects on which light is shed by the multi-level model is the friction resulting from more than one actor in the line at one level and that both have formal-hierarchical competences. This is illustrated in the figure below.

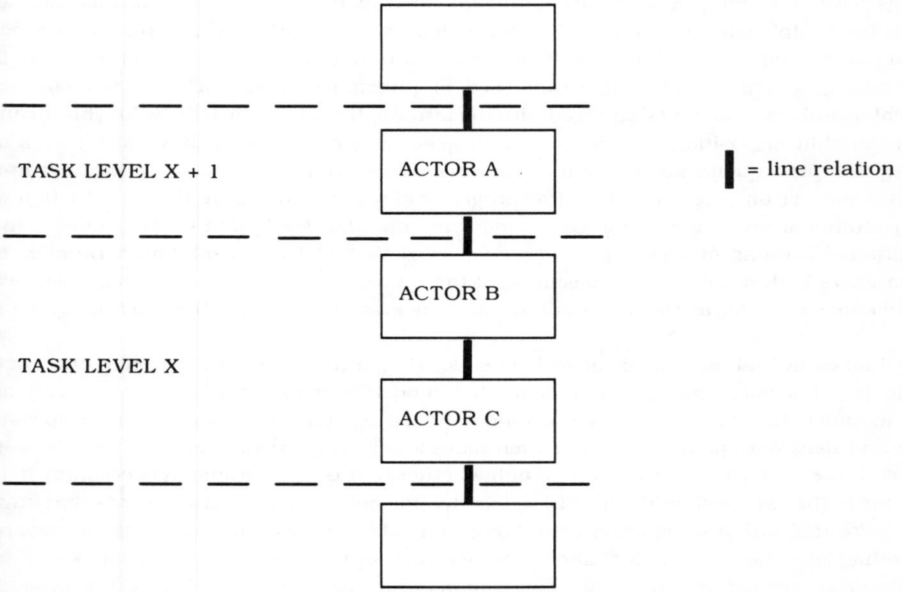

Suppose that in a particular system there is a position with formal-hierarchical responsibilities towards another actor at the same level – B towards C in the figure –, while in actual fact B carries out the same tasks as his formal subordinate C. In practice we would see the following happen: if C requests assistance or advice from B, B – so as not to go beyond his competences – will have to respond with: I'm afraid I must consult A (his superior) on this. This will prompt the following reaction from C: then I would be better to approach A direct. Thus, if two actors at a single task level have a formal hierarchical relation it leads to processes of elimination. We shall return to this phenomenon in more detail in the NWO case study (Chapter 6).

In the above we introduced the term 'primary output'. Rowbottom and Billis (1987, p. 56) refer to the level which produces the primary output as 'basic expected work level'. Which level this 'basic expected work level' is varies with the type of output produced by the specific system. In most systems this can be either level one or level two. The primary output of systems in which a service is provided is generally at level two.

One of the specific characteristics of the research system – as a system carried by 'professionals' – is that the primary output is produced at a relatively high level in the system. The basic expected work level in the research system is at level two to three, and there is a quite clear trend towards a shift in the direction of level three. Practice, and the view that the products of research are the results of individual, creative researchers who set no limits on their scientific inquisitiveness are gradually losing ground. Economies of scale, working with costly facilities such as laboratories and automated data files, etc., means that the trend is towards research as the work of research groups within the framework of a coherent research programme. Over the years, the task of the professor has thus shifted from that of researcher/teacher to the manager of a research group. Certain things have long changed in science and medicine (this trend was pointed out as early as 1905 by Adolph von Harnack in his prestigious work entitled "Von Grossbetrieb der Universität"), indeed the character of the arts and humanities and the social sciences is also changing. This trend is also expressed in government policy. The phenomenon of 'teaching and research units' emerged with the introduction of the WUB in 1970. This meant a formal shift in position from individual professors to collectivities in a specific area of study. The perception that research is the work of research groups working together in a specific area or on a certain subject or programme was reinforced by the introduction of the conditional funding scheme. One important condition set by the government for the conditional funding of research programmes was that at least a minimum number of researchers had to work on the execution of these programmes. We are therefore tempted to indicate level three as the one that produces the primary output in the research system.

One final point that must be dealt with when looking at the multi-level model in operation is the question as to what extent an actor should operate at a *fixed level*. In the classifying explanation of the model it is always assumed that each actor corresponds with one specific level and does not operate on two or even more levels. The question is whether this is in line with the practical situation, and if not, whether that is undesirable. It is certainly true that the higher we climb in the multi-level model the more we come across actors that have been allocated with a set of tasks containing elements from several task levels (downward extending jobs), both conceptual and executory work for instance, or making both strategic and tactical decisions (cf. the KNAW, for example, which operates at level six as the national advisory body but which also fulfils a level five task as the umbrella organization of several research institutes). In such cases it will need to be established quite clearly what the highest level is at which an actor operates. This also determines the job requirements to be set with regard to an actor. If the system's scale of operation is large enough, from the viewpoint of efficiency alone, preference should be given to delegating those tasks to a lower level. The most obvious example of a 'misfit' is that of organizations where managers or researchers type out their own manuscripts.

A totally different aspect of the 'fixed level' of an actor is the requirement that he has sufficient empathy for the functioning of actors at other levels. An actor who adopts a defensive attitude towards all the initiatives taken at higher levels and refuses to cooperate in the thinking process, or refuses to think ahead, is functioning inadequately. The same applies with regard to the attitude towards lower levels: it is a poor general (minister, manager, etc.) who fails to visit his troops and chat with the men, fails to call into the laboratory to hear what is happening on the shop floor, etc. This latter phenomenon is referred to by the term 'zooming' (Rowbottom and Billis, 1987, p. 46). Zooming can be regarded as an intrinsic part of an actor's conscientious fulfilment of his task. In doing this an actor remains to operate at his own level (he must not take over command or issue orders in the laboratory). Such informative visits are aimed at optimizing the actor's function. It makes the actor better equipped to optimize the workings of the lower level by exerting a direct influence.

3 Generating research

The sociological characteristics of research and its economic implications

3.0 Summary

In this chapter we shall deal with the initial processes that take place in the research system: how research results are generated, measured and valued; and how are these processes controlled in terms of industry; what are the variables aimed at and by which actors?

Research is a creative process. It is the search for the unknown. Nevertheless, research can also be seen as a production process, aimed at the production of certain results (achievements; outputs). It was already pointed out in the two previous chapters that this is a process with a very unique characteristic; it differs entirely from the production of motorcars or bicycles. In order to do full justice to the typical character of research and researchers the sociology of science is taken as the starting point in this chapter. Sociology of science teaches us that the conduct of the producers of research is determined by a number of quite specific norms and values. These norms and values are described in section 1. This is then translated into economic conceptions. Section 2 sets out the characteristics of public goods. Given its sociology of science characteristics, fundamental research generally has the economic characteristic of a public good. One of the problems involved in the provision of such goods is that their efficiency and effectiveness cannot be ascertained in the relatively easy way in which market goods can. The public sector has therefore its own mechanisms of accountability. Production indicators will need to be either pointed out or developed. Section 3 describes the possibilities for measuring production results in the public sector on the basis of micro-economic theories on this subject. In section 4 certain aspects are then applied to the scientific research produced in the public (in this case, university) sector: which indicators are eligible for the measurement of research results, and how, and by whom can they be applied?

3.1 Values and rules of conduct in science

This chapter culminates in an analysis of the various possibilities of indicating the primary outputs of the research system. Before discussing the problems this section deals with the *process* aspect of scientific research: how is the primary output achieved in the research system?

Research is not a normal production process but a search process. Researchers do not carry out their work on an assembly line, they do not work on a prescribed output, sometimes their efforts are based on pure chance; in short: the production process of scientific research is the epitome of a complex and obscure process. Nevertheless, it is referred to as a process, which suggests that that process is regulated in one way or other. In order to find out which regulating mechanisms are in working in the world of research we can take advice from the sociology of science. Science sociologists (including Hagstrom, 1965; Merton, 1973; Gaston, 1978) investigated the question of which unwritten rules of conduct apply to researchers and on which norms and values they are based.

Why do researchers carry out research? What are their driving forces? Assuming that they are rational human beings there must be a certain *reward or exchange mechanism* in working. Gaston (1978, p. 1) describes this reward system as follows: "The reward system in science involves the relationship between how well scientists perform their scientific roles and what they receive for that performance". By the reward system is not meant reward in the restricted sense – financial reward (although this can be a consequence) – but a reward in terms of ultimate motivations: recognition, prestige, status, etc. These are the aspects which are distributed by the scientific community, the forum. However, it must also be pointed out that the 'scientific community' is not an entity but the abstract representation of a large number of sub-communities in (sub)disciplines and their respective forums.

Researchers gain recognition, prestige and status in their discipline the more their colleagues consider them capable of advancing knowledge and insight in their field of study. In order to be able to make such contributions young scientists are socialized in the role of researcher by their more experienced colleagues. This process is in fact no different than the process of socialization a young businessman goes through in trade and industry, or that of the young civil servant in the civil service. The ingenuous learns what the prevailing etiquette is: the written and unwritten rules of the game. The difference between science, trade and industry and the civil service lies in which values are thought the most highly of. The main concerns in business are profit, turnover, market share; in a bureaucratic mechanism the (budgetary) size of the service in which one works, the official position and status, the hierarchical position; in the scientific community one is judged on how he contributes to the relevant discipline or specialism in the form of new theories and/or empirical support in explaining a theory.

Several norms and values are observed in the world of science when striving towards this goal. Merton (1973, p. 267-278) exposed these rules of conduct in describing four basic norms which regulate the conduct of researchers. These four basic norms are: 1) universalism, 2) organized scepticism, 3) communality, and 4) disinterestedness. He who goes against these rules calls upon the wrath of the scientific community. These four basic norms, and the related conduct of researchers, are described as follows.

Universalism implies that no significance at all may be attached to the race, gender, age, religion, political colour, nationality or any other personal trait of a researcher when assessing the value of his or her scientific contribution. Only technical and subject matter criteria are of significance in this assessment process. Universalism also implies that each publication is critically checked by peer review, whether the author is surrounded by an aura of prestige or not. The norm of universalism is linked directly to the fact that scientific knowledge is international by character. Once discovered, a scientific law is accepted worldwide, no matter where that discovery was made. Even though researchers, being human beings, may have chauvinistic traits, when assessing the work of colleagues they must not allow themselves to be prejudiced in any way. Discoveries made by a Russian scientist will also apply in the USA and vice versa. Universalism implies orientation towards the international scientific community. It also implies that contributions published in an international magazine (particularly in a language accepted internationally in the relevant field of science) is held in much higher esteem than contributions in the researcher's national language.

Organized scepticism implies that all scientific claims on research results must be able to withstand the critical inspection of other researchers before one can speak of certified scientific knowledge. It requires that researchers must accept that their statements are subjected to a process of verification. This is the basis of Popper's principle of falsification.

The mirror image of organized scepticism is that a researcher must always present himself as a modest and detached person in the sense that he opens himself up to criticism from his fellow researchers. This reserved attitude is expressed, for example, in formulas such as 'the outcomes of the study are provisional, tentative', 'much more research is needed', etc.

Organized scepticism is also institutionalized in the form of editorial staff and referees of scientific periodicals whose task it is to screen incoming manuscripts. The more severe a periodical's screening procedure is, and the more difficult it is to get one's manuscript accepted, the higher the esteem for that contribution by fellow researchers. Yet the fact that a contribution has been published does not automatically mean that it is true. The researcher can have been mistaken. Editing and refereeing contributions is also the work of man. It is therefore important that all claims and research results, and the way in which they were reached, are always controllable; that they can be tested against the scepticism of fellow researchers.

The criterion of *communality*, is the direct result of the above. Communality, implies that when a researcher makes a scientific contribution he does not attempt to lay individual claim on the underlying new conception, data, theory. The researcher who makes a magnificent discovery and keeps it to himself doesn't count for much. Acquiring prestige among fellow researchers is only possible if a researcher is prepared to stand in the witness box. This is done by publishing his discovery. The other side of the coin is that having done this his fellow researchers can use that material as input for their own work. However, reference should always be made to the source when making appropriate use of the results of other's research. This is the scientific etiquette that applies in exchange for property rights. Quoting another researcher is proof of recognition of his original contribution. In *exchange* for this recognition it is assumed that researchers will not withhold any crucial information about their research, at least for no longer than can be considered reasonable. Communality, promotes efficiency in the research system. It boosts the tempo of scientific progress. There is no need for others to carry out the same research but they can build on the results of research carried out by fellow researchers. The element of exchange when generating research results was formulated by Hagstrom (1965, pp. 12 and 13) as: "Manuscripts submitted to scientific periodicals are often called 'contributions', and they are, in fact, gifts. Authors do not usually receive royalties or other payments, and their institutions may even be required to aid in the financial support of the periodical. On the other hand, manuscripts for which the scientific authors do receive financial payments, such as textbooks and popularizations, are, if not despised, certainly held in much lower esteem than articles containing original research results".

Disinterestedness implies that researchers give priority to the 'scientific interests', the search for truth, above all other considerations; in other words, that these aspects carry far more weight in the totality of their objectives. We have already stated that researchers aspire towards prestige and recognition among fellow researchers. This is not done at any cost: a researcher does not constantly think in terms of which research will gain him the most prestige. The area of conduct possibilities (choice options) is, in fact, very restricted. The conduct of researchers, as so many rationally acting actors in a world of uncertainty, is characterized by satisficing rather than by optimizing. The norm of disinterestedness is not so much connected with the noble characteristics or noble motives of researchers; their disinterestedness is much more a question of quasi-altruism. Researchers are the same as other people; they are driven by a vector of ultimate goals with both good and less pleasing motives, but it is especially a number of "practical principles and objections" which prompts the satisficing conduct of researchers. Three of these can be mentioned.

In the first place, a researcher cannot simply stop work on the research he is conducting to undertake something else which might seem to be more promising. On the one hand this would be a waste, while on the other hand there is a great risk attached: what might seem more promising could lead to nothing. A relatively heavy onus of proof lies on the researcher wishing to switch over to a new, more promising line of research towards the body or bodies making that research possible (external principal, faculty, teaching and research unit, supervising professor, etc.).

In the second place, researchers seldom carry the material baggage (laboratories, data files, etc.) to engage in work in a field other than that in which they are presently engaged.

Thirdly, the intellectual baggage is also often lacking. Although on reflection one can feel that a different problem might be more challenging and important, whether a researcher truly has the capacity to catch up and make a contribution in a different area of research is open to question given the high level of specialism required in modern day research.

The altruistic attitude of researchers is therefore based on several de facto limitations in the options open to them. A continually further disciplinary deepening is thus the best strategy for a researcher to score on the ladder of prestige and recognition. Avoiding risks and disciplinary division are thus the reverse side of disinterestedness.

Together, universalism, organized scepticism, communality and disinterestedness, form a set of values which nurtures a type of researcher conduct functional to disciplinary scientific progress. Disinterestedness implies that the vector of the potential goals of researchers is reduced to such an extent that 'for the sake of science' becomes the main objective. The results which then emerge in consequence are scrutinized by fellow researchers. This is the organized scepticism of the forum of peers. Universalism implies that this peer review is carried out on the content of those results. The personal traits of a researcher are not taken into consideration. This public check by peer review is only possible if researchers choose to divulge their findings through publication, lectures, etc. Fellow researchers can then build further on the results of research that has been made public by making citations or references in their own work. Thus the exchange is complete: the researcher makes his contributions without immediate quid pro quo but with the incentive of gaining his colleagues' esteem and recognition.

Translated into economic terms, an exchange mechanism is also at the basis of the production process of scientific research. This makes it possible to describe researchers as rationally acting actors: they perform with a view to obtaining something in return (esteem, recognition, status). Researchers hope to be quoted; their disinterestedness is a form of quasi-altruism. It is for this reason that researchers do not wish to exclude fellow researchers from becoming acquainted with the results of their work. Publication is therefore in the interests of both the researcher and the scientific community.

Thus, apart from application-oriented research (where patents, licences and other forms of intellectual ownership can be part of market transactions), in the research production process exchanges are not made in terms of quid pro quo of the power of disposal as is the case for market goods. Esteem and recognition cannot be enforced by the research producer. These are always uncertain blessings. In other words the exchange process is imperfect; an imperfection which often makes research – especially fundamental research – a so-called *collective good*. The most obvious characteristic of research as a collective good is the public access to research results. The production of such goods is, as a rule, guaranteed through the budget mechanism. In that case we speak of public goods.

In the next section we shall go more deeply into the specificities (described in economic terms) of public goods. These characteristics are illustrated by examples of various kinds of research.

3.2 The economic public goods theory applied to scientific research

3.2.1 Market goods and public goods

Likewise any other market good the results of research can also be analyzed in terms of supply and demand (demand in the broader sense; the community can also be the demander). The key question for economists is always on the link between supply and demand; in other words, which allocation mechanism is in play.

In principle, every economic order has two mechanisms for the allocation of economic goods: the *market mechanism* and the *budget mechanism*. In order to make a choice between these two mechanisms we first of all have to answer the question whether a good is (or could be) marketable (in the abstract meaning giving to the term by economists), or whether there are any arguments that could be put forward for financing by the general fund. Within the framework of our definition of the problem, the question is whether research is a market good of a public good. At this general level this is a question to which there is no answer. Scientific research is a far too heterogeneous category to be able to do that. Although our intuition clearly tells us that certain application-oriented development work is more than capable of achieving success in a commercial set-up, pure scientific research will often be dependent on state funding. However, intuition alone is inadequate if we have to indicate the most appropriate allocation and funding method for the wide area between these two extremes. In order to make it plausible that it need not be that ideology, force of habit or the issues of the day necessarily have the upper hand in the practical situation, it would seem appropriate to analyze the motives for bringing the budgetary mechanism into effect. Moreover, we follow the economic theory of (quasi) public goods. This theory looks on economic goods on the basis of a taxonomy of two characteristics: *(non-) excludability* and *(non-) rivalry*.

Before discussing these general characteristics of economic goods in more detail and applying them to scientific research we shall first describe them in more detail.

By non-excludability is meant that a producer is not always able to (fully) enforce the right of ownership on production results. Others can get a piece of the pie (make use of the results without being forced to pay). Non-rivalry means that, compared with the demand, the scale of production is so large that additional use of the results, or extra provision of the results, does not result in extra cost, or only to a small extent.

The question of excludability is whether a juridical title can be upheld. If not, the market mechanism cannot be applied. If it can, the question arises whether to implement the market mechanism or whether financing by general funding should be chosen on grounds of policy (concerned with the distribution of incomes for example) or the previously described patterns of motivation according to the sociology of science. The question of which options in respect of provision should be used is therefore ultimately decided by the social objectives.

Excludability is a matter of effectiveness. Rivalry, on the other hand, is an issue of efficiency: with the aid of micro-economics and the welfare theory, an insight can be gained into the pricing of a good, given the specific market and production structure (scale).

These two characteristics will now be dealt with in somewhat more detail in a general sense and subsequently applied more specifically to various forms of scientific research. These facets of rivalry and excludability are illustrated in the table below (adapted from Wolfson, 1988a, p. 19).

DIVISIBILITY OF THE PRODUCTION STRUCTURE (RIVALRY) / EXCLUDABILITY	NO (TO A LIMITED EXTENT)	YES (TO A GREATER EXTENT)
NO (ONLY WITH SOME DEGREE OF DIFFICULTY)	(1) COLLECTIVE GOOD: DIKES, AIR DEFENCE (GOVERNMENT TASK)	
YES (RELATIVELY EASY)	(2a) PRIVATE GOOD: PATENTS (MARKET TASK)	(2b) PRIVATE GOOD: DRIVING LESSONS (MARKET TASK)
	(3a) QUASI-COLLECTIVE GOOD: RESEARCH (?) (GOVERNMENT POLICY)	(3b) QUASI-COLLECTIVE GOOD: EDUCATION (?) (GOVERNMENT POLICY)

The above taxonomy of economic characteristics can provide us with a certain basis on which to determine the mix of mechanisms for justification, regulation and who should bear the cost of scientific research. The proportions of this mix can vary to a great extent depending on the degree of excludability and rivalry. Another factor of importance is that the greater the limitation as regards excludability and rivalry, the less applicable is the market mechanism and the motive for public financing wins in validity. This method is also suitable to make policy-makers aware of the information costs and transaction costs which can be involved in failing to legitimize property rights. A contribution can thus be made to the rationalization of policy options. The method subsequently forces us to indicate, or develop indicators for accountability in those cases where the research production process fails to result in marketable products. This mix of management mechanisms must therefore inevitably latch on to the options available for influencing the input and preconditions (environmental factors) of the production process. Those options relate, for instance, to quality checks of the chosen production factors and the activities during the processing phase (assessment procedures, peer review, the scientific forum, etc.), as well as the assessment of the organization structure (the allocation of relative competences: which management tool at which level?).

The above theories of non-excludability and non-rivalry will now be dealt with in more detail and applied to various forms of research and development.

3.2.2 Non-excludability and externalities

The market mechanism leads to a system of provisions which is based on exchange of power of disposition, claims or property rights. For example, in the transport market travellers exchange money – as an intermediate power of disposition – for train tickets. To ensure the sound working of the market mechanism it is essential to have *exclusive* property rights, i.e. that it must be possible to exclude those who do not wish to pay from making use of those rights (that the passenger without a ticket will be put off the train).

If products can be marketed on an exclusive basis it implies a saving on information costs as to the benefit they provide: the sales results express the benefits derived from the production, and this is also apparent from what the customer is prepared to pay. The sales prices achieved provide information as to the revealed preferences of the users. If the price covers the cost, the continuation of production is guaranteed.

Markets are based on these mechanisms of sounding individualized preferences and by using price control as a method of exclusion. Occasionally the government makes use of the market as a system of provision by implementing the benefit principle for services. That the output of the production process can be determined as physically recognizable units is an *essential condition* for marketability. This condition must be met to make forms of internal settlement possible (among, or in, various government bodies for instance). On the other hand, the level of determinability of the production result is no *adequate condition* for undertaking the introduction of exclusion measures and a system of provision in conformity with the market. There are situations in which, basically, the ownership rights can be made totally exclusive but in which the producer or the government (as the representative of the community) regards such a method of "settlement" as too expensive or undesirable or unsatisfactory. In the restricted sense, exclusion is virtually always possible, also with regard to fundamental knowledge, but this can involve extremely high exclusion costs. Any person, for example, wishing to make use of the formula $E = MC^2$ (Einstein's conclusion from the theory of relativity) could be charged a fee (as a sort of copyright fee). It will be obvious that the implementation of such an option is unrealistic given the high costs involved.

If a production process does not lead to physically recognizable and marketable units of output the market mechanism is unable to guarantee continuity of supply. Although users can take advantage of the production results they cannot be forced to (co)finance them. In such an event we speak of non-excludability. Non-excludability leads to '*externalities*' (spill-overs, third-party effects). Externalities can be described as the positive or negative effects emerging from economic activity external to the individual exchange mechanism, on the production or consumption requirements of other economic actors. Elaborating on the example of the transport market, externalities can be illustrated as follows: the rail network is not only beneficial to the traveller that makes use of the train and purchases a ticket to do so, but also to the motorist who, thanks to those who use the rail services, is less confronted with road congestion and thus requires less time to reach his destination. The latter is a (positive) externality. The quintessential feature of an externality is the lack of a financial settlement. If, in one way or other, the motorist was forced to pay for the indirect benefit he gains from the railways the externality would be eliminated (internalized). Whether or not to take measures to internalize the externalities where possible is a matter of (often implicit) policy considerations.

With regard to goods with positive externalities, if supply and financing is determined completely by the market mechanism it could lead to less than optimal production and higher than optimal price. The case of negative externalities is naturally the counterpart.

Goods with 100% externalities are referred to as *collective goods*. These are goods which offer benefits from which no one can be excluded, moreover, the benefit for the one is not at the expense of the benefit of the other. An often given example of a collective good is the Dutch dike structure. The person refusing to help pay for the upkeep, etc., of such a good cannot be threatened with individual exclusion from this security system. The building and maintenance of dikes is a matter of communal action and financing. In more general terms, the provision of a collective good will therefore not generally be realized through the market mechanism. The appropriate method of financing is some form of apportionment, either voluntary (contributions, donations) or mandatory (taxes). Given that in these cases the validity of the preferences of those who use these goods is not checked out, the possibility is opened for strategic behaviour: the users speculate their need for the good in the knowledge that the cost will be divided among all the members of society. The fact has already been pointed out that although there are also cases where, in principle, exclusion sanctions are possible they are not brought into effect on grounds of policy. In that case, we speak of *quasi-collective goods*. Abandoning the option of implementing sanctions to exclude individuals from use leads to a loss of information regarding the ultimate willingness to pay, and thus possibly to strategic behaviour in order to avoid payment of the individual contribution.

3.2.3 The excludability characteristic applied to scientific research

If we apply the concepts outlined above to scientific research it becomes apparent that as far as the collective aspect is concerned we can distinguish between a number of slightly different forms. The surgeon who describes a new operating technique in 'The Lancet' places the results of his studies at the disposal of his colleagues as a collective good. On the one hand, this emanates from his professional ethics – which rules that for the good of patient care such matters are not withheld (the scientific and social importance of publication), and on the other hand, from the quasi-altruism of researchers to stand in the limelight (the individual advantage of publication; to show that he also counts in the field and therefore does not wish to exclude anyone from becoming knowledgeable of that fact). In research, however, it is slightly more complex if one is a little more closer to the application side. To stay within the realm of medicine let us imagine a medical faculty research group which has developed an improved and less expensive medicine for diabetes. They can take the same course as the surgeon and publish their findings in a medical journal. The pharmaceutical industry can then start production of the drug without the need to pay a licence fee to be allowed to manufacture. In such a case, all diabetics are able to benefit from the results (positive externalities). However, this is not an inherent pure collective good but positive externalities generated by a policy decision. After all, the externality could also have been internalized if the research group had applied for a patent on their discovery. To be able to start production of the medicine in question, the pharmaceutical industry would have had to pay for the patent and could have charged that price on to the users in the cost of the drug. In such a case we can no longer speak of an externality.

In general, the more fundamental the nature of the research and the more uncertain the valuation of the results, the higher the need for public access to the assessment of the quality of that research by fellow-researchers. Conversely, the more research is oriented towards application, the greater the stimulus of the production process thereof if exclusion sanctions can be enforced (patents, licences, right of intellectual property). The connection between the sort of research, the degree of uncertainty, how that uncertainty is dealt with (policy options), the nature of the research as an economic good and the allocation mechanism, is illustrated in the figure below.

kind of research:	fundamental	←——→			application -oriented
relative degree of uncertainty:	large	←——→			small
policy options vis-à-vis the results:	publicness	←——→			protection (establishment of property rights
distinguishing features as economic good:	collective good	←→	quasi-collective good	←→	private good
allocation mechanism:	budget mechanism	←——→			market mechanism

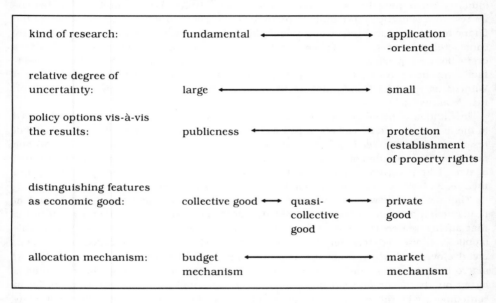

We shall now go deeper into the case of research as a collective good.

Research as collective good

The characteristics of a collective good are very much present in pure scientific research. This type of research is not (primarily) application-oriented. Generally speaking it is impossible to know ex ante whether the activities will result in marketable results, the cost of which can be made good by charging a price. In other words, the output of the production process cannot be predicted from the inputs. Risk and uncertainty is a substantial component in the production process. This implies that to be able to establish and promote scientific progress it is essential that researchers publish their results. When all is said and done researchers could still withhold their discoveries from the scientific forum but they would in that case be shirking out of the production of knowledge. It would then be impossible to verify whether there is an advancement in the state of knowledge. Verification is lacking and, as explained above, publicness is more important in the case of fundamental research than applied research given that the value of the research results is surrounded with so much more uncertainty. This makes it even more important that the results achieved in research can be either confirmed or disproved by other groups working in the same field. The veracity of the research is thus benefited. Given that publicness is an inherent component of the production process of fundamental research, this type of research is typified as a collective good.

Although influenced by the tendency to shorten the knowledge path (from discovery to application), we could say that trade and industry is showing more interest in fundamental research (biotechnology for instance) only few companies are willing to finance fundamental research themselves. One exception here is the large multinationals, which work on such a scale that the fruits of fundamental research can sometimes be internalized. The Netherlands has no tradition of private organizations, financed either by individuals and/or industry, concerning themselves in this area (as in the USA). In the Netherlands fundamental research is carried out mainly in (para) university institutions. The lion's share of the financing is by public funds. Government, as the largest societal collectivity, is apparently considered the most capable to bear the financial risks of such research. Co-financing does occur however, particularly in the field of medical research, from funds which are maintained through private gifts and donations, such as the *Koningin Wilhelminafonds* (Queen Wilhelmina Fund for Cancer Research) or the *Nierstichting* (Foundation for Research on Renal Diseases).

In addition to the above argumentation a different one has been developed with regard to the humanities as to why research has the nature of a collective good. Certain kinds of research can be regarded as a cultural good and can be put on a par with certain artistic products. The valuation of works of art is also uncertain and only develops over the course of time. Like government grants for the preservation of museums, the opera and genre theatre, it also has a similar function in respect of certain types of research.

The above dealt with the ex ante vagueness as to the (valuation of the) output of fundamental research. A second, related argument in favour of government involvement is that such research is essential in order to continue generating immediately applicable (application-oriented) research. Pure scientific research is therefore regarded as a societal, creative overhead which functions as a breeding ground for technological innovation. At macro-level this argument is also used as the motive for public funding. This reasoning is based on the *linear innovation model* (science – technology – market). Conversely, in contemporary literature on innovation, emphasis is laid on the *interactive model* of many links between science and the market sector. Rosenberg, on the basis of several examples (including the development of an aircraft), made a reasonable case that technology development is often ahead of fundamental research and that in many cases fundamental research plays a role in the underpinning of technological progress. In other words: technology development is increasingly setting the scientific agenda (instead of the other way around).

Within the sphere of government, TNO and the large institutes of technology (so-called GTI's) are examples of organizations which demand a solid fundamental basis to be able to fulfil their primary mission of carrying out applied research. The government guarantees this in the form of the base subsidy to TNO and grants for background research to the GTI's. In doing this, government expresses the social value it attaches to the existence of these institutions between universities on the one hand and commercial research institutes on the other.

Fundamental research is also carried out in commercial research institutes and (especially large) companies in the form of background research. In this respect the results are not of direct benefit to an external or internal principal. There are various reasons why this background research is considered essential. It can serve to keep the level of knowledge of the institute or research department up to date and also function as the basis for procuring new assignments. Such research is then regarded as a necessary investment to be able to continue to generate tangible results in the long term. Maintaining the level of such capital-intensive investment is a matter of 'good business practice'. In the case described above the risks attached to fundamental research can be limited to the unit in question. The financing of this research is not primarily a matter for the community but a problem of internal pricing of a business.

Research as a quasi-collective good

Research as a quasi-collective good with positive externalities can be envisaged, for example, at industrial branch level. A certain research effort can be of definitive significance for maintaining the level of external competitive power of an industrial branch as a whole. The realization of that effort is a collective good for that branch of industry. It is especially the structure of the branch which is the decisive factor as to whether that good will be realized or not. If the branch in question is typified by the existence of a single, or only a few, large companies which are faced with fierce international competition, these companies generally feel pressurized into making the required research effort under their own steam. Special governmental stimuli are, as a rule, unnecessary. This is the case in the main Dutch multinationals. A special motive for the government to grant financial support can lie in the aim towards avoiding that the multinational in question misses the boat as regards a major innovative development and thus prevent the competitor from building up a monopoly position.

Another extreme is a branch of industry comprising a large number of companies, all of which are too small to provide an adequate basis for the required research effort. In this case the atomistic structure induces *collective research*. A successful example of such a branch of industry which, thanks to its collective research structure, operates innovatively and competitively, is the agricultural sector. In so far as government subsidies are not forthcoming for this collective research it is referred to as a 'club good' and the only issue relevant here is how the costs are realized by the group that benefits.

The problem of attaining an adequate level of research effort is apparently the most evident in those branches of industry which, in terms of market structure, are positioned somewhere between the two extremes outlined above. On the one hand there is too much competition to organize the teamwork required to carry out research in all the companies of that branch, and on the other hand, the individual companies are too small in relation to the total size of the market to be able to form a sufficient basis for the research effort without joining forces.

Government mainly becomes involved in application-oriented research if the relevant risks and uncertainties form a threat to industrial activity. Risk and uncertainty play a major role in the implementation of research results in a product or production process. Only a relatively small number of discoveries are eventually found suitable for commercially successful application (sometimes only after a few decades). The financial risks of unsuccessful research can form an obstacle for industry in maintaining an adequate effort in the area of product and process innovation. Other than is the case in pure scientific research it would seem at first sight that (total) financing by the government is by no means an automatic procedure. The government could suffice with forms of risk sharing. For example, this could be done in the form of a contract (cf. the incentive contracts used in the USA for defence projects; see Moore, 1967). Government can also offer risk capital (e.g. development loans). Other methods to reduce the market risk for the innovative entrepreneur are: subsidizing research costs (e.g. the INSTIR subsidy scheme, a scheme provided by the Ministry of Economic Affairs to stimulate innovation), domestic market protection measures or guaranteeing a slice of the market via the government's acquisition policy. We can also refer in this context to the United States of America, where government defence orders provide business concerns with the opportunity to develop advanced products with a guaranteed sale and limited financial risks.

3.2.4 Non-rivalry

If definability and excludability (in the sense described above) of production do not give rise to problems one can generally charge a price for the product. However, charging a price can be rather complex if users exert a non-rival demand on the production result. *Non-rivalry* is when little or no extra costs (marginal costs) ensue from additional usage of the capacity of a facility due to an extra user. Such a situation arises in the event of lumpiness in the production structure and can be illustrated by the example of the railway network. The railway network is faced with two quite different problems of rivalry. If we distinguish between the normal network and the intercity network we see that the normal network is faced with a problem of structural over-capacity and the intercity network with a peak-hour problem. For the normal network the rivalry problem is the result of a technical lower limit: many lines can easily cope with the daily peak; they are structurally loss-making given that, because of technical indivisibility, it is impossible to reduce the supply (as long as there is a connection, at least one line is essential).

Conversely, the intercity network is not loss-making. Here the problem is not one of technical indivisibility leading to a structural non-rivalry of transportation claims, but a rush hour problem. Seat occupancy goes through a daily cycle of off-peak - peak - off-peak - peak - off-peak. There is a fluctuation in claim and rivalry over the course of time. Such services are referred to as *'part-collective goods'* (Tinbergen, 1984). The solution to the peak problem lies in weakening the sine curve of seat occupancy by implementing a system of differentiated fares (cheap-rate tickets, etc.).

Rivalry is concerned with the optimal control of the *usage* of a good. As a rule this is dependent upon correct pricing. The traditional comparative-static price theory prescribes the rule of marginal costs: the price of a good should be based on the marginal costs. Why the marginal costs and not the average total costs or average variable costs for example? The answer lies in the idea that the function of the price system is to have some form of control over the allocative decisions taken by both consumers and producers, and to bring these decisions in line at the optimal point in society. This search for an equilibrium is made in the form of marginal decisions, i.e. decisions concerning the question whether the consumer or the producer will or will not expand his consumption or production respectively by a single (theoretically infinitesimal) unit of product (Wolfson, 1988, p. 59). The point of departure for the analysis is the pure form of a market of absolute open competition. In this model it is assumed that because of the fierce competition producers will not be able to influence prices. They adapt to quantity; i.e. they will continue to produce extra units of product as long as the costs involved (marginal costs) remain below the current price.

In a situation of pure non-rivalry the marginal costs are zero: the train still has to travel from a to b; why charge an extra passenger if the train isn't full? In this case the marginal costs rule leads to the conclusion that setting tariffs would be ineffective given that (extra) use does not give rise to additional cost. The consistent application of the rule of marginal costs would lead to financing the provision by public funding given that it is socially unacceptable to charge the present user for the continuity of an existing basic capacity.

The comparative-static theory of pricing is by nature only partial; it is only valid for short-term market equilibrium. Adding dynamism to the definition of the problem brings up the question of how depreciation and the running costs of such services can be recovered if they are not (fully) brought up by the group that makes use of that service given that the continuity of the financing is thus endangered (cf. Demsetz, 1969 and Wolfson, 1981 and 1988). This problem is most evident in exclusive, and consequently tariffable supply situations, where high research and development costs were involved. Implementation of the rule of marginal costs and the financing of such a provision from public funds also has major administrative consequences. These relate particularly to the lack of 'sound', obvious information as to the consumers' valuation (in the form of a price that one wishes to pay). The lack of such information can frustrate the verification of policy options when setting up the provision (cf. Wolfson, 1981, p. 8-11). This is a factor which is not taken into account in the traditional theory of pricing because it simply assumes that information is available free of charge.

The rule of marginal costs therefore offers only a guide-line for the short term assuming that the capacity of a provision is a constant factor. This does not allow us to escape from the policy dilemma that depreciation and running costs are not recovered by those benefiting from that provision if the fixed prices fail to cover the costs. If we were to accept that the deficits were compensated out of public funds, or satisfy ourselves with complete public funding, then we simply deprive ourselves of the possibility of using prices as an instrument of preference identification and exclusion sanctions. Against this background, the literature has volunteered various options to cut back on the losses. The option that least violates the rule of marginal costs is price differentiation. This can be applied if the production of a provision is linked with a varying degree of utilization and the demand depends on different categories of users (cf. Oort, 1958). This approach emerges from the (welfare) theory of *the second best* (cf. Lipsey and Lancaster, 1956) which comes far closer to the real situation than the free market competition model by assuming segmented markets and partial competition. By adopting a range of tariffs one can obtain the best of both worlds by recovering the costs (as much as possible) from the user groups. The numerous fare systems in force by NS (Netherlands Rail) in the form of different season-tickets, cheap-rate tickets, weekend return tickets, family tickets, student rail tickets, senior citizens rates, etc., and by the airline companies are the most obvious examples of this.

The (potential) benefit from fixed rates must obviously be constantly balanced against the respective exclusion costs (the ticket collector's salary, the ticket clerk's salary, etc). This applies à fortiori to price differentiation: the complexity of the tariff structure will have to be set off against the costs borne by the users and the producer in connection with obtaining or providing information.

In those cases where it is impossible to apply a system of price differentiation, the literature (Hotelling, 1938) suggests the option of adding a proportional, extra charge to the marginal costs as a reasonable compromise between the marginal costs rule – which applies to the short term – and the long-term consideration which prescribes cost-covering. The underlying idea is that distorted marginal costs still form a better basis than a fundamentally wrong one such as the average costs.

3.2.5 *The rivalry characteristic applied to scientific research*

As we have already seen, the question of rivalry is primarily one of optimal pricing. However, we must distinguish between the long term and the short term.

Considering long-term pricing the first question that arises is whether the operation can be expected to run profitably. If this is not the case then we must opt for a pricing system and tariff structure that will keep down the losses. In the case of research organizations aiming at carrying out contracted research it is therefore appropriate to increase the marginal costs when setting prices. This increase offers the best possible way of recovering the investment costs. On-charging of investment costs must be based on a level of utilization which can be regarded as normal with a view to the market structure and market situation. Some aspects do not apply to research institutes alone but equally to universities where personnel and material is made available for contracted research.

Short-term pricing can be done on a basis of the marginal costs rule. In situations where there is only an occasional call made on the existing (over) capacity, the double cost of providing staff and materials for research can be less. However, the tariff policy must take into account those costs of potential disturbances in competitiveness (social costs) which fall outside the business economic calculation.

The above was based on situations where exclusive research results are generated and as a rule can be offset by payment from a third party. In many cases, especially when concerned with fundamental research, this will not be the case. The basic norm of the public nature of research results in the production of fundamental research not generally being left to the market mechanism. Fundamental research in the Netherlands is funded for more than 85% by government. This government-funded fundamental research is carried out for a good 80% in universities and it is this category of research which is the subject of this study.

3.2.6 *Scientific research as a public good*

Based on the above we can explain in short when it is theoretically possible to produce scientific research for the market or when there is a valid motive for the production of research in the public sector. The criterion for guaranteeing the continuity of a marketed economic good is that a price can be charged on to the users of that good or those who benefit from it. When applying this criterion it becomes apparent that fundamental scientific research can not as a rule be produced as a market good given that it is essential for research results to be made public for the reason of peer review. The economic criterion of non-excludability is therefore intrinsic to the nature of the production process of this sort of research. Should an exclusion sanction be enforced it would be impossible to establish whether there is a cumulation of knowledge. Additionally, given the non-competitive nature of knowledge, the application of an exclusion sanction would be inefficient as the social value would then be lost. This potential benefit for those who would like to become acquainted with that knowledge, but who are unable to afford it, is referred to as deadweight loss or deadweight burden.

However, in those cases of research which by nature are not necessarily collective goods, and where it is feasible for a price to be charged for research results, there can also be motives for public supply (research as a quasi-collective good). In the first place, the (potential) proceeds from charging a price must be weighed against the related exclusion costs. Account must also be taken with those costs ensuing from disturbances in competitiveness (social costs) which fall outside the business economic calculation. Also, when implementing price differentiation the proceeds from a segmented tariff structure will need to be weighed against the information costs of the users and producers resulting from such a complex structure.

Finally, it should be pointed out that the possibilities of charging a price for the results of research is limited by the personal nature of those results. Scientific knowledge is not only embodied in economic goods but in human capital as well. And humans are free beings. If a nation, or organization, strives towards an all too rigid total covering of the cost of producing research results by charging users and others who benefit from those results, it could happen that not the research products will leave the country or organization at a price, but the researchers themselves. In order to prevent a brain-drain it is essential that tariff policy and job motivation are brought into line (think of the debate on the issue of who should receive any financial proceeds from the publications of researchers in the employ of a university). That institutions created in an adequate fashion should take into account the behavioural reactions of the actors also applies here.

Up to now we have treated research as an independent category. We can also regard university research as input for university education (teaching and research as the warp and weft of the same fabric). The motive of externalities, on which government funding of university education is based, is thus also extended, mutatis mutandis, to university research. These two motives for government funding of university research are expressed in the fact that the financing mechanism is partly student-dependent and partly student-independent. See Ritzen (1988) for a more indepth explanation of the consequences of these two motives.

In conclusion, we see a number of quite valid motives that can be put forward as to why scientific research will be produced as a pure or quasi-collective good in the public sector. On the basis of insights offered by the micro-economic theory on this subject the following section goes more deeply into how, in general, the production processes and production results can be dimensioned in the public sector where there is a lack of 'sound' market standards as data carriers. In other words: which indicators can be used in the public sector within the framework of justifying, controlling and managing the processes? In section 4 certain aspects are applied to the research production process in the public sector. What standards are conceivable in which accountability can be given for creativity? How can monitoring and accountability be organized? Also dealt with in this section is the value of indicators such as published articles, defended dissertations, citations, and other proof of quantitative interprofessional verification. The limitations of such standards are also discussed. In the assessment of research processes and results there will always need to be sufficient leeway available for incommensurable elements.

This brings us yet again to the adequate institutionalization of the research system: with a view to the fact that the production of research is impossible to control by a top-down approach with the assistance of 'sound' output criteria, there is a need for actors at various levels that are capable of handling information pertinent to their own level.

3.3 A micro-economic approach to production processes in the public sector

In production processes resources (inputs) are transformed into results (outputs). Inputs are labour and material resources which can be broken down further and placed in categories. A price can be charged on these different physical inputs. In business economics terminology we then speak of type of cost. The goal of production processes is adding value. The question whether this goal will be achieved is the easiest to answer if the results are traded on a market. The proceeds from the results can then be compared with the cost of the required inputs. The added value is the profit. In this case of market goods the value can normally be read from the revealed valuation of the users/payers.

If production processes do not lead to results that can be traded on a market, then the value of those results – and thus the added value – cannot be determined accurately. In that case, it is also far more difficult to quantitatively underpin conclusions with regard to productivity, efficiency and effectiveness. This problem is characteristic of the production processes in the public sector. Given that the university system falls within the scope of dimensioning and evaluating production processes in the public sector, this subject will be dealt with in the remainder of this section. Micro-economic insights will be used to investigate which production standards are possible in the public sector.

When searching for such standards the first place to look is in the statistics. Government production is part and parcel of the National Accounts of the CBS (Central Statistical Office). The CBS 'solved' the problem of evaluation by equating the production value of the public sector to the cost of the means of production (output = input). The added value is thus by definition zero. Such implementation of statistics is inadequate for our purpose. It provides us with no information whatever as to the results of the production processes we are interested in, how these results are realized, and how they are valued by the users/stakeholders. Nor can questions as to efficiency and effectiveness of production processes in the public sector be answered satisfactorily with this approach.

An additional complication that can arise in respect of quantification in this most primitive approach to value assessment in the public sector emerges if different (categories of) results are produced within a single production process. For example, this is the case in respect of universities which, as a result of their legally established goal, produce both research and education as the warp and weft of the same fabric. What then is the value (cost) of education, and what is the value of research? In the CBS system this problem is solved by taking the personnel effort as the standard and then assigning it to the two output categories mentioned above. Assignment is based on surveys held among university staff into how their time is spent. However, these surveys are only held every ten years, implying that assignment in the years between must be viewed with caution. The most recent survey (1982/1983) showed that the time spent by university staff on research had increased to 50%, approximately 9% more than in 1972/1973. This resulted in a break in the statistics.

The use of statistics is both appropriate and necessary. Yet they serve statistical goals. Measuring *inputs* can not, however, provide information about production *processes* (performance, activities) or the *results* (outputs) thereof, let alone information about the *effects* (outcome) on the users of the results and the *valuation* of those effects. The latter relates to a 'subjective perception', something that the actors (users) have and which cannot be measured. Activities, results and effects form three alternative measuring points to indicate the output of production processes in the public sector. The corresponding indicators are referred to as process indicators, performance indicators and effect indicators.

Such indicators serve to bridge the gap between theory and empiricism. The various alternatives are shown in the figure below which illustrates the transformation processes in the valuation procedure (adapted version, derived from Wolfson, 1988, p. 320).

VALUE TRANSFORMATION PROCESS / APPROACH	PRODUCTION HOUSEHOLDS →				CONSUMER HOUSEHOLDS
BUSINESS ADMINISTRATION	CAPACITY →	ORGANIZATION ACTIVITIES →	PROJECT/ PROGRAMME →	USERS →	THOSE WHO DERIVE PLEASURE
ECONOMICS	TYPE OF COST →	COST CENTRES →	COST OBJECT →	BENEFIT →	UTILITY
SYSTEM THEORY	MEANS USED (INPUT) →	PRODUCTION PROCESS (THROUGHPUT) →	RESULT (OUTPUT) →	EFFECT (OUTCOME) →	SATISFACTION
	- labour - equipment	- literature read - congresses attended	- scientific articles - books	- citations - applications	
INDICATORS	INPUT INDICATORS →	PROCESS INDICATORS →	PERFORMANCE INDICATORS →	EFFECT INDICATORS	

Before dealing with the differences between process, performance and effect indicators it must be pointed out that each of these indicators must satisfy a common criterion for them to be used as the output standard in an empirical demand analysis or in a process of allocation and management of budgetary means. This common criterion is that the indicator must be linked to a controllable variable. In this context *controllability* is seen as the power to ensure that a process runs parallel to its objectives (Wolfson, 1988, p. 92). Two important variables are involved in controlling a process: *observability* and *controllability*. Observability implies that the variables can be observed and measured. The criterion of controllability goes one step further. It implies that an output standard can serve as a control variable in decision-making on the allocation and control of the production process. An appropriate indicator must therefore be able to serve as an instrument for measurement and control.

A *process indicator* describes either certain productive actions (activities in the production process) or a certain intermediate or semi-manufactured product. Measurements could, for instance, be the number of house calls, the number of passengers, the number of operations, the number of trees planted, etc. Such an indicator is thus related to the production process as such. In some cases production processes are aimed at maintaining the provision of a service. The availability of the *capacity* is then the main objective, as applies to the fire brigade. In such cases activity and performance go hand in hand. A process indicator is thus a suitable variable for indicating the value of availability. The main point is that the fire brigade exists – in case of emergency – and not how many times it's called out.

Process indicators in scientific research are, for example, the number of books and articles one has read, or the number of congresses one has participated in. These are activities which are of importance in maintaining the level of one's knowledge. In the production process therefore they are essential steps in order to be able to generate results.

yet it is not the results in themselves that research organizations aim for in pursuing their goal. Apart from such a case where the goal of an organization is aimed at the availability of a capacity, process indicators are therefore unsuitable to be used as the markers for production results. We are thus left with two ways in which to determine the results of public services:

a) by quantifying the goods and services produced; the *performance* (results) produced;
b) by quantifying the *effects* resulting from that performance or which can be expected from that performance.

In the former we refer to *performance indicators*, in the latter, to *effect indicators*.

The difference between performance and the effect produced by performance is – following Bradford, Malt and Oates (1969) – referred to in the literature as the D-output and C-output. The D- or *direct* output is the end product as produced by the production economic unit, while the C- or *effective* output relates to the usage in which the consumer households are interested. As used here, the term *consumer households* covers not only consumer households but also other production households using the product (the D-output) of the production households in question as input (in statistics terminology the latter refers to intermediate supplies). Consumers are therefore customers – whether they are paying customers or not.

In the case of the product 'research' relatively little is supplied direct to consumer households (non-specialist articles in newspapers and magazines, for instance); research results are mostly used at an earlier stage along the knowledge path as input for other production households. This use by other production households can be in the form of:

- another researcher making reference to an article, book, etc.;
- patents, licences, programmes, etc., being purchased;
- companies implementing a discovery (product development).

From the above examples we see that usage by subsequent production households along the knowledge path sometimes has to be paid for. That producers of research often make their products available free of charge can be due to the 'technical' difficulties involved (implementation would involve prohibitively high costs) or that asking for a fee is regarded as inexpedient (publicness; see section 2). The implication of this in economic terms is that research is characterized as a (quasi) collective good.

The difference given above between activities, results and effects can be illustrated by the production of transport services by the railway. The most important activity of the organization in this example is to ensure that trains are run from a to b, etc. The total number of kilometres a train travels should then be able to serve as a process indicator. Activities are concerned with the alternatives (a combination of production factors) for generating results. The number of ticket inspectors can be reduced and the finances subsequently available becoming available are used to put in extra trains, or vice versa.

The results are concerned with the railway's primary output: not the number of trains in service but the number of passengers transported (differentiated in accordance with distance travelled). A good performance indicator is the number of passenger-kilometres produced. This is the D-output; the variable which the organization can use to express its production results.

The next question is what effect this variable has on the utility functions of the users. The consumer households' demand for transport services is determined by the effects expected from the D-output. The C-output, for example, is concerned with transportation over a specific distance as quickly as possible. This is co-decisive for the user when deciding whether to take the train or other means of transport. D- and C-outputs are interrelated, but the relation is not mono-causative. Other (closely-related) factors also influence the C-output: if the train is delayed due to bad weather there is no change to the D-output but the C-output is reduced.

If we wish to construct an effect indicator in this example we could take the number of passenger-kilometres divided by the cumulated travelling time. By using such an effect indicator, the output required by consumer households can be *objectified*. This is essential because the ultimate individual users' evaluation – the degree of satisfaction one experiences from the train journey – has a subjective character and is therefore unsuitable for use as a variable in an empirical study. In this context Wolfson (1988, p. 13) differentiates between two concepts of utility:

a. *utility* as subjective rationalization: the individual *subjective experience of utility* (satisfaction) by virtue of the 'internal terms of exchange' used by actors to order their preferences; and
b. utility as a positivistic, falsifiable concept: *benefit* as *objectifiable* 'external terms of exchange' as apparent from the price ratios in trade.

This objective concept of benefit is important when selecting or constructing an effect indicator. Falsifiable elements in the perception of bridging distances must be objectified as well as possible. In other words: they must be expressed in size and number. In the above example we suggested inclusion of travelling time in the indicator. The effect indicator could be differentiated even further on a basis of the comfort experienced (if this is objectifiable): has the passenger travelled first or second class?

As stated earlier, there is a link between the performance (D-output) produced by an organization and the effects of that performance (objectified valuation of usefulness; C-output), but that this is not mono-causative. In addition to the transformation process on the supply side (from means to performance), which can be described with the assistance of a production function, a transformation process also takes place on the demand side. This second process of transformation (from performance to effect) can be described with the assistance of a household production function. Such a function illustrates that the effect of the goods and services used in a household will depend on:

a) environmental factors;
b) skills (capabilities or functions) of the user (cf. Sen, 1985);
c) the specific purpose of a good or service in the household process.

Let us explain these three factors in short.

We can illustrate the significance of *environmental factors* by using the police services as an example (cf. Clotfelder, 1977). Suppose that a crime index is used as the effect indicator. It is important that not only the police performance and market substitutes (the D-output that forms the input for the household transformation process) are taken into account but also the environmental factors which have an influence on the crime level as recorded in the statistics, e.g. changes in population composition, the general economic conditions, the attitude of civilians (proportion of law-abiding citizens), etc. In the 'ideal' effect indicator a correction will therefore have to have been made to allow for such environmental factors if we are to obtain a reliable picture.

An empirical example of such an approach is to be seen in the series of studies carried out by the Netherlands Sociaal en Cultureel Planbureau (Social and Cultural Planning Office) and Centraal Planbureau (Central Planning Office) into usage indicators of public services. If, for example, one attempts to establish the effectiveness of the health services over a period of time, a measured worsening of the average health of the population is adjusted to the level of the ageing population (cf. SCP/CPB, 1986, p. 21). Another example is given by Van de Kar (1987, p. 87), namely: government policy aimed at increasing road safety, in which among other measures subsidies are granted to organizations to provide information about road safety. The number of informative meetings or pamphlets distributed could serve as process indicators in this context. The ultimate policy effect could be indicated, for example, by a weighted average of the number of road accidents in each period. The causal relationship between this latter index number and the number of pamphlets distributed is in actual fact virtually impossible to establish given that road safety is quite obviously influenced by numerous other factors. Therefore, if the indicator of the number of road accidents is not adjusted for these environmental factors it is a performance indicator and not an effect indicator.

If we want to avoid premature policy conclusions, the influence of these environmental factors must be indicated by showing the changes in the most influential factor(s). In the case of road safety this could be traffic density, for instance, or changes in the average annual alcohol consumption per capita. An effect indicator can be constructed by taking these factors into account.

Different consumer households will evaluate the same supply of goods and services differently given that they each have different skills. The person who has not learned to listen to classical music, or who has a hearing problem, or simply dislikes classical music, will derive less pleasure from a performance of Don Giovanni than the true lover of opera. Differences in the individual evaluation of an achievement or performance can only be objectified in part. Effect indicators can hardly take individual differences in taste into account. Categorial, group differences in skills (e.g. the educational or language disadvantage of ethnic minorities, disability) can be objectified. One example is to break down government-subsidized opera visits into the various categories of the population (social class, age, sex, region, etc.). Does cultural dissemination really exist? The collection of such differentiated data makes it possible to retrace government policy.

Finally, the specific destination of a good or service in the housekeeping process is of importance in a household production function. This insight originates from the modern theory of consumption wherein goods and services are seen as sets of characteristics (cf. Lancaster, 1971). These characteristics are the different features of a good or service to which the consumer households attach value (utility in an objectified sense). Both privately and publicly produced goods and services can have several functions which can be fulfilled simultaneously (the motorcar as means of transport and the motorcar as status symbol, the train as means of transport and the train as providing the opportunity to read through documents, the telephone to both make and receive telephone calls) or to the exclusion of the other (the newspaper which has to be saved so that it can be re-read at a later date cannot be used as wrapping paper). It is these functions that create the demand for the good or service, either individually or in combination. Different consumer households can therefore strive towards different effects when acquiring goods and services, either individually or over a period of time. Also, the one function can be exclusive by nature (the dam as motorway; exclusion is possible) while the other function can be non-exclusive (the dam as sea wall; exclusion is not possible).

The above makes it clear that extremely stringent criteria must be set in respect of effect indicators. The question then is whether we cannot suffice by measuring performance. This is a method considered satisfactory in the market sector and is based on spontaneous feedback of information from users who have paid their dues. If, contrary to what one is promised, the new detergent does not wash whiter, the consumer will think twice the next time. The purchasing conduct thus revealed does give a good indication of the consumer's valuation of a product in the market sector. Hence there is no reason for us to delve deeper into the household transformation process from result to effect.

The budgetary mechanism does however have a handicap here given that the effectiveness of public services cannot be accessed in the same way as in the market sector. Moreover, public services are not generally under pressure from a competitive supply and the feedback via the opinions of the electorate is not geared towards the evaluation of specific public services but to a large package of facilities (the political programme you choose once every so often).

Conclusion: in the market sector the indication of performance is generally sufficient; in the public sector, however, there are sound reasons for also gathering indications as to the ultimate effects brought about by the production processes.

The next section will deal with the system of concepts developed above, geared towards scientific research produced in the public (in this case: university) sector.

3.4 Output indicators in the scientific research production process

Since the sixties we have seen an international increase of interest shown in the development of output indicators for scientific research, the so-called *science indicators*. This development started with the international accurate and comparable definition of inputs but over the years the trend has turned more towards 'performance indicators' (results and effects). The OECD (OECD, 1980) has had a pioneering role in this.

Although interest in science indicators was relatively slow to take off in the Netherlands it was nevertheless quite distinct. The RAWB and a research group at the University of Leiden (Moed, et al., 1983; 1989; supported financially by NWO and the Directorate General for Science Policy of the Ministry of Education and Science) deserve special mention in this context.

Interest in research performance received a strong stimulus in the Netherlands through the implementation of the so-called conditional funding of university research. Through the introduction of this scheme, the minister presented the universities with the prospect of budgetary reallocation among the various universities on a basis of research performance (productivity, quality). In the policy paper entitled 'Higher Education; Autonomy and Quality' (Ministry of Education and Science, 1985) the minister pressed for the development of evaluation criteria as a necessary means to establish the quality of the products of the universities. The minister himself then set the example by initiating the first HOOP (Higher Education and Research Plan) (Ministry of Education and Science, 1987a): in the HOOP addendum Proeven en Achtergronden (Tests and Backgrounds) (p. 150-152) the Ministry needed all the letters of the alphabet to list a wide range of different indicators. These indicators by the way refer to education, research and personnel (percentage of female research personnel, for example), the latter being input indicators and not performance indicators. The science indicators in this alphabet relate especially to the number of theses, number of research products, how much NWO research and how much externally assessed research within the framework of the conditional funding scheme.

Finally, it must be pointed out that in recent years a number of disciplinary evaluating committees have taken to measuring outputs in scientific research. These reports fuelled the debate on the practicability of output indicators in scientific research. The most significant conclusion to be drawn from this is that consensus among fellow researchers as to the primary communication media in their discipline is a prerequisite which must be met by judging quality on a basis of bibliometric material.

It was pointed out earlier in this chapter that the quality of scientific output can seldom be judged as 'good' in the short term. Studies have shown that it sometimes takes many decades before a scientific result is rated at its true value, at least from the present perspective. Philosopher of science, Lakatos, spoke in this context of a minimum period of fifty years. However, outside the philosophical framework it is of little use to study the quality of scientific work from an angle of eternal value. Decisions have to be made daily on scientific quality by scientists themselves, and also by those engaged in decision-making on policy and management at various levels. It is against this background that we investigate in this section which performance and effect indicators are conceivable in scientific research and discuss the pros and cons of those indicators. On a basis of this analysis we end with the conclusion that there is apparently no single indicator which is suitable as the *only* management variable in the process of (allocation) decisions in research. All indicators appear to be defective to a greater or lesser extent. In short, when measuring research performance we may not suffice with either a weighted or unweighted number of publications, number of pages or number of citations as the only standard in the same way as the production result of the bicycle factory can be measured by the number of different types of bicycles produced.

"Scientific output is the whole of scientific knowledge ensuing from research, presented in such a *form* that it is accessible to others" (ZWO, 1979, p. 45). This definition makes it clear that knowledge which is not shared with others leads to a scientific output of zero. With regard to the form, it is important to point out that this is closely connected with the goal and nature of the research in question and cannot therefore be established on a universal scale. The research project, discipline, or type of research organization determines the appropriateness of the form of the unit of output.

Usually, the less market-oriented the goals or tasks (or in other words: the reason for carrying out research) *of a research organization, and thus the more fundamental the nature of the type of research will be, the more the most appropriate indicator is likely to be an effect indicator rather than performance indicator.*

It is important to stress this pattern given that many actors, particularly those working in the field of less market-oriented research, are not sufficiently aware of this (e.g. faculties deploying a simple performance indicator in their annual report as the unweighted total number of publications over the relevant year and, in the event of an increase in that variable, conclude that the research production in that faculty has increased).

The pattern formulated above is best illustrated by TNO and other application-oriented and market-oriented research organizations. The goal of such organizations is to perform applied research, preferably for existing customers (or to go out and search for new customers). The research carried out in these organizations is geared towards finding new applications, developing prototypes (product development), etc. Although their findings can be published (this is not always the case: aspects of secrecy) the goals of such organizations are not oriented towards publication. A patent, or a protected form of intellectual property is in this context a more appropriate variable against which to measure output. Given that this part of the knowledge path borders directly on the market, an indicator, such as the yield from assignments or cooperation agreements, is the most suitable for implementation as the performance indicator. Because the market mechanism works here, the research organization has a direct, obvious indication of the effects of its products. In other words, there is little reason to worry about separate effect indicators.

Although the differences between university and non-university research are by no means absolute (and seem to diminish in recent years) it can be stated that the research goals of the university system are to be found more in the sphere of fundamental research. This means that research is also partly embodied in trained people and thus leaves the organization via a teaching output variable. As a rule, universities operate in an early stage of the knowledge path, which does not border directly on the market. Nevertheless, there are obviously certain developments which can be directly applied in industry or elsewhere. However, this is more the exception than the rule. It is also of importance that the university goal for each discipline has a different accent; we will return to this at a later stage in this section.

What then are feasible performance indicators in the university research system? To answer this question we shall discuss the pros and cons of a number of performance and effect indicators based on the studies and reports referred to above.

Publications are usually referred to as the most important performance indicator. Other examples of potential performance indicators, which we will not deal with here, are:

- lectures one has given;
- congresses one has organized;
- editorship of journals.

Publications form an extremely heterogeneous category. Every publication (category) differs from the next. To be able to develop a performance indicator an assessment of quality will need to take place. The question here is to what extent can quality be objectified; be expressed in size and number. Past attempts to achieve this show that little consensus has been achieved on this matter, even though this process takes place within one discipline (and the problem of comparing apples and oranges is thus brought down to the disciplinary level).

The first step to be taken to objectify the value of publications is to make a break down into several rough publication categories:

1 theses;
2 books;
3 edited compiled works;
4 reprints;
5 articles in scientific journals;
6 articles in non-specialist magazines (i.e. other than scientific journals);
7 reports (research memoranda, working papers, etc.);
8 annotations, etc., (of particular importance in the juridical discipline);
9 book reviews.

Generally speaking there is no scientific value attached to book reviews, reprints and articles published in non-specialist magazines (while on the one hand, a reprint does say something of the effect of a book). Neither are research memoranda and working papers generally regarded as being of the same status as final publications. Such 'grey publications' serve to elicit commentary from colleagues about current research. As a rule they are regarded as the unripe form of final publications.

The most important media for new knowledge is regarded by most disciplines as being: articles in scientific journals and theses; in the humanities a great deal of value is attached to publication in book form. Characteristic of articles in scientific journals and theses is that a system of refereeing has developed in connection with these two forms of publication. The judgment of quality by the scientific forum is made more explicit in one way or other. A thesis is approved by a tutor and a graduation board. In the theses category we also see a rough differentiation in quality: one graduates cum laude or not. Nevertheless, there are major differences in graduation tradition between the various disciplines. There is a higher level of graduation in some disciplines than in others. Another difference is that especially in science and medicine theses are often a compilation of related articles in which the researcher reports his findings. Although one can graduate on a compilation of articles in the humanities, such a thesis is held in less esteem. In these disciplines the value of a thesis is partly to show that the Ph.D. student is capable of writing a book. Scientific journals uphold a system of assessing submitted works by editors and referees; the latter by international journals in particular. The one journal being more selective than the other. The stringency of the assessment procedure determines among scientists the perception of the quality of the journal. A second measure for the quality of a journal, which is more open to objectification, is the extent to which the articles published in that journal are cited in other periodicals. This is referred to as the impact factor of a periodical (cf. Liebowitz and Palmer, 1984).

International publications are generally regarded with higher esteem than national ones. The reason for this is that only contributions to international literature carry any weight from a scientific point of view (the basic norm of universalism). The scientific forum is bound to neither language nor national frontiers. This applies in particular to those disciplines which do not have a socially-oriented dimension. It is, however, more discerning with regard to law and the social sciences, which to a large extent consist of analyzing and commenting on constantly changing social developments. In such disciplines, both forum and media are more national by character. The performance indicators used must do justice to this.

The above illustrates quite clearly that it is neither possible nor desirable to attribute equal significance to the various publication categories described above. This can apply even *within* a discipline because the various subdisciplines and their media are often difficult to compare (e.g. fiscal economics and econometrics as two different subdisciplines of economics). Only at the relatively low level of aggregation of a subdiscipline is one able to conceive that consensus can be achieved among scientists on the significance of various publication categories.

Attempts to construct performance indicators on the basis of various categories of publications are unavoidably linked with many hypotheses. The most significant is the assumed homogeneity of scientific quality in the different categories. Naturally, the reality is that theses do differ, books differ, and publications in one and the same scientific journal differ. What can be objectified in practice is the length (number of pages, taking into account the number of words per page) of a book or article, yet this is obviously not a 'proxy' of (variations in) scientific quality. In order to say something about this we must first of all establish the role a publication in the discourse between colleagues; or in other words: what valuable knowledge and insights have other researchers gained from that publication, expressed in scientific output.

This brings us to the role set aside for *citations* in establishing scientific production (Garfield, 1979). The role of citations is based on the idea that the better the research or researcher the more it, or he/she is cited. Citations are the expression of the scientific indebtedness of later work to earlier work. On a basis of this reasoning, citation indexes are used as a performance indicator. This brings us to the end of publications as performance indicator and we now move on to an effect indicator. One must however pay attention to the scope of the effect: the main point is the effect on other researchers in the scientific circuit to which publications are submitted as an intermediate product.

Material available from the Institute of Scientific Information (ISI) in Philadelphia, USA, is a source for citation analyses. This institute publishes three citation indexes: the Science Citation Index (SCI) for the natural sciences, the Social Sciences Citation Index (SSCI) covering the social sciences and the Arts and Humanities Citation Index (A&HCI) for the humanities. For the purpose of compiling these indexes, note is made of the references contained in all the articles of an enormous number of periodicals. Also, a limited number of books are investigated, usually compilations of congress papers. The Science Citation Index is far more extensive than the other two.

Both a number of indicator problems and objections of principle are attached to the use of an effect indicator such as a citation index. The most important indicator problems are:

- the publications used represent the established order; new magazines, journals in multi-disciplinary areas, radical publications (representing a new or underlying paradigm) are not usually included;
- as a rule, non-English (for instance Dutch) scientific publications are not included;
- in the case of publications written by more than one author only the first mentioned is named.

Objections of principle against citation analyses are:

- they do not give an impression of recent output but of past performance; age is rewarded; the prestige of the established order is measured; citation analyses have a conserving effect;
- citations are not generally interdependent; it is apparent that networks of citations exist (in a specialism and/or concerning a specific journal) in which researchers cite each other and raise their prestige (the mutual admiration society). Outsiders run the risk of being ignored;
- another form of misrepresentation is that citations are not necessarily founded on the importance or benefit of the relevant work, but that social effects are borne in mind, e.g. ceremoniously citing those people considered to be influential;
- a reference to a person's work need not necessarily imply agreement, it can also imply critique. This is inherent to the verification process of research. According to critical rationalism, critique is even the motor of scientific progress. It does mean, however, that a citation index is not only one-dimensional;
- there is no balancing of the quality of the magazines in which an author is cited;
- after a period of incorporation, significant doctrines (paradigms) start to take on a life of their own; after that the original genius is often not cited (in the words of Newton: authors are sometimes completely unaware of who's shoulders they are standing on when looking out on their scientific vistas);
- certain trends in areas of research can receive attention which is out of all proportion. It can also occur that researchers deploy strategic behaviour in an attempt to increase their chances of publication and to be cited by using trendy key-words in (the titles of) their research products (e.g. in economics 'rational expectations', ' property rights' and 'agency theory' all tend to score well at the moment).

The above gave the pros and cons of publication and citation analyses. Publication analyses are used in scientific research as the most important performance indicator. Citation analyses go one step further and can be regarded as an effect indicator. An effect indicator describes the objectified valuation from the demand side (the consumers) of the production process. When dealing with performance indicators the consumers' evaluation is generally out of shot. There is, however, a distinction between grey publications and 'official' publications (articles, books with an ISBN number). Grey publications are usually issued at one's own expense and through one's own channels (a series of publications issued by an institute, faculty) and therefore avoid the selection mechanisms of the field; in the case of 'official' publications a publishing body acts as intermediary which evidently has a (positive) perception of the consumer evaluation.

Performance and effect indicators are *instruments* in management processes. Which is given preference depends primarily on the goal of the output measurement. If the output standard used plays a role in the processes of allocation and the control of resources, the standard will need to meet the previously mentioned criteria of *observability* and *controllability*. The output standard must be able to serve as an instrument of measurement and control (management variable).

There are two major objection categories to using a publication standard as a management variable. The first category is connected with the fact that scientific research leads to very heterogeneous outputs. As we have seen, the quality of these outputs is difficult to assess objectively and capture in a single indicator. Flying blind with a publication standard as a management variable can encourage various forms of strategic behaviour. It is therefore necessary for researchers to have as much of their work published as possible. Raising the number of publications is then effective from the viewpoint of the researcher. He is stimulated to increase his 'score' ("publish or perish").

From the viewpoint of the funding government, which in fundamental university research ultimately represents the community as the demander of research results, this behavioural stimulus can also be *ineffective* given that a steady and constant quality of research outputs is not guaranteed. For instance, a researcher who has made a number of interesting discoveries during the course of his research can increase his production by reporting those discoveries in not one, but several articles, each dealing with a separate component. From a social point of view, no one benefits from such production of paper. The pressure to publish can also lead to researchers protecting their own material rather than trying to achieve progress through cooperation with other researchers.

Finally, the combination of organizational and behavioural insights, the angle of this book, leads to an important conclusion within the area of multidisciplinary research. The consequence of increasing the pressure to publish is that it will strengthen a researcher's natural inclination to 'score' in his discipline. Looking beyond the boundaries of one's own discipline usually requires an investment in time and effort. Multidisciplinary research will thus be repressed (even further). These examples of ineffectiveness result from the fact that the motives of the decentralized levels (levels three, four and five) fail to run parallel with the aims of government at level seven which, to an increasing extent, requires that the research system proves itself in measurable terms.

A second category of objections to the use of a publication standard as a management variable is connected with the previously mentioned curriculum and organizational interweave of university research and teaching. This objection has come to light since in recent years universities have been put under pressure to make their research performance more perceptible (annual scientific reports, conditional funding, disciplinary evaluation committees, etc.). The problem facing the universities is that teaching and research results are not measured on the same scale and that, with regard to teaching results, it is apparently more difficult to find a clear 'sound' standard than is the case for research results. In other words: a research result can be appropriated, a teaching result can not. The literature on property rights (e.g. Furubotn and Pejovich, 1974) makes it quite clear that this is at the expense of the factor for which there are no incentives. An indication that such a process is under way was illustrated by the previously mentioned CBS survey into how scientific staff spend their time, which showed, quite surprisingly, that, despite the enormous increase in the number of students, more time started to be spent on research during the period 1973-1983.

What happens if the pressure to produce is increased in a production process which results in measurable products (in this case: research performance) and outputs which are less easy to capture in an unambiguous standard (in this case: teaching performance) was formulated by Newman: "Easily measurable factors tend to receive too much weight, and intangible factors too little (. . .) short-run results tend to be over-emphasized compared with long-run results" (Newman, 1975). Economists are faced with this phenomenon in a different guise: "bad money always drives out good money".

As far as the development of new citation indicators in scientific research is concerned, much promising work has been produced by the previously mentioned Leiden research group (Moed et al., 1983; Moed, 1989). Over the years this group saw chance to develop a method by which a number of the pitfalls of citation analyses are avoided. This research group performed citation analyses in a number of the exact sciences (mathematics, physics, astronomy, chemistry, biology, medicine, pharmacy) using the Science Citation Index of the Institute of Scientific Information. The citation scores of the various research groups that correspond with the subdisciplines of the various faculties of the University of Leiden were then calculated (the 'Basic Leiden File'). These citations were subsequently weighted with a factor indicating the quality of the publication in which an article was quoted (Journal Citation Score; JCS). Finally, the score of each research group was set off against the average score of all other research groups in the field in question worldwide. The latter shows how the performance of a research group compares with the world average. The introduction of such a reference value allows a comparison to be made between research groups from different (sub)disciplines in an indirect manner by implementing the criterion of how much they count in their particular field. By applying this method the 'apples and oranges' problem is solved. Yet it is important that the two can be distinguished. Research groups engaged in fundamental research in a particular field can compare themselves with each other just as can those groups engaged in applied research, but what should be done with quinces? If both fundamental and more applied research is typical of a specific area of study, and the various research groups apply both in a different mix, it appears that the indexes always show a bias in favour of the more fundamental groups, while the goal of more applied groups need not necessarily be less valid. In such cases the indicators derived from the SCI, SSCI and the A&HCI cannot be used without additional data.

The outcomes of the Leiden study were then presented to the research leaders of the relevant faculties. This resulted in a feedback of the quantitative material to judgment by peers which, in turn resulted in verbal statements as to the results found: the score of one group went up after the appointment of a new professor, or conversely, the score dropped after a study group had been disbanded after arguments among its members. Another function of this qualitative validation is to bring errors in measurement to light. For instance, a prominent biology journal which published a great deal of the work produced by this Leiden research group, was only included in the SCI file in 1979 (Moed et al., 1983, p. 30). Publications in this journal prior to 1979 were therefore not included in the Basic Leiden File. This illustrates that the 'sound' figures never speak for themselves but must always be scrutinised very carefully.

Five conclusions can be drawn with regard to the functionality and policy relevance of citation analyses. These relate to (1) the period during which citations are counted (the 'measuring glass'), (2) the aggregate to which the analysis relates, (3) differences in functionality per discipline, (4) the use of citations indexes for secondary analyses, and (5) the most appropriate level for performing citation analyses.

In the first place, the resulting citation analysis illustrated that in the majority of subdisciplines there is a reduction in the number of times a publication is cited after a period of three years. This implies that the analysis can be limited to the first three years after the publication of an article (short term impact). This makes reporting on relatively recent work possible. A citation analysis can therefore provide the research management of a faculty with relevant information.

Secondly, it is important that in the research in question the citation analysis is applied to research groups and not to individuals. A number of potential objections against citation analyses are thus removed given that the law of averages is applicable. Two objections which loose in significance are:

- that in the case of publications written by more than one author, only the first mentioned is named;
- a citation does not always imply agreement, it can also imply critique.

If a citation analysis is made of the aggregate of (sufficiently large) study groups then it is a worthwhile exercise. In the previous chapter we explained that today it is more often research groups rather than individual researchers that can be regarded as the basic expected work level of the system. Faculty management tools must be geared to this especially. It will be quite clear that in view of this, citation lists of individuals (such as the top 30 economists as used in the Netherlands) serve rather to confirm individual status than they are of relevance to policy.

Thirdly, it is important for us to point out that the material issued by the Institute of Scientific Information can only be used if the journals contained in their files adequately cover the publication behaviour in the relevant discipline. This can be measured against the percentage of coverage: the percentage of English language publications of the investigated research unit included in the SCI file. In the exact sciences this percentages is generally high enough to guarantee reliable analyses. For these disciplines the Leiden project would be eligible for modification to the Dutch dimension.

In those disciplines where books or national periodicals are regarded as the main media for passing on scientific knowledge, the ISI files do not provide reliable information. ISI coverage of publications on the humanities and social studies is only in the region of 10%, implying that citation analyses in these disciplines cannot result in reliable figures. This lack of coverage is not a purely technical problem but it reflects the bipartite goal of these disciplines. The function of research in both the humanities and the social sciences is not only aimed at scientific progress but also in lighting the way for people other than one's fellow colleagues. This 'Aufklärungs' (or enlightenment) function is held in high esteem: in the humanities a great deal of value is attached to the dissemination of culture, an important form of the transfer of knowledge in management science is to provide managers with a system of terminology, well-wrought annotations may be expected of university law professors which can be of benefit to practising lawyers, the professor of public finance is expected to be able to explain the secrets of the state budget to the general public in newspapers and on television, etc., etc. The practice of science in these disciplines is therefore a mixed business. This also entails a greater degree of 'local' orientation, as well as a lesser degree of consensus on the importance of scientific work, theory or empiricism, and which, for example, is expressed in the absence of consensus as to the relative importance of journals and other forms of knowledge transfer. The conclusion that emerges from this is that unrestrained bibliometry, derived from physics, in the humanities and the social sciences leads to a distorted picture.

Fourthly, it must also be pointed out that with the assistance of citation files so-called *cluster analyses* can be performed (cf. Small and Sweeney, 1985). The most well-known form of cluster analyses is the *co-citation analysis*, developed by the ISI. In co-citation analysis an investigation is made into whether certain sources can be cited in pairs significantly often (above a certain citation threshold). This technique is based on assumptions in respect of the communication characteristics of fields of research. Co-citation analyses are aimed at determining specific innovative patterns in research.

Finally, it is also important to point out that citation analyses can be a useful tool at faculty level (level four) in monitoring the performance of research groups. We have already pointed out that 'sound' figures often require further interpretation. At faculty level information is generally available for dealing with the outcomes of citation analyses. Citation analyses provide information on aggregates at level three which are focused on policy pursued at level four. Faculty science committees, assisted by bibliometric material, could advise their faculty boards on the assignment and/or continuation of research projects and programmes. However, it is most undesirable that levels five, six or seven concern themselves with this sensitive material. On the one hand, those working at these levels lack the background information on specific research groups and will therefore have a slight tendency to set their policies on 'automatic pilot'; on the other hand, policy at these levels should be concerned with strategic affairs.

This brings us back to the main line of this book. Given that the output of scientific research cannot be established unequivocally (the question of method) it is difficult to achieve top-down management of production processes in the research system. The management of the system therefore demands an adequate level of institutionalization of the various levels. There is a complementary link between the question of method (what) and the question of the forum (who): the higher the level of consensus on the institutionalization of competences, the lower the importance of the question of method.

The conclusion to be drawn from the above outline of publication and citation indicators is that a measuring system for scientific production can never function as an automatic pilot. However, a pallet of more or less *objectified* standards, such as performance and effect indicators, serves as a *tool* in *intersubjective assessment processes*; they must not however be allowed to take their place. Scientific quality and progress simply cannot be fully captured in size and figures. Yet judgment by peers, the scientific forum function, can take advantage of the availability of a number of objectified standards as input. Additionally, publication-counts are particularly characterized by a production standard, while a citation index is a measure of quality (effect, evaluation by fellow colleagues). Citation-counts can in fact be regarded as a second-order peer review. Apart from that, publication and citation measures are not completely independent variables but are closely connected (Cole and Cole, 1973).

Finally, it is of importance in this framework to point out that the current trend – encouraged particularly by the Ministry of Education and Science – for the academic world to express itself where possible in performance indicators, is indicative of an implicit policy option (hidden agenda). The result is namely that practical and applied areas of study (where the 'Aufklärungs' function is given special emphasis in the disciplinary goals) find it more difficult to prove themselves in measurable units in terms of bibliometric standards than the more fundamental subjects. This has repercussions on various levels of the university system. Not only do individual researchers and research groups (levels two and three) receive an impetus to put pen to paper, it also has an effect on the staff appointments policies of levels four and five. The question is whether this system-provoked behaviour is efficient from a societal point of view. Especially for the social sciences and the humanities it is very much a question of whether the initiated change in the character of science does justice to the empirical object of these disciplines.

PART II
CASE STUDIES

4 Case study 1: The Netherlands science policy

The institutionalization of science policy at central government level since 1963

4.0 Summary

This first of the chapters dealing with case studies is devoted to the institutionalization of the Netherlands central government science policy. The multi-level system is applied to the relations and developments relating to the highest levels of the system. Various periods, and the relevant actors, are distinguished in the development of science policy.

As far as the different periods are concerned, the first contours of a science policy started to form in the sixties, more than quarter of a century ago. It gained momentum in the seventies, a period in which there was a strong belief in social reform. Amongst other things, there was the pretension of a synoptic and coordinated science policy. This trend came to a halt in the eighties and science policy took on a more down to earth character: more fragmentary, selective, dispersed and decentralized. The ambition to accomplish a strategic orientation remained but the universal concept failed to materialize. During this period a significant component of science policy was also concerned with technology policy.

The division into separate periods relates to the change in relationships between the main actors at the level dealing with science policy: the Minister of Education and Science, the Minister for Science Policy (in the seventies) and the Minister of Economic Affairs. With regard to the institutionalization of the echelons immediately below the political level we note that although science policy did give attention to the importance of a stronger organization structure at level five, little interest was shown in the function and position of level six. The danger in this is an inadequate buffer function between science policy and the research system.

4.1 Introduction

In this second part of the study the model developed in the previous chapter is checked against the practical situation. This is done on the basis of three case studies of a number of administrative developments in the Dutch research system. The analysis is focused on what happens if a certain level is institutionalized more strongly because certain tasks and responsibilities are transferred to a lower or higher level. In the event of the former we speak of a centralizing movement; in the case of the latter, a decentralizing movement.

The case studies have been selected in such a way to enable the analysis of various components and different levels of the (para)university research system. Case study 2 investigates the universities at level five in relation to the bodies at levels six and seven. The relations between the various levels under the NWO umbrella are looked at in the third case study.

This first case study deals especially with levels seven and six: the development of science policy by the Netherlands government over the past twenty-five years. Characteristic of a science policy is that an attempt is made to bring developments in the realms of science into line with economic or social trends outside science. It is important to stress that science policy at level seven is not limited to a single government body but that there are several points of initiation. This applies throughout this entire period. The most important initiators are the Minister for Science Policy, the Minister of Education and Science and the Minister of Economic Affairs.

There are two significant points in time in the institutional development at level seven: the year 1971 saw the first appointment of a minister (without portfolio) for higher education and science policy at the Ministry of Education and Science; the separate ministership for science policy was abolished in 1981. These breaking points can be used to make a further breakdown into three sub-periods:

period	*most distinctive characteristic*
1963 - 1971	the first contours of a science policy at levels six and seven
1971 - 1981	the institutionalization of a coordinated science policy at level seven
1981 - the present	diffusion, dispersion and decentralization of science policy

This period classification will be discussed in the remainder of this chapter in three consecutive sections. It is a division which runs more or less parallel to the breakdown made by Blume (1986) in his study of the development of the Netherlands science policy in an international perspective. Blume looked into science policy against the background of the political and social value orientations (perceptions, opinions) with regard to the role of scientific research in social development. In the period reviewed these value orientations were never consistent factors but changed quite radically, both in the Netherlands and in other countries. The predominant orientation in the sixties was described by Blume as "science as the motor of progress", that of the seventies as "science as problem solver" and that of the eighties as "science as source of strategic opportunity". In this chapter we also show how, in the terms of our model, changes in predominant value orientations translate into changes in institutional structures.

4.2 The first contours of a science policy at levels six and seven (1963-1971)

It was the Organisation for Economic Cooperation and Development (OECD) which, early in the sixties, started to stress the importance of policy development in the field of science and technology. In 1963 the OECD convened the first conference of ministers on this subject. It was a period in which the budgets for scientific research were increased quite substantially. In the first place, this was founded on society's faith in the beneficial effect of the results of science and technology. Public opinion was widely influenced by a number of spectacular, big science projects such as the American and Russian space programmes. Secondly, these budgets were allowed to grow because of the fear of lagging behind the USA (the American challenge).

Also characteristic of this period was the belief in a synoptic science policy with unambiguous goals, objective criteria as regards options, etc. This belief in rationality was also recognizable in other areas of government policy. For example, the emergence of planning and budgeting techniques such as the American Planning-Programming-Budgeting System. The deployment of such techniques should be seen in the light of trends towards centralization in decision-making (Van Gunsteren, 1976) and for the first time we see a call for coordinated government policy in the area of science studies. When the Marijnen government came into power in 1963 it was stated that the aim would be towards promoting a powerful national science policy and international scientific cooperation. This subject was also incorporated in the government policy statement of the Cals government which came into power in 1965. It was also in this period that the Minister of Education and Science was designated with a more or less coordinating task in respect of all scientific research.

The institutional contours of a science policy were given shape during this period in the form of the establishment of new bodies of representatives at levels six and seven: the Advisory Council for Science Policy (RAWB, 1966), the Interdepartmental Consultation on Science Policy (1966) and in informal ministerial consultations on science policy (1969), resulting several years later (1972) in the Council for Science Policy as a ministerial sub-council. The RAWB comprises nine members who are appointed by government à titre personnel. The task of this Council is to advise the government on matters of scientific research, taking the general interest into account.

In the explanatory memorandum to the draft bill on the establishment of the RAWB, the government stated their intention to pursue a national coordinated policy on matters of science. The Minister of Education and Science assigned himself to the task of stimulating and adjusting.

Another level six body, for which the preparations were made during this period and established some years later (1972), was the (Interim) Scientific Council for Government Policy (WRR). The establishment of the WRR was seen as a form of expansion of the government's planning instruments. It was designated to perform three tasks:

1. with a view to government policy, to provide the government with scientifically-based information on those developments which could have an impact on society in the long term, at the same time to point out any conflicts and anticipated problems, to formulate the issues in respect of major policy issues and to present policy alternatives;
2. to develop a scientifically-based framework to help the government set its priorities and pursue a coherent policy;
3. with a view to the duties in the area of perspective research and planning in the longer term, to present proposals, both within and outside of the sphere of government, with

regard to removing structural deficiencies, to promote certain studies and to improve communication and coordination.

Another step towards a government science programme in this period was the proposal to bring together all the relevant budgetary items of the various ministries in a separate budget overview. This is the annual *Science Budget* which has now been published since 1966 (see also section 4.3).

During this period other discussions were also held, both in parliament and elsewhere, on scientific research at universities and colleges of technology and how this should be organized. Very soon after the RAWB had been established it was requested to advise on the most efficient method of funding university research. This took a long time to produce and in its 'Provisional document on the organization and funding of scientific research performed in universities and colleges of technology' (RAWB, 1971) it was stressed that university research should play a more significant role in a national science policy: non-teaching-linked university research should be incorporated in a national framework of priorities which would be subjected to the approval of the minister responsible for national science policy.

Parliament was convinced that there was insufficient insight into the appropriateness of expenditure for university research. This led in 1970 to the Auditor's Office being requested to carry out an investigation into this. The Auditor's Office came to the conclusion that none of the universities pursued a coordinated research policy, realized through careful consideration of the priorities of the highest governing body. Research projects are determined by the individual professors (Minister for Science Policy, 1974, section 6.3.3.2).

OECD examiners also denounced the negative aspects of the Dutch university research policy (Minister for Science policy, 1974, section 6.3.3.2): "... there does not exist any uniform set of mechanisms or procedures for ensuring:

a. that the funds are spent efficiently
b. that areas of real scientific promise are supported
c. that funds are allocated on the basis of scientific merit and design of proposed projects
d. that some of the research undertaken will produce information which will ultimately contribute to national economic, social and educational goals."

During this period, attention given to the emotional, intellectual and administrative side within the university system was to a large extent swallowed up by the high level of unrest among students and the subsequent aftereffects. Partly as a result of this, the university administrative structure was strongly democratized (University Administration Reform Act, WUB, 1970).

Not only the universities, but also the national science council (the Netherlands Organization for the Advancement of Pure Scientific Research, ZWO), was strongly criticized by, amongst others, the OECD examiners, as being too passive and not having stimulating policies.

Conclusion: Between 1963 and 1971 there was a growing need to develop a national science policy. This was expressed particularly in the creation of a number of new institutions at levels six and seven. It was felt that the research organizations at level five (universities, ZWO) had, for various reasons, little to contribute towards science policy. Very few initiatives were taken by those involved in direct and indirect funding to enter into consultation and to specify the priority areas in research. Policy-forming during this period was therefore carried out mainly outside the realms of these organizations.

Towards the end of this period it was generally accepted – also outside parliamentary and government circles – that measures would have to be taken for a more distinct and more strongly coordinated science policy. The science offices of political parties had already carried out studies on this subject, scientific associations were working on it and articles started to appear in scientific journals and newspapers (Minister for Science Policy, 1974, appendix 3). There was an explicit faith in the possibility of a synoptic science policy. Such faith in synoptic decision-making was based on the assumption that the policy information required was easy to generate and apply (i.e. free of charge). That the former was debatable had already been brought to the fore in the thirties and forties during the debate on the logical (im)possibility of a centrally managed planned economy. In that debate both Von Mises and Von Hayek had pointed out that a central planning system would require a virtually endless flow of information to be able to generate the same allocation result as the price and market mechanism.

In the sixties and seventies Simon (e.g. Simon, 1976) – and even before that, Lindblom in 1959 – added a second argument based on a psychological approach. It is not only the generation of information by one (central) actor that is problematic, but dealing with that information too. Simon explained that by the very nature of an actor, the capacity of an actor to handle information is limited. A rational actor imposes limitations on his own capacity to absorb information. This virtual incapacity to achieve total synoptic thinking and acting was reason for Simon to substitute the traditional economists' assumption of the optimizing behaviour of actors for the assumption that actors aim towards levels of satisfaction in their drive towards their objectives (*satisficing* behaviour).

Looking back it is remarkable to see how during this period these views on limitations, which cling to the generation and handling of information, have come to stand in the shadow of an overpowering belief in controllability (termed by Von Hayek as *'constructivism'*).

4.3 The institutionalization of a coordinated science policy at level seven (1971-1981)

Just as a national science policy starts to emerge in the Netherlands we see a change in attitude towards the practice of science in the late sixties. Scientific and technological progress is no longer considered to be downright beneficial for society. In the public debate the disadvantages of progress are stressed in a number of areas: degradation of the environment, the arms race, the waste of natural resources, medicalization of the population (the Club of Rome, Illich, etc). Arguments were put forward in favour of zero-growth and the benefits of science and technology were contested. Researchers were confronted with the question of whether their activities were of any social relevance at all. Academic freedom was no longer a self-evident right, and this aspect was brought into discussion. Both public and political opinion refused to acknowledge the monopoly held by scientists to select research topics themselves. The general attitude was that the demand side should take on a more prominent role. The consequences of this were that less emphasis was laid on fundamental research during this period and that researchers and scientists had less influence on the formulation of research policy (Blume, 1986, p. 37).

At level seven the increased interest in pursuing a science policy was reflected in the appointment of a minister for science policy and higher education (Minister De Brauw from the conservative democratic-socialist party DS'70, 1971-1972; cf. the overview of governments and ministers since 1963 in the addendum to this chapter). The reason for including higher education was because DS'70 (a right-wing party) felt that science policy alone carried insufficient weight for their minister. Moreover, the main item in the DS'70 election campaign was retrenchment and reorganization in the area of public funds. In this respect De Brauw had set his mind on university education in particular.

The socialist-confessional Den Uyl government came into power in 1973. This government gave added stimulus to science policy. A ministership for science policy was created and given the backing of the administrative machinery, in this case the Directorate-General for Science Policy headed by a Director-General (DGWB). The Directorate-General for Higher Education and Scientific Research (DGHW), charged with matters concerning the universities, remained under the Minister of Education and Science. This was to remain so under the government that followed.

The first Minister for Science Policy was F.H.P. Trip, a member of the small Radical Political Party (PPR). As stated: a minister *for* science policy and not *of* science policy. This subtle difference had far-reaching consequences in the Netherlands government administration. The Minister for Science Policy is, likewise his predecessor, the Minister for Higher Education and Science, a minister without portfolio. He therefore does not have his own budget even though he does have certain budgetary items at his disposal from the Ministry of Education and Science for the purpose of initiating new developments. The status of the Minister for Science Policy is that of a coordinating minister. Minister Trip launched the 'joint action model' as a coordination model. The starting point he took was that an objective position was a prerequisite for sound coordination. Executive tasks should therefore be kept to a minimum.

One of the most significant policy documents produced by the then Minister for Science Policy was the Science Policy White Paper (*Nota Wetenschapsbeleid*; 1974). One of the strong features of this document was the belief in a rationally planned science policy epitomized in the form of long-term planning. The minister's main instrument for financial coordination was the annual *Science Budget* which should grow from being simply a financial survey to become a "long-term plan for science". The Science Budget is part of the National Budget and, since 1976, is made public on the third Tuesday of September every year. This is not essential given that the Science Budget lacks the official status of a budgetary law. Its status is that of an addendum to the Explanatory Memorandum on the Ministry of Education and Science budget. Although the Science Budget is presented to parliament by the Minister for Science Policy, as the coordinating minister, each specialist minister is responsible for his own policy.

The Science Policy White Paper aimed at achieving wider coordination of research to bring it into line with the priorities in society. It is therefore quite remarkable to note that in the political perception of the social priorities at that time (still) very little concern was shown for the interests of trade and industry. Several structural changes were suggested for the organizational structure of the research system in order to improve coordination. The intention of the proposed organizational structure was "... on the one hand, to break down the – sometimes – too great autonomy of the universities and increase government's influence and on the other hand, to strengthen, within that structure, the influence of the researchers themselves and that of those groups in society with an interest at stake" (p. 9; one could ask whose influence would then deteriorate, C.A.H.). Characteristic of the Science Policy White Paper (and the competences of the minister responsible) is that it virtually ignores university research. The two, most significant, structural changes proposed in this document were the establishment of *sectoral research councils* and the restructuring of ZWO into a Science Research Council (RWO) which would have to operate more stimulatingly (see the section on ZWO in Chapter 6).

The concept of a system of sectoral research councils was based on the idea that the scientific research infrastructure could be organized not only via disciplinary (not very accessible for government policy) lines, but that a second organization system could be applied in which research was categorized according to its area of application. This makes it possible to envisage a matrix organization of the research system.

The White Paper suggested the establishment of sectoral research councils for each social priority area under the responsibility of the minister(s) most involved. The sectoral councils would be given the task of advising the minister(s) on all research carried out in that area and of presenting concrete proposals for government research in this field (long-term plan). These are typical bodies, operating at level six, and each having the task of coordination and planning. The sectoral research councils should be made up of representatives of government, science (research institutes in the relevant sector, possibly from universities) and the 'users'. The sectoral research councils should not be designated with a role of allocating funds; this role is set aside for other bodies, particularly ZWO which was to be reorganized.

The long-standing National Council for Agricultural Research (NRLO; 1957) was taken as the model on which to base these sectoral research councils.

Below is a list of the sectoral councils established in this period.

Year	(pre)sectoral research council
1976	Research Council for the Urban Environment (VRA-OGO)
1978	Advisory Council on Development-related Research (RAWOO)
1980	Energy Research Council (REO)
1981	Research Council for Environment and Nature (RMNO)
1981	Programming Council for Environmental Planning Research (PRO)

Much later, in 1987, the Health Research Council (RGO) was established. In the years between the system became somewhat inert. The concept of an all-embracing system of sectoral research councils was quickly dropped and the system remained fragmentary. A number of the sectoral research councils were reorganized, some were even disbanded, and the parliamentary discussions on a framework law to govern sectoral research councils took many years.

In the years after the publication of the Science Policy White Paper the minister's tasks and responsibilities were expanded somewhat. This was especially the case during the Peijnenburg/Van Trier era (1977-1981). The Minister for Science Policy was given budgetary responsibility for the most important organization for applied research, TNO. A financial and organizational restructuring operation took place within TNO under his direct responsibility and a new TNO law came into being. Also, the Minister for Science Policy was provided with an incentive fund (in 1979) for the purpose of encouraging research which went beyond the boundaries of the various departments and/or were of a long-term nature. This resulted in a shift in the activities of the coordinating Minister for Science Policy from being mainly organizational-oriented (in the Trip period) to content-oriented. Also during this period (one of the occasions being during the discussions on the Ministry of Education and Science Budget for 1978 and the Science Budget 1978) the Lower House urged for a widening of the scope of responsibilities held by the Minister for Science Policy. It was argued that the Minister's scope of action should be extended to include technology, innovation, information technology and automation. This was adopted by Minister Van Trier who, during the formation of government in 1981, published a 'political testament' in which he argued for a separate departmental Minister *of* Science, Technology and Information Policy.

This minister would be responsible for ZWO, KNAW, institutes of education and research and the large research institutes such as the ECN (Netherlands Energy Research Foundation), WL (Hydraulic Laboratory), NLR (National Aerospace Laboratory). He should also have a greater involvement in the conditional funding scheme for university research. Should this be out of the question, as an alternative the minister chose for the continuation of the ministership without portfolio, but under the Ministry of General Affairs. He felt that this construction emphasized the faceted character of science policy and limited any lack of clarity in the relations with specialist ministers to a minimum. Should this construction also prove impossible he would be satisfied to maintain the existing situation on the understanding that the tasks, responsibilities and means were expanded and that the system was enlarged and made more independent. However, very little, even of this least demanding wish, was to materialize.

Conclusion: The most dominant perspective on science in the seventies was that the developments should not be allowed to have free play. Science should make a more direct contribution to solving societal problems. This was where the relevance of science lay and the government would have to do more in this direction. This interventionist attitude was expressed in the reinforcement of levels seven and six. A separate ministership for science policy was introduced at level seven and a number of sectoral research councils were established at level six. The Minister for Science Policy was a minister without portfolio and his tasks were mainly to coordinate. The responsibility for university education and research remained with the Minister of Education and Science. Science policy was pursued on the basis of a long-term perspective. There was still very little attention given to the short-term wishes of trade and industry. The position of the Minister for Science Policy did change to some extent. His original wish was to be given coordinating tasks only and not to have his own budget (Trip period) but this turned out to be too weak a position. A minister with coordinating tasks alone apparently had too little real influence given that the specialist ministries regarded many of his efforts as interfering in their policies. The 'joint action model' and its inherent interdepartmental political and official consultation procedures often resulted in lengthy struggles for power. The more it became apparent that coordination (of the policy of other ministers) was a difficult process, the more he started to yearn for his own finances for science policy.

During this period the intention was to achieve a greater involvement of the direct and indirect funded research (universities and ZWO, both on level five) in national science policy yet very little happened in this respect. The universities failed to be brought under the Minister for Science Policy and, moreover, they placed great emphasis on their autonomous position vis-à-vis the government. ZWO showed very little enthusiasm to react actively with regard to national, socially-inspired research priorities. It was only in 1979, when the Minister of Education and Science presented his Policy Document on University Research (BUOZ), that the universities and ZWO were confronted with radical plans concerning research planning, the shaping of research centres, etc. De facto, the government continued to pursue a favourable policy towards universities and ZWO during the period 1971-1981. On balance, we can conclude that in this period levels six and seven were moderately reinforced, partly because levels five and lower managed to sidestep a science policy.

4.4 Diffusion, dispersion and decentralization of science policy (1981 - the present)

This third period is characterized by three main developments: the development of a government technology policy geared to trade and industry, a general trend to set the organizational infrastructure of research more within the framework of greater efficiency, and particularly the restructuring of the university system, aiming at greater efficiency and effectiveness. These three developments have repercussions on the science policy institutions.

The reason for the first development was the change from economic growth into economic stagnation in the seventies. After having originally fought this economic crisis with economic means the awareness gradually grew that this standstill was due to friction in the economic structure itself, not only nationally but on a world-wide scale. Late in the seventies the conclusion was finally drawn that growth in the services sector would have to be restrained and that latitude would have to be created for *reindustrialization* of the economy to allow renewed economic growth (Blume, 1986, p. 52). In the eighties, under the influence of the changing economic policy pursued by the government, the predominant orientation in science policy shifted more towards technological aspects, particularly those aspects which were in the interests of trade and industry. This change of direction was expressed in a number of policy documents (see e.g. the Ministry of Education and Science White Paper on Innovation (Innovatienota), 1979 and OECD Reviews of National Science and Technology Priorities; the Netherlands, 1986).

This reorientation was the basis of the technology policy which started to develop in the Ministry of Economic Affairs during this period. The main concept being that a science and technology policy is of *strategic* importance for renewed economic growth. The term 'strategic' indicates the future possibilities that can be generated through research; it is not concerned with (direct) applications in industry. In terms of policy instruments and the financial interpretation of this technology policy, the greater part of attention was devoted to the supply side of the technology innovation process: direct support for innovation in trade and industry and market-oriented support from the technological and scientific infrastructure. The policy pursued emphasized the generic incentive measures which were aimed at reducing the high costs and risks involved in R&D activities for trade and industry. Policy on the technological and scientific infrastructure was aimed on the one hand at advancing that knowledge which is important for the market sector, and on the other hand, at improving the contacts between the technological infrastructure and the market sector.

The above reports also argue that research will need to be based more on a clearly specified *goal*. The main question here is: "Can one identify those areas of curiosity-orientated research in the process of being transformed into 'strategic areas', i.e. that are beginning to show promise of constituting a knowledge base that, with further funding, might eventually contribute to the solution of important practical problems?" (Irvine en Martin, as cited by Blume, 1986, p. 56). One major task of government policy is to select and fund such strategic areas of research. This 'specific' policy took shape in the Netherlands especially in the form of *Innovation-oriented Research Programmes* (IOP's). These programmes, originally proposed in the White Paper on Innovation, produced under responsibility of the Directorate General for Science Policy of the Ministry of Education and Science, and brought into effect by the Ministry of Economic Affairs.

Finally, within the framework of the development of a technology policy geared to trade and industry we must point out the emergence of a number of international programmes in which government and industry cooperate such as BRITE (Basic Research in Industrial Technologies for Europe), ESPRIT (European Strategy Program for Research and Development in Information Technologics), EUREKA (European Research and Coordination Agency) and RACE (Research and Advanced Communication in Europe).

The second main trend in the eighties concerns the organizational developments in the research infrastructure. Partly under the pressure of financial, economic circumstances in this period more attention was given towards questions of effectiveness (goal-orientation, strategic policy-making, long term planning). This is also evident in other areas of government policy: privatization, self-management in (sections of) ministries and local government, budgeting in the health care and welfare sector, etc., etc. In the non-university research sectors this increase of interest in questions of effectiveness was manifested in TNO for example. A new law governing the TNO is enacted, giving it a new organizational structure and a new funding system. The intention of this restructuring exercise is to make TNO a more market-oriented organization rather than the 'professorial organization' it had become.

Characteristic of this second trend were the statements made by the Committee on Financing Structures for Research and Development (CFSOO), established by the Minister for Science Policy. In its final report – given the title of "Accounting for Creativity" (Commissie Financieringsstructuur, 1985, p. 61-62) – the Committee recommended that the government devoted more attention to demarcating the spheres of activity of diverse organizations (the physical structure of the research system). In this context the committee argued that the government should issue guide-lines on the goals and tasks of the various research organizations. The government did turn its attention towards goals in respect of the university system. This was demonstrated in the Higher Education and Research Plan (Ministry of Education and Science, 1987a).

The wider attention given to matters of effectiveness is manifested in government policy in a more specific demarcation of the roles and responsibilities between specialist ministries and research organizations. This was evident in the HOOP, the long-term requirements plan of the Ministry of Defence, the document Landbouwkundig Onderzoek in Perspectief (Agricultural Research in Perspective) and the research plans of the Ministry of Housing, Regional Planning and Environment. Characteristic of these policy documents was that the big research organizations and heavy users were to play a greater role, not only in the implementation but also in the development of policy.

A possible consequence of improved cooperation between specialist ministries and research organizations is that a better dialogue can take place between specialist ministries and the Directorate General for Science Policy: on the main tasks of research organizations, on the demarcation and shifts in goals and important innovations.

The third main development during this period concerns the restructuring of the university system. Given that this is discussed in more detail in the following chapter only the main developments in policy will be touched upon here. Up to the end of the seventies government's concern for university research was mainly focused on growth in research capacity. This favourable policy was realized on the one hand by automatically coupling this growth in capacity to the rapid increase in the demand for education and on the other hand, by setting up new disciplines, faculties and institutes. Partly because of the pressure of the general economic situation and the resulting, changed budgetary conditions, this favourable policy was gradually transformed into a policy aimed at planning research. The most significant initiative for this change in policy was the Policy Document on University Research (BUOZ, 1979) produced by Minister Pais. The BUOZ explained the main lines of the Science Policy White Paper in terms of university research. The inadequacies in university research needing to be improved by implementing the proposals put forward in the BUOZ were:

1. Teaching and research tasks are linked in the customary funding model. The funds available for research in a certain area are linked to the number of students that have enrolled for that particular study. This method of funding implies that the amount of funding for research is determined by the lesser or greater preference of students for certain studies: other criteria cannot be made operative.
2. The second inadequacy is that only a low level of task allocation has been achieved at national level. Given the above method of funding it is also impossible to use the instrument of fund allocation.
3. Personnel policy is not geared towards task differentiation, nor does it lead to the required level of mobility among researchers.
4. The choice of subjects for university research is inadequately fuelled from within society itself.
5. There is a lack of visible outputs of what has been achieved with the funds that have been provided.

Improvements are sought in the development of a different organizational and funding structure and research planning has a central role in this. There are, however, other important aspects: making the effects of research visible, assessing the research effort and the quality of research, plus the production of an account.

The basic principle of the proposed funding structure is that the allocation of funds should facilitate steering, and that the availability of funds should be able to be made dependent on the quality of the relevant research.

The main message of the BUOZ is that the universities should be motivated to pursue their own research policy. Basically, this should also open the possibility to gear university research towards the science policy pursued by government.

In the eighties, partly as a means of breaking down the BUOZ policy concept into separate areas, and partly as an independent measure, the university system was restructured and slimmed down by implementing the following policy operations:

- shortening the duration of studies, achieved by introducing the *two-phase structure*;
- specifically shaping the (selective) second phase by creating the position of *trainee research assistants* (aio): a low-salaried member of staff given a period of four years to complete his/her thesis. The introduction of trainee research assistants also had organizational consequences: special institutes were founded to provide shelter for this doctoral degree research. These institutes were the forerunners of a system of research schools announced by the minister in 1990;
- the introduction of the *conditional funding* scheme (VF) which makes provision for a conditional allocation of research funds by the Ministry of Education and Science on the basis of research programmes which have been judged favourably by boards of representatives with a disciplinary composition. This system implies the separate financing of research;
- the *Key document on policy proposals concerning university academic staff* (BUWP document; Ministry of Education and Science, 1981) which provides for a restructuring of scientific staff grading. This restructuring operation aspires to give a certain hierarchical structure to staff grading. The grades of university lecturer and senior university lecturer are introduced. Strict requirements are set in respect of senior lectureships. This restructuring of academic teaching staff also leads to a reduction in the average

costs per member of staff and helps to create financial leeway for the introduction of trainee research assistants;
- two major economy operations, the *Distribution and Concentration of Tasks* (TVC; 1982), which over a number of years was to make a cut-back of 258 million guilders net, and the *Selective Shrinkage and Growth* (SKG; 1986) which on balance was to effect a saving of 130 million guilders;
- the setting up of a *University Education Inspectorate* (Ministry of Education and Science, 1985), which must ensure that the quality of the curriculum and research programmes is evaluated;
- the introduction of a new planning procedure for the system of higher education. This procedure is given shape in the *Higher Education and Research Plan* (HOOP), a government publication issued every two years. The HOOP is both the channelling document for planning and financing teaching and research sectors of universities and colleges of higher vocational education (direct funding) and the planning and funding of NWO (indirect funding);
- the change-over from *ZWO* to *NWO*; with the intention of creating an indirect funding organization more capable of innovating and initiating research programmes (see Chapter 6).

The implications of the three main developments in the science policy of the eighties described above mainly affect level five and the lower levels. We will not go into the critique from the university community here; our main concern in this context is the repercussions for the relations at level seven.

Characteristic of the seventies was that at level seven the government's science policy was shaped mainly by the Minister for Science Policy. In the eighties however, the Minister for Science Policy became the victim of his own policy: he was caught up with and overtaken on both sides. On the one side, by the Minister of Education and Science (i.e. DGHW), who did all in his power to mould the mass of university research – which was unreceptive to policy influence – into recognizable and traceable segments. In a number of steps, university research was made 'salonfähig' for a government science policy, initiated by the Minister of Education and Science. By intensifying policy in this way, the attempt made by Minister Van Trier in his political testament of 1981 to transfer the most interesting parts – from the angle of science policy – of the Ministry of Education and Science to a new (to be established) department for Science, technology and information policy, was thus thwarted.

On the other side, the Minister for Science Policy was overtaken by his counterpart from Economic Affairs. Thanks to the revival of interest shown in the interests of trade and industry, the Ministry of Economic Affairs could once again move forward in the eighties. In 1979 the Minister for Science Policy had seen the creation of the White Paper on Innovation (Ministry of Education and Science, 1979b), but the Ministry of Economic Affairs adopted the initiative as regards policy on applied science in the form of a technology policy geared towards the market sector. Certain matters led to the gradual disintegration of the central science policy. When forming the government in 1981 the separate ministership for Science Policy was abolished and coordination was again placed in the hands of the Ministry of Education and Science. In the formation of government in 1982, technology policy was separated from science policy and brought under the Ministry of Economic Affairs where a Directorate for General Technology Policy was set up.

Conclusion: In the eighties, science policy pursued in the Netherlands was adjusted pragmatically to the changed economic and social situation. The pretension of a science policy centrally coordinated by government was dropped and replaced with a general market-oriented technology policy, plus a policy geared towards the selection of research sectors which offered strategic possibilities (e.g. biochemistry, information science, new materials). The Minister of Education and Science, as the coordinating minister for science policy, retained his tasks of initiating and stimulating in respect of the whole of science policy, yet the incentives policy for industrial innovation started to predominate in this period. Also, the links with science policy and wider social issues became weaker. Simultaneously, the innovation policy pursued laid a quite definite emphasis on stimulating market-oriented technology.

4.5 Conclusions in the light of the model

We can trace back the beginning of a science policy to be pursued by the Netherlands government to about twenty-five years ago. In this relatively short time scientific research has undergone a quite remarkable 'Werdegang'. Whereas in the sixties research was in the interests of economic growth, in the seventies the focus was on social welfare and in the eighties the pendulum had returned to research in the interests of economic growth. Both policy and the institutions have undergone the most evident change since the sixties. Up to the sixties there had been no articulated science policy pursued as such. The most important achievements since the days prior to science policy were the establishment of TNO in 1932 and ZWO in 1950. Yet science policy has by no means been a non-compartmentalized policy over the past twenty-five years. This policy has always been based on several starting points. At present the main roles are played by the Minister of Education and Science with regard to university research (except for the University of Agriculture which comes under the Minister for Agriculture, Nature and Fishery) and the Ministry of Economic Affairs with regard to technology policy and the research relevant to that policy. In the seventies the Minister for Science Policy was faced with difficulties. This period was dominated by the pretension of a synoptic science policy. In retrospect, it is quite remarkable to see that the known range of ideas from the economic theory (Von Mises, Von Hayek, Simon, Lindblom) on the limitations relating to the generation and handling of information had been completely disregarded in this period. Conversely, the science policy of the eighties is fragmentary and selective by nature: geared towards the selection of likely areas for research in the Netherlands. Awareness emerges as to the importance of making strategic choices in science policy. Such policy is more suited to the nature of scientific research, which, by definition, is a complex of activities with uncertain outcomes which cannot be influenced by blueprints. This applies all the more to a small country in a relatively large international setting.

The need, and the possibilities, to administer specific planned stimuli to the research system through various channels have strongly increased over the past twenty-five years. Generally speaking, this can be regarded as a welcome development which must be steered on the right lines of the structure of responsibilities of the various levels of the model. Science policy, especially in the eighties, has been in the light of the institutional channelling of the need to give planned stimuli. To take the wind out of the sails of direct traffic between level seven and level four (and lower), or to declare it forbidden territory, science policy was geared in particular to giving an added significance to traffic between levels seven and five – obviously after upgrading or specifying level five (restructuring TNO, starting discussion on bringing the large technological institutes (GTI's) up to level 5; the HOAK document, with its emphasis on university autonomy, and subsequently the HOOP as the framework for dialogue between the government at level seven and the universities at level five).

Despite these initiatives, there is still a danger of imbalance in the science policy pursued at present, especially with regard to the points set out below.

1. the danger of *over-steering* through funding. This gives a direct link from level seven to level five and lower. Attempts are made to programme the steering of research through direct funding (conditional funding), indirect funding (NWO areas of priority) and also via the various funds of the Ministry of Economic Affairs and other ministries.
   The consequence of too high a level of steering by way of the funding mechanism can be that too little leeway is left open for fundamental research. A too rigid programming of research suppresses the tendency to take risks in research and thus encourages researchers to avoid risks in their work. It is also at absolute right-angles to the obligations of universities and faculties;
2. at present there is a strong leaning towards the *interests of trade and industry*. The danger here is that encouragement is given particularly to research which has a pay off in the short term and that long-term strategic research is given too little attention and too little funding;
3. both of the dangers outlined above are reflected in the institutional sphere: at the moment too little interest is shown in the crucial tasks which have to be fulfilled at *level six*. The RAWB and the sectoral councils are now on the defensive. There is also the lack of a directive body at supra-university level. Due to the relatively weak position of the buffer function at level six, the research system is now in the unfavourable position of being directly dependent upon the whims and fancies of the (science) policy system at level seven. The way in which changes in social norms and values are brought over in the research system is too harsh. This leads to some university institutions and sections presently developing a bias towards trade and industry which is in sharp contrast to the stand they took five, ten or twenty years ago. Such a trend gives rise to the question of what the goal of the university system exactly is. This question is dealt with in the next chapter.

Appendix

Overview of governments, ministers of Education and Science and ministers for Science Policy (1963 - the present)

period	*government*	*political colour*	*Minister of Education and Science*	*Minister for Science Policy* [1]
1963-65	Marijnen	Confessional / Liberal	Bot (KVP)	–
1965-66	Cals	Confessional / Socialist	Diepenhorst (ARP)	–
1966-67	Zijlstra	Confessional	Diepenhorst (ARP)	–
1967-71	De Jong	Confessional / Liberal	Veringa (KVP)	–
1971-72	Biesheuvel I	Confessional / Liberal / DS'70	Van Veen (CHU)	De Brauw (DS'70)
1972-73	Biesheuvel II	Confessional / Liberal	Van Veen (CHU)	–
1973-77	Den Uyl	Progressive / Confessional	Van Kemenade (PvdA)	Trip (PPR)
1977-81	Van Agt I	Confessional / Liberal	Pais (VVD)	up to 1979: Peijnenburg (CDA) 1979-81: Van Trier (CDA)
1981-82	Van Agt II	Confessional / Progressive	Van Kemenade (PvdA)	–
1982	Van Agt III	Confessional / D'66	Deetman (CDA)	–
1982-86	Lubbers I	Confessional / Liberal	Deetman (CDA)	–
1986-89	Lubbers II	Confessional / Liberal	Deetman (CDA)	–
1989	Lubbers III	Confessional / Socialist	Ritzen (PvdA)	–

1) Minister De Brauw was minister without portfolio charged with science policy and university education. Ministers Trip, Peijnenburg and Van Trier were ministers without portfolio charged with science policy.

5 Case study 2: Dutch universities on their way to more autonomy

The significance of raising the level of university autonomy for the relationship with central government and for the supra-university level

5.0 Summary

Government tends to shackle the universities with numerous administrative and financial cords. In recent years however, the government has finally become aware that the optimal functioning of the university system is best served by less government interference. The autonomy of universities must be strengthened and the government must adopt a policy of management at arm's length. This change in philosophy of the Ministry of Education and Science towards policy was first formulated in the policy document entitled Higher Education: Autonomy and Quality (HOAK) of 1985.

This chapter examines what changes will have to brought about in the university system in order to introduce the HOAK philosophy. The conclusion is that to ensure successful implementation of the HOAK concept it is not sufficient to develop adequate management capacities at level five only, but that it is equally important to have an adequate set of administrative tools to perform the tasks at level six in the system. Various modalities are compared within this framework. We argue that a solid and independent council will have to be set up at level six for the purpose of organizing the decision-making processes in the university system concerned with concentration, distribution of tasks, cooperation between universities, coordination, discontinuation, setting limitations on the intake of students with regard to subjects and sectors, the establishment of research schools, etc. Certain responsibilities regarding the allocation of the budget can also be placed in the hands of this council. The most far-reaching variant is a body based on the English University Funding Council which determines de facto the budgets for the universities.

Nevertheless, it is clear that if the introduction of such a council at level six fails, the universities will continue to be the plaything of the Ministry of Education and Science.

5.1 Introduction

In October 1985 the Minister of Education and Science published the policy paper 'Higher Education: Autonomy and Quality'. The draft version, still bearing the subtitle 'a different way of steering', had already been issued six months earlier. The word 'different' can also be stressed with regard to the definitive version: the HOAK concept implies a breakaway from the long-standing trend of growing government regulation of university education. The line set out in the HOAK concept has been carried through into the Higher Education and Research Plan (Ministry of Education and Science, 1987a) and the Higher Education and Scientific Research Act (WHW; Ministry of Education and Science, 1988), which was presented to parliament as a bill in 1989.

In the policy concept according to the HOAK document, the main points are formed by the following elements:

- more *diversity* in the higher education system;
- a higher level of *market-orientation* and *flexibility* of institutes of higher education;
- an adequate system of *quality assurance*;
- government management more at arm's length and a greater degree of *autonomy* for the universities.

The HOAK philosophy implies radical changes throughout the entire system of higher education. From the perspective of the universities this implies that on the one hand they will be partly faced with a different *environment* (in which the government's presence will be less evident) and on the other hand, they will again need to give a different form to their *internal functioning* (administrative organization, etc.).

Although the HOAK philosophy relates primarily to teaching, the wider principle has been adopted here in order to think out the concept in terms of education, research and also the supporting administrative processes.

The HOAK philosophy is geared towards the entire system of higher education, including higher vocational education and the open university. Here, we shall only deal with the significance of this policy concept for the universities.

In this chapter we will not go into the detailed measures and proposals ensuing from the HOAK policy document. The main point of concern is to reflect on the philosophy that universities are given more freedom of policy. What, therefore, are the consequences for the university system and the fulfilment of those tasks at supra-university level? In section 2 we will therefore look into the question of whether the HOAK is going to take us into a different university system. As a heuristic exercise we have outlined a model in which the universities are given far more autonomy than suggested in the HOAK document. A central problem, in both this heuristic exercise and the HOAK system, is how supra-university coordination and the distribution of tasks within the system can be regulated (or not). Section 3 outlines the history of how this sixth level has functioned and describes a number of modalities related to a more adequate institutionalization of this particular level. This view can be regarded as the next logical step in the HOAK concept. Section 4 closes with a number of conclusions in the light of the multi-level system.

5.2 The HOAK policy document: towards a new university system?

By producing the HOAK policy document the government has chosen to entrust the university system with a greater degree of autonomy. This choice was not based on a blueprint of the optimal organization of the university system. Such organization is always dependent on time and place. Of crucial importance is that the university system's structure and mentality is sufficiently adaptive so as to prevent it from obsolescence and malfunction. The system must at all times be able to absorb any changes which occur in its surroundings. In this light, the HOAK document should be seen as a single step in a (search) process with an open ending; a process of tâtonnement in which the dimension of time should be measured in decades rather than in years. We have reached an interchange, and a certain well-considered course has been taken by introducing the HOAK. However, this course also leads to another interchange which, in turn, leads to another, and so on and so forth. It is impossible at this point to say where the journey will end; that depends on the choices made at each intersection. It is quite possible that on reaching the next one the government might be dissatisfied with the increased autonomy of universities and decide to retrace its steps. Nevertheless, it is equally conceivable that the government will continue to take steps along the road to even greater university autonomy.

The first subsection gives a summary of this 'HOAK step'. In section 5.2.2 we explain the course which comes into view if the course decided upon at the next interchange is one of a further increase of university autonomy. Finally, as a heuristic exercise, in the last subsection we sketch out the final destination we will arrive at if the choice to increase university autonomy has been made at each interchange along the way. This model of complete autonomy for universities can thus be regarded as one of the possible destinations we will arrive at if no other turning is made, but have consistently followed the one road towards increased university autonomy. This conceptualization is based on an 'if-then' argumentation without making any statements as to the desirability or probability of that course. It is for the particular purpose of illustrating that the real possibilities of changing the system at any given time depend on the time path that has been followed prior to that. This line of thought is sometimes referred to with a term used in physics: *hysteresis* or *path-dependence*. Hysteresis can be defined as the general condition in which "the steady-state or long-run equilibrium position of the system will not be a function only of the long-run values of the exogenous variables but also of the initial conditions of the state variables and of the values assumed by the exogenous variables outside the steady-state. Hysteretic or path-dependent systems are therefore 'historical' systems: how you get there determines where you get to" (Buiter, 1987, p. 24).

5.2.1 The small steps of HOAK

In summary, the most significant system-transgressing measures announced in the HOAK document were:

- a system of planning and funding will be introduced which will have a far wider effect than the present one (fewer regulations beforehand but more quality checking afterwards);
- a board of inspectors will be set up to assess, per discipline, the quality of teaching programmes in the system of higher education;
- should the quality of a discipline be found insufficient (and remain so) the government can stop funding.

5.2.2 Further increase of university autonomy

The measures outlined in the above do not provide us with a description of the final destination. The objective of the HOAK document is to completely reverse the trend that has been followed for many years now. If it is possible to take these small steps of the HOAK satisfactorily, then the dialogue between government and the universities can be shifted to the subsequent limitations of university autonomy. This keeps the perspective open to increase university autonomy even further. The following could be considered:

- the government withdraws its involvement in the personnel policy pursued by the universities (hierarchical structure, grading regulations, etc);
- in turn, the universities adopt a more flexible personnel policy in order to react effectively to changes in its surroundings (grading on a basis of achievements and labour market situation, fewer permanent positions, increasing the opportunity of relocation, more part-time jobs and dual appointments (part at university and part in trade and industry), more secondment opportunities, etc.; (Commissie Financieringsstructuur, 1985);
- the introduction of internal systems of quality valuation, differentiated according to the type of teaching and research and attuned to the needs of the various stakeholders;
- faculty and university boards are given heavier responsibilities; the tasks of the councils are limited to supervisory tasks; the board becomes more professional (cf. ARHO, 1988).

5.2.3 A heuristic model: complete autonomy for universities

The HOAK is only a very small step towards greater autonomy for universities. To obtain a counterfactual against which to measure the HOAK model we could give consideration to a model in which universities operate as completely autonomous companies. In such a heuristic exercise the universities compete against each other, each having a differentiated and customer-oriented supply of research and advice products. The institutes are expected to act as businesses from a strategic and financial economic point of view. In this approach the government has the task of optimizing the functioning of the market mechanism. This implies that in the system of higher education there must be *(monopolistic) competition* as in the market place. In that case a relatively large number of producers compete to win the consumer's goodwill (Florax and Van Vught, 1987). The monopolistic element lies in the fact that each university will stress the features of its own specific products. In the area of teaching, the universities can compete in terms of study fee, length of course, teaching method, curriculum content, and possibly denomination. Major differences in quality could emerge between the universities. Top universities/faculties will only want to accept top students, and this will lead to the introduction of student selection procedures. Although this entrepreneurial model can lead to even fiercer competition it can also lead to various forms of cooperation (market sharing between the universities, etc). Nevertheless, the government, as the guardian of the proper functioning of the market mechanism, must thwart such situations where one or two producers monopolize the market. The protection of consumer sovereignty is also a task for the government.

In this model the government can only exert influence as the purchaser – with a great purchasing power – of the products of education and research (which can also include setting loosely defined tasks in the area of fundamental research) and no longer acts as the owner/director of the universities. The ratio of the right to appoint university governers is irrelevant in this model. Funding of the universities is direct from the government by way of contracted research and the funding of scientific research. Direct funding can be replaced by a system of issuing vouchers to students, companies or other bodies requiring university products. By doing this the government contracts out part of its demand. These customers can exchange their vouchers at the university which serves them best (in terms of price, quality and other product specifications). The customer is always right and the producer wanting to survive will make sure that he caters to his customer's needs.

We have already made it quite clear that the destination of complete autonomy for universities, described in this subsection, can only be reached after having passed a series of intersections where the choice has been consistently taken for increasing university autonomy. We have used the term 'path-dependent' in order to illustrate that it would be very naive to presume that such a model is a real possibility at this stage without having passed the successive intersections along the way.

If we return from the heuristic to the reality we see that the first interchange was not crossed without problem. The HOAK philosophy is threatened both at level seven and within the university system itself. With regard to the former, we see that in the HOAK document, and in the parliamentary debate, it was stressed on numerous occasions that the increased university autonomy will have to be limited by conditions set by the government. The creed of the HOAK catechism is hybrid: although there is the intention to take a small step on the road towards more university autonomy, when the next interchange comes into sight there is still a great deal of hesitation to make the same choice of increasing university autonomy again. The government lacks faith that the increase in university autonomy, brought about by the HOAK, will lead to a permanent process of innovation, differentiation, distribution and concentration of tasks, of which the logical resultant is the profiling of institutes.

The HOAK philosophy is also threatened from within the universities themselves. The reaction of the universities to the Selective Shrinkage and Growth operation (SKG) and their reluctance to cooperate in the VSNU context do not exactly illustrate university independence and self-confidence. The universities were also very hesitant in their reaction to the plans of a VSNU study group (VSNU, 1988) in which they were to play a major role in setting the terms of employment. They showed the same hesitancy with regard to the ARHO recommendation (ARHO, 1988) in which the argument was put forward for a more decisive administrative structure.

The 'garbage can' type of decision-making (cf. Cohen et al., 1972), characteristic of university organizations, makes it extremely unlikely that the heuristic model described in this subsection will be quick to develop. It is a model which assumes rigid, hierarchical organizations, clear-cut entrepreneurial objectives, team spirit, decision-making dedicated to commitment, smooth cooperation, etc. In general, such characteristics fail to correspond with professional organizations. It is the specific behavioural characteristiscs of the actors which characterize an organization as a professional one. Behaviour can therefore be regarded as a mechanism to retard system changes.

We have described the world of continually increasing university autonomy as one which, basically, is conceivable. In this section we have used the term path-dependent in an attempt to make it clear that in the progress of a process, in which the time dimension must be measured in decades, a number of successive interchanges will need to be passed. In such a process of adapting the system to the changed environment the main point is to progress step by step, continually expanding the perspective. However, if we expect to arrive at our destination at top speed, while the road is only suitable for driving in second gear, then there is a high risk of accidents happening along the way. This can be illustrated by the plans of a discussion group (Rinnooy Kan, et al., 1987) for an 'entrepreneurial university' in answer to the challenge formulated in the HOOP. The discussion group describes a model in which the government steps back to an even greater distance. The main elements of this model are:

- the government funds universities on a basis of the number of students only (no more basic funding per discipline to cover the fixed costs);

- the universities can collect tuition fees which can be different for each faculty (these fees are given as ranging between 1,600 and 10,000 guilders);
- the universities can take out loans on the capital market using those properties which have been transferred to them as security;
- the entrepreneurial university can undertake new disciplines and pre-select students themselves;
- the university can be regarded as the holding company and the independently functioning faculties as working companies; basically, a faculty would be able to detach itself from the university.

The interchange at which the choice for such an entrepreneurial university becomes a viable option is by no means in sight yet. The first road – leading to stronger university management – will have to be travelled first of all. Time and space will be required to allow a generation of research managers to develop. The university administrative organization will have to be reinforced.

Once this road has been travelled the following problems will have to be dealt with in the next part of our journey towards an entrepreneurial university (cf. Groenewegen, 1987, p. 1148):

- if the responsibility for decision-making is transferred from the ministry to universities, faculties and teaching and research units, it must be ensured that adequate information is available at these levels and that the judging bodies are able to scrutinise proposals;
- all persons at the various levels must be motivated to take initiatives and act in accordance with the organization's goals. This tends to hurt a professional organization where it hurts most and will therefore require a great deal of internal missionary work to be carried out by the governors of entrepreneurial universities;
- personnel policy will need to be freed of its present rigidity; a far wider diversity in salary structure must be possible so that incentives can also be applied at micro-level to encourage entrepreneurial behaviour;
- also required is an administrative structure which makes more flexible financial reallocations between growth and shrinkage activities possible between the various entrepreneurial universities; it must be plausible to shift budgets from those teaching and research units which do not fit in with the institute's profile to those units that do;
- finally, the main problem is the staffing of those organizations within the university which have to ensure that the spirit of enterprise is in line with the goals of teaching and research. The danger of bureaucracy, lobbies, the implementation of easily effected standards, etc., is distinctly present through a 'market organization'.

The conclusion of this subsection is that the heuristics of completely autonomous universities, or the presented heuristics of the entrepreneurial university, will remain at a utopian distance if one makes the mistake of thinking that this model will immediately come into sight after the HOAK has been realized. Ensuing from the concept that systems are path-dependent is the fact that the climate will need to be made ripe on a daily basis to be able to make the right decision when reaching tomorrow's interchange.

5.3 The missing complement of the HOAK policy concept: a stronger supra-university level

5.3.1 Culture as a pre-condition for the possibilities to change a system

In the above section a heuristic model of complete autonomy, competing universities based on the American model, was sketched as the counterfactual for the HOAK proposals. In that model the government's only influence – either direct or indirect (through grants or vouchers) – is via the demand side of the production process of teaching and research. The government has been relieved of its role as the owner/director of universities. It no longer fulfils what we see as the typical role of a government but becomes the customer of university products redressed to one of the actors within the environment of the university system. Decisions about concentration, distribution of tasks, profiling, cooperation between universities, coordination, the closing-down of production units (faculties), setting limits on the intake of students in disciplines or sectors, etc., are made through the price and market mechanism. In the heuristic model described in section 5.2.3 levels seven and six are no longer necessary to deal with this type of regulation. The research system is thus decapitated to five levels, similar to the earlier example of the production line for the manufacture of vehicles, which also reaches no higher than concern level.

Since the eighties we have seen the quite distinct trend of universities being more market-oriented and generally more responsive to their surroundings. A more aggressive approach is taken in their advertising with the purpose of attracting students. Nevertheless, there is little reason to assume that these trends will progress to such an extent that the model described above will become reality in the foreseeable future. Even in the initial phase of the HOAK government stated quite explicitly that higher education would continue to be both the concern and instrument of government policy with a somewhat more general government involvement at most. As far as the government is concerned the journey goes no further than the first interchange.

This brings us to the cultural limitations of our higher education system. Our present state and social culture has also followed a time path. Before the Netherlands became a welfare state, higher education was not regarded as one of the main tasks. However, in the welfare state the government's main tasks were defined more loosely. In the welfare state that has developed in the Netherlands the government has taken a large number of tasks upon itself, including the provision of a system of higher education. Characteristic of a welfare state are the relatively egalitarian relationships and when applied in the system of higher education this implies that income, origin, etc., may never form a barrier for acceptance. The manner in which we in the Netherlands have shaped our attitude towards educational rights is, for example, illustrated in our system of study grants which is totally a-selective. This contrasts sharply against other wealthy, developed countries such as the United States and Canada where potential students have to compete to win a grant and obtain themselves a place in one of the better universities. The British system is in this respect also more competitive than the Dutch system (cf. Pratt, 1987, p. 25).

Nor is it appropriate in that egalitarian culture for universities to select their students for initial teacher training courses. Equality is therefore related to the supply. Dutch universities, or faculties in a certain discipline, can not be categorized according to quality (as is the case in the USA) . In general they are all considered to be equally good and all lead to the same attainment targets. This is why we have a uniform, government fixed, tuition fee for all universities.

The above illustrates how institutions (systems) are embedded in an environment of norms and values. In the United States of America the norm of "equal opportunities" is operationalized in terms of formal initial opportunities (every newspaper boy can become a millionaire and/or president); in the Netherlands the concept of equality leans more towards an equal outcome (cf. Wolfson, 1988, p. 290-296).

In this book we have made no value judgments on these and similar differences in culture. We simply make note of the fact that culture is a pre-condition for the opportunity to bring about changes in the system. A system reflects a culture. This implies that elements taken from another system (the American system for instance), and the goals inherent in that system, cannot simply be brought into the Dutch university system.

To analyze government policy on science and higher education we take the existing culture of the welfare state in the Netherlands as the given factor (*if*). In this section we ask ourselves, within the framework of the institutional design of that policy (which institutions, instruments, administrative arrangements), what (*then*) are the options for shaping the relationships between levels seven, six and five in the research system. How is decision-making on the distribution and concentration of tasks, profiling, coooperation and coordination organized? What role should be set aside for level six? We devote particular attention to the tasks of level six because we think that the strong emphasis laid in the HOAK document on the do's and don'ts of the government (level seven) and the universities (level five) neglects the role of level six.

In subsection 2 we outline the way in which supra-university cooperation was shaped up to a few years ago in the Netherlands. It is the story of the rise and fall of the Universities Council (Academische Raad). The Universities Council had the double task of advising the minister and looking after the interests of the universities. Nevertheless, the Council's recommendations were often divided and the discussion about the common interest failed to result in binding decision-making. The Council was therefore not really successful in operating at level six. The Universities Council was dissolved in the mid-eighties and its tasks dissipated. Since then the task of giving advice has been designated to the Advisory Council for Higher Education (ARHO) and looking after the common interests of universities is now structured in the Association of Universities in the Netherlands (VSNU). Subsection 5.3.3 goes into the ARHO and its connections with the longer standing advisory body for science policy, the RAWB.

The role of the VSNU, the body which presently acts in the interests of all universities, is discussed in subsection 5.3.4. In subsection 5.3.5 we summarize the above in a reflection on the optimal institutionalization of the sixth level, passing in review a number of options for its adequate institutionalization. Our most significant conclusion is that there is the lack of an independent board with an administrative function and authoritative powers at level six in the Dutch research system. We regard such a board to be the logical complement for the HOAK concept to become a success.

5.3.2 The rise and fall of the Universities Council

The supra-university level has never been strongly institutionalized in the Netherlands. Ideas have been put forward, and have indeed caught on since World War II, especially those suggested by the State Commission headed by Reinink. The task of this commission was to advise the government on the reorganization of higher education. The commission gave consideration to two different administrative systems for what was considered the essential coordination and cooperation in the world of the universities.

The first system (the 'Universitas Neerlandica') entailed the designation of autonomous competences to the joint universities in the form of an inter-university coordinating body. The competences of this body would lie in the area of the budget (that this body would be responsible for dividing a lump sum – in the national budget for higher education – between the universities) and the right to appoint professors.

The second system was clearly less far-reaching. Autonomy (even if only limited) would be granted to the individual universities. The government would remain responsible for the university budget. Nevertheless, there was still the need for a consultative body with advisory tasks: a High Universities Council (HAR). The State Commission ultimately gave preference to this second system. Yet even this less far-raching system ran up against objections from the universities as they saw no need for a body imposed upon them by the powers that be (the government). It was emphasized that such a communal body should in no way affect the character and independence of individual universities and polytechnics. It was on this basis that the universities and polytechnics structured their joint consultation in the fifties (in the Inter-university Liaison Organization). The High Universities Council was never realized.

The reform of the higher education system was finally accomplished in 1960 with the University Education Act (WWO'60) which also made provision for the establishment of a *Universities Council*. This body was given a less powerful status than (the HAR) proposed by the Reinink Commission.

The Universities Council existed up to 1986. The legislator had earmarked three tasks for this council:

- *advising* (the government and universities);
- *consulting* (between the universities and with government); and
- *coordinating* (in the distribution of tasks between the universities).

The council had no authoritative powers in respect of coordination, hence the little success it had in this area. This was because of the formal status of the council, which was such that in performing its duties it was completely dependent upon the latitude it was given by the individual institutes on the one hand, and the government on the other. Obtaining this latitude was a necessary condition for the Universities Council to be able to function properly. Sad to say, this latitude was generally lacking. Both the universities themselves and the government were the cause of this.

When assessing the fulfilment of the council's two main tasks – advising and consulting – it can be said that its position in the administrative system had shifted over the course of time. This was evident from two points. First, it can be pointed out that during its initial period the Council took the initiative on a number of important aspects of policy. Later however, it became more a case or reacting to the initiatives taken by government. The reason for this was the general tenor that the government and the ministries started to undertake more in the sphere of developing policy for higher education and stopped acting primarily as managers. The role of the Universities Council in preparing policy tended towards a monitoring, defensive and criticising role.

Second, the effect of the WUB (introduced in 1970) on the position and the functioning of the Council. It was established in the WUB that decision-making by the Council should be on behalf of the universities. Each university was given one vote; the Government-appointed members of the Council had only an advisory vote. The consequence of this was that the essence of decision-making in actual fact came to lie outside the Universities Council. Given that many university councils gave their delegates binding mandates, decisions were not taken at the meetings of the Council itself but during university council meetings at which the relevant mandates were established. This resulted in the Council's advice being no more than an accumulation of the various stands taken by the individual universities themselves. In other words: the introduction of the WUB brought about a shift from advice given by experts to advice from the stakeholders. In the actual performance of its tasks, the Council thus evolved to become primarly an advisory body *to* the government as the voice of the joint universities. This development resulted in an even bigger gap between the policy preparatory work carried out by the Universities Council and the establishment of policy by government and parliament. In other words: the more it became evident that the Universities Council had little to say by virtue of its own authority, the less the government took notice of its advice. In terms of our system the conclusion must be that the level of operation of the Universities Council was degraded from level six to (a supporting role) at level five.

In conclusion, it can be established that the Universities Council failed to develop into a powerful and directorial body in the system. Its advice was often divided and its task of consultation failed to lead to binding decision-making. Because of the complex structure of the Council's organization (a large number of sections corresponding with the various disciplines) recommendations and decisions took a long time to reach. Many wheels were involved in the preparatory work leading up to the formulation of recommendations. On the one hand there were the sections and the various committees of the Council; on the other hand, the universities. The procedure generally taken was as follows. The universities, and possibly the sections and committees, were asked to comment on a particular policy proposal. These comments were then compiled into a preliminary recommendation on which the universities could submit their amendments. Having completed this procedure it was then discussed in a Universities Council plenary, often preceeded by a discussion in the Executive Council. This procedure was so time-consuming that the level of the Universities Council formal efficiency was generally very low.

Upon analysis, the shortcoming of the Universities Council can be exlained by using the economic theory of public choice. Among other aspects, this theory is concerned with the conditions under which the common interests of multiple actors can be promoted.

The effective promotion of interests can be seen as the common interest of the universities. Such a common interest is referred to as a 'group good' (cf. Olson, 1965). The decision-making theory followed here shows quite clearly that it is a misconception to think that a group good will be realized simply because it is in the interest of all (in this case: in the interest of each university). The most important factor as to whether a goup good is formed or not is the group's *size*. If a group is too large, organization and decision-making about that group good will not be achieved on a basis of voluntary collaboration. Uncertainty as to whether the other participants are willing to share in the cost (in whatever sense) of a joint activity tempts the individual participant to withdraw from the group's decision-making if it goes against the grain. This is the prisoner's dilemma that constantly faces each of the thirteen universities and polytechnics within the framework of the Universities Council. The prisoner's dilemma is a game theory model of the behaviour of a number of prisoners who have jointly committed a crime and are now isolated from each other. Each prisoner is promised a reward (in terms of a shorter sentence) if he betrays his accomplices (their sentence will then be increased). Because each prisoner is unaware of the sentiments of his accomplices, each prisoner is tempted (rational) to cooperate, resulting in the paradoxical situation that each prisoner is thus given the maximum sentence. Conversely, if no one had 'talked' then they would all have received a shorter sentence. The group good (a shorter sentence for all) is not achieved because the prisoners have no authoritative sanctions at their disposal in order to reach an agreement, and stick to that agreement. The universities in the Universities Council were all in a similar position and thus unable to face government as a solid front in order to promote their common interests.

When the first Lubbers government came into power in 1982 a project group 'External Advice' was established. This project group was set the task of investigating the conglomerate of external advisory bodies of the government. The Universities Council was assessed as follows:
- the effectiveness of the advice given by the Universities Council is limited;
- the recommendations drawn up by this body are often no more than a collage of the viewpoints of the individual universities;
- the recommendations of the Universities Council play an extremely small role in the government's preparation or establishment of policy;
- advice is slow in forthcoming and is not very efficient;
- a great deal of funding is involved.

As a result of this assessment the Universities Council was disbanded at the end of 1985 and replaced by a new administrative structure. As proposed by he project group this structure involved separating the advisory and consulting tasks. The Association of Universities in the Netherlands was established for the purpose of taking over the consulting task (see 5.3.4). The Advisory Council for Higher Education (ARHO) was set up to advise on matters of policy in higher education (including higher vocational education).

5.3.3 The Advisory Council for Higher Education

The term set for the ARHO is four years. Its members (eight, two of whom are appointed in an advisory capacity) are nominated and appointed in their own right; they do not represent universities or other organizations. The chairman and secretary are appointed on a full-time basis and the rest perform their tasks in part-time service, the majority of them in addition to their regular work. In general, the council is geared towards individual projects and third parties can also be invited to participate in the work of a project group, either on a temporary or permanent basis. The decision can also be taken to request preliminary advice or studies from outside experts. In all cases the council checks the actual formulation of questions and provisional viewpoints with outsiders who are required to bring in specific expertise in certain areas.

The establishment of the ARHO gives rise to the question of how this body measures up to the RAWB with its broad advisory task within the system (which in 1991 is to be expanded even further when the RAWB will be transformed into the Advisory Council for Science and Technology Policy; AWT). The tasks and status of the RAWB have already been discussed in Chapter 4. Past history has shown the ARHO to be a body which is aimed primarily at the Directorate-General for Higher Education and Scientific Research of the Ministry of Education and Science, whereas the RAWB is mainly oriented towards the Directorate-General for Science Policy (and to an increasing extent towards the Ministry of Economic Affairs). The organization of level six therefore reflects the organizational structure of level seven. The ARHO is targeted towards higher education, including higher vocational education; the RAWB is targeted towards research, including non-university research. It is also of importance to know that advice given by the ARHO is concerned especially with the early stages of policy delopment. Despite these differences it can be stated that there is quite a large amount of overlap in the subjects on which both ARHO and RAWB give advice.

This gives rise to the question whether the scope of ARHO advice is wide enough to justify the independent position of this board alongside the RAWB. It would therefore seem only natural for the ARHO to be absorbed by the RAWB, possibly in the form of a separate section.

5.3.4 The Association of Universities in the Netherlands

The Association of Universities in the Netherlands (VSNU) was established for the purpose of carrying out the task of consultation. The necessary separation of the tasks of advising the minister (by the ARHO) and consultation and promotion of the common interest (by the VSNU) can basically be seen as an improvement of the institutionalization of the sixth level. Nevertheless, the question still remains whether the VSNU is capable of fulfilling level six tasks and of effecting decision-making on those tasks.

It would seem that the VSNU is faced with the same problems as the Universities Council. Also in the VSNU we see the same thirteen institutes of university education consulting with the minister and there is still no collective autonomy. It must be feared that the level of the VSNU's effectiveness will be low given the non-commital nature of its decision-making. It would also seem that under the VSNU the interests of the institutes themselves take precedence above the common interest. The consequence of this is that the ministry is able to play the universities off against each other. We still see the ministry using its position of power to influence developments in certain universities at micro-level. Examples of this being the way in which the ministry manages innovation funds, and the way in which it has attempted to accomplish networks of trainee research assistants (by inviting prominent professors to develop proposals outside the realms of the existing frameworks). From the point of view of supra-university coordination, decision-making would benefit from this if an organization operating at level six is able to play an important role. We shall return to this subject later on.

As far as the functioning of the intermediary level six is concerned we see a remarkable difference between the university world and the institutes of higher vocational education. In the latter there is a much clearer division of roles between the institutes and the intermediary body (in this case the Council on Higher Vocational Education (HBO-raad)). Contrary to its university counterpart, this council functions on level six. The Council on Higher Vocational Education performs those tasks which are above the capabilities of the individual institutes. This is an accepted pattern in the field of higher vocational education; the institutes have neither the inclination nor the scale to deal directly with the Ministry (and vice versa). This Council functions as a sort of umbrella, sheltering the government and the institutes to ensure that when the rain does fall it is scattered about. The reason for this is that – resulting from the economies of scale operation in the eighties – institutes of higher vocational education were given a different funding and administrative structure. Since then, institutes of higher vocational education have had far greater financial freedom. They also have the freedom to choose their own administrative structure (board of governors or directors). The power of self-regulation is therefore much more evident in these institutes. Their preoccupation with ministerial affairs is proportionately less. Given that they are not constantly under the pressure of having to deal with the government they give the Council on Higher Vocational Education all the administrative leeway required for it to function as the level six organization.

Conclusion: the VSNU, like its predecessor the Universities Council, threatens to become the plaything of the the government at level seven and the universities at level five. This is mainly because of the lack of authoritative competences. The number of members of the

VSNU is such that it is a large group in which the individual members are inclined towards *strategic behaviour* without that behaviour being able to be sanctioned effectively. In reality, this strategic behaviour is to be found in the fact that the individual universities jointly impede decision-making, or avoid it, as soon as they feel that they must disagree with the resulting (expected) decision. The universities then tend to think that better arrangements can be made with the Ministry on a bilateral basis.

Secondly, it is important that the government is always tempted to make direct arrangements with the universities if it feels that such action is more beneficial than dealing through the VSNU. From this point of view, relations in the field of higher vocational education are exemplary: direct contact between the Ministry and the institutes of higher vocational education has been minimized and is of a more general nature. This makes it possible for the Council on Higher Vocational Education at level 6 to fulfil its role of intermediary.

5.3.5 Optimal institutionalization of the sixth level

We already stated in Chapter 2 that the institutionalization of level six was the least crystallized of all the levels in the system. This is because of the level of abstraction and complexity of the tasks at level six. In the practical situation in the Netherlands several institutional modalities have developed alongside each other; all of them sophisticated by nature: consultative platform, advisory bodies, plus some budgetary instrumentation (budget as the lubricant).

Yet our argument here is for a more far-reaching modality, one which we shall explain in more detail. An independent administrative body should be created at level six (alongside organizations which have strategic advisory tasks, such as the RAWB) in which binding decisions are taken on the distribution and concentration of tasks, the discontinuation and establishment of disciplines, centres of excellence, etc. There are also various options open to designate level six with competences regarding the allocation of budgetary funds to the universities.

The presence of a strong insitution at level six with sufficient powers to take decisions and impose sanctions would basically render the above described strategic behaviour of universities and government – the consequence of non-binding decision-making – impossible. It could contribute towards solving the problem of structure in the university system. This implies that both institutes and government would sacrifice part of their autonomy and subject themselves to decision-making at level six. Such a structure is quite the opposite to those administrative structures which have been developed in public administration in the Netherlands to date.

Under the pressure of major cut-backs in expenditure something similar had already happened temporarily in the university system in the past (1982/1983) within the framework of the so-called Distribution and Concentration of Tasks exercise (TVC). A body was then created (the TVC body) which was given far-reaching tasks, and although these tasks were of an advisory nature (advising the minister) agreements were still made by the universities' representatives which placed the institutes under certain obligations. Adopting a game theory approach, Grondsma (1987) explains the success of this 'arena of consultation' on the basis of two factors:

1. there is sufficient information available and none of the players (university representatives) has more information than the others, in other words: a monopoly on information is avoided; and
2. the time limit imposed by the minister, plus the threat that if this time limit is not met he will put forward his own economy plan, reinforces the element of harmony in the

game. The game played here is a so-called variable sum game: by entering the arena the players are better off working as a team than if they simply stand at the side and watch on.

The TVC operation illustrates that when subjected to heavy pressure (to economize) the universities become malleable. Nevertheless, the same administrative arrangement was not used for the next retrenchment operation (Selective Shrinkage and Growth; 1986). The minister took it upon himself to make the decisions after obtaining advice from small, fast-working external committees which had investigated the quality of the disciplines at various locations. Despite the difference in the arrangement chosen by the ministry there is still a quite clear parity between the TVC and the SKG: in both cases the existing consultative body of the joint universities – the AR and VSNU respectively – were considered too weak to be able to perform this level six task.

Problems of scale, cost, labour market perspectives for students, etc., tend to turn the distribution of tasks, concentration, cooperation, coordination, establishing the main areas of disciplines, into permanent problems in the university system of today, apart from the budgetary (economizing) aspects which at times gain the upper hand. These problems cannot be 'solved' by repeating a TVC or SKG operation once every few years. An open university system must have a regulating system at its disposal by which the management system and the output is kept in line with the changing surroundings. Adequate fulfilment of the level six task in the system is therefore of the utmost importance. Below is a comparison between four models of potential institutional orders in research and science policy:

1. the bureaucratic order: the government as the director/owner of universities. Level six bodies perform advisory tasks only. This model comes closest to the present reality;
2. the market order with completely autonomous universities as outlined heuristically in subsection 5.2.3. In this model the government is only one of the actors connected with universities. The system has been decapitated to a maximum of five levels. There is no longer a need for level six;
3. strong institutionalization of level six. Level six also has the power of the purse with regard to the allocation of funds to universities. In reality, the system closest to this model is to be found in Great Britain where the University Funding Council is established at level six;
4. strong institutionalization of level six, yet with far more restricted budgeting competences than in the previous model, for instance only for that part of the budget which is of strategic importance.

In the choice between these models for the institutional design of government's research and science policy we again adopt the if-then approach. *If* we may be allowed to assume that the government's most important administrative goals are:

a on the one hand, to manage the universities more at arm's length; but
b on the other hand, that higher education and research continue to be both the concern and instrument of government policy;

as acknowledged in the HOAK and the HOOP, what *then* is the most suitable model for realizing that government policy? We shall now discuss the above four models. The first two will be discussed in somewhat lesser detail given that these two extremes were dealt with more explicitly in section 5.2.

The bureaucratic order

The government fulfils the role of director/owner of the universities. If decisions need to be taken with regard to the distribution of tasks, concentration, cooperation between universities, discontinuation of production units (faculties), setting limitations on the intake of students in certain sectors, etc., then those decisions are made at level seven. Bodies at level six or five can be required to give their advice on these matters. The advantage of this unambiguous line relationship between government and universities is that it enables government to give maximum justification to parliament for the policy it pursues given that no competences have been delegated to a level six body. The most bureaucratic model is therefore also the most democratic one in terms of external legitimization. The main disadvantage of this model is that, if the outcomes of decision-making are to correspond with the goals of government, the government has to generate a great deal of information and must be able to use it in the correct aggregates. Central management (at level seven) of the university production processes therefore involves extremely high information costs and transaction costs. Knowledge of production processes which are difficult to measure, such as scientific research, is generally stored at work level and thus a large degree of involvement of the lower levels in decision-making remains necessary.

The market order

In the previously outlined heuristic model of completely autonomous universities the universities compete against each other to win the favours of the customers (students, trade and industry, the government as principal). Each university will attempt to find a '*niche*' in the form of typical characteristics specific to its own institution. In the area of education, the universities will compete against each other in terms of price, for instance, or the duration of a study, teaching methods, curriculum, and possibly denomination. Enormous differences in quality can therefore arise between universities. There is room for both Harrods and Marks and Spencer. Top institutes/faculties will only want to accept top students. Therefore, various selection procedures occur in this model.

In this model the government does not fulfil the typical role of government but is the customer of university products, redressed to one of the actors within the environment of the university system. Decisions about concentration, distribution of tasks, profiling, cooperation, coordination, the discontinuation of production units (faculties), setting limits on the intake of students in disciplines or sectors, etc., are made through price and market mechanisms. Levels seven and six are no longer necessary to enforce this type of regulation. The research system is decapitated to five levels, comparable with the earlier example of the vehicle production line which also does not reach higher than a concern level.

This model is not dealt with here. As we explained in the previous section, if this model is to come into sight as a real option, a certain time path will first have to be taken. The second government aim – that higher education and research continue to be both the concern and instrument of government policy – indicates that we are not yet on this path.

A level six organization with far-reaching competences (the UFC model)

A powerful and directorial body is established at level six. The relevant body is independent and can make binding decisions. In this option we suggest that this independent administrative body should also be given power of the purse. The level six body thus has the maximum competences to be able to function in a managerial capacity in the university system. This weighty allocation of competences to level six is naturally at the expense of budgetary and other tasks, presently performed at levels seven and five. This board could also be given the responsibility of setting up evaluation committees. Debate is under way at present as to whether evaluation committees should advise the minister or whether they should advise the joint universities (VSNU). It will be quite clear that the former is less desirable given that it would impede 'management at arm's length'. On the other hand, the VSNU is far too inadequately equipped to be able to enforce recommendations of evaluation committees in the event that some universities be against them.

This third model is especially based on the structure of the British university system. In Great Britain the distribution of direct funding is in the hands of such a body: the University Funding Council (UFC) which replaced the University Grants Committee (UGC) in 1989. We will discuss the differences between the UGC and the UFC and the backgrounds that led to this institutional change later. The most important aspect here is that both the UFC and its predecessor are level six bodies.

The UGC was established in 1919 to advise the government on the funding of universities. In practice, advice given by the UGC on the distribution of funds between the institutes has always been followed and thus we can speak of a de facto budget allocation organization. In order to explain why the UGC advice has always been followed we must point out that in Great Britain it is traditional that the funding of individual universities is not a matter for politics. Maintaining a safe distance between government and universities is part and parcel of British political culture. The British Department of Education and Science has therefore only a relatively small office which deals with the university sector.

The UGC comprised 24 members, of which only the chairman and vice chairman held full-time positions. The majority of its members were from the academic world; the rest from trade and industry. All were chosen from a wide range of disciplines and were appointed by the Secretary of State for Education and Science. The UGC also had a number of subcommittees in the various disciplines; each subcommittee being chaired by a member of the main committee.

The most important task of the UGC was to draw up a report containing recommendations on the allocation of the annually recurring grant for research and education between the various universities. Long-term figures were also used to assist in this. The allocation criteria adopted by the UGC were not made public. Funds allocated were generally block grants, although earmarking did take place for specific subjects. The UGC did however couple its allocation with advice and guidelines as to how the funds should be spent. Review committees were also established by the UGC.

Up to 1981 an incremental policy had always been adopted with regard to the criteria for the distribution of funds among universities and it was in this year that the first change was seen. In 1981 the UGC was informed that its budget was to be cut by more than 10%. This resulted in the UGC passing on this reduction to the universities, not proportionately but selectively. The outcome was a cut-back in the budgets of universities varying from 6% to 44% (cf. Pratt, 1987, p. 47). The criteria used for this selective division of the reduced budget were never made public. However, it is important to note that the UGC, as a typical level six organization, was apparently capable of making selective decisions, even if did cost it the trust of the universities. The Netherlands government never dared to give such powers of decision-making to a level six organization, consequently ad hoc decision-making arrangements were made when necessary (TVC, SKG).

In 1989 the UGC was replaced by the University Funding Council. This was a consequence of the Education Reform Bill which was passed in 1988. This bill established that a Polytechnics and Colleges Funding Council (PCFC) would be set up in addition to the UFC.

This PCFC would perform an analogous function with regard to non-university higher education – a sector which prior to that had been tackled by local government.

This major change in the British system of higher education was announced in the white paper issued by the Secretary of State for Education and Science in April 1987 entitled 'Higher Education: meeting the challenge'. The main differences between the UFC and its predecessor, the UGC, are:

- the UFC comprises only fifteen, also independent, members, half of whom are from the university community and the other half from trade and industry. The members of the UGC were predominantly representatives of the university community;
- the UGC also had an important role in advising on matters of policy and calculated for the government how much funding was needed for the university sector; conversely, the UFC is only concerned with the allocation of the budget between the universities and does not have the task of advising on the overall government policy on universities. "The UFC's essential responsibilities should relate to the allocation of funding between universities rather than to its overall amount, which is a matter for Government to decide after considering all the evidence" (Secretary of State, 1987, p. 38). It should be pointed out however, that over the years the government had on many occasion deviated from the recommendations put forward by the UGC on the total amount of funding required for the universities; this undermined the authority of the UGC (Shattock, 1987, p. 481-482);
- the government issues the UFC with rules for its task of allocating the budget. The system of block grants is brought to an end and the UFC must enter into contracts with the universities in which they agree to a set standard of performance. As yet this contract concept has not been worked out in detail.

The switch-over from UGC to UFC can be regarded as a form of centralization in the British university system. Over the years the government had become increasingly dissatisfied with the protective role played by the UGC in the university system; dissatisfaction which culminated under the present Conservative government. Although the UGC was able to meet the large cut-backs enforced in 1981 by adopting a selective policy of retrenchment this undermined its position in the academic world. The UGC – and the buffer principle it represented – adopted a progressively more defensive attitude and eventually led to its replacement by the UFC. Despite the clear shift in accents (at a greater distance from the universities, stronger influence of trade and industry, more emphasis on efficiency) the system of management at arm's length remains effective in Great Britain through the intermediation of a body at level six.

A level six body with strategic budgetary competences (a somewhat weaker version of the UFC model)

The supra-university processes of coordination in this fourth model are also regulated by a level six organization, yet this differs from model three in that it does not have full power of the purse. In this model only strategic budgetary competences are set aside for level six. One can think here in terms of national centres of excellence, research schools for post-graduate courses and other strategic developments which lead to the profiling of universities. The power of decision on the allocation of funding between the universities for such strategic objectives could be placed in the hands of this level six body, while the existing normative funding mechanism used by the government to fund universities remains intact.

The HOAK document fails to answer the question of how supra-university processes of coordination should be regulated if the universities are given a greater degree of autonomy. This section can therefore be regarded as the logical complement to the HOAK proposals. We will now end this section by comparing the four different options, checking them against the objectives of government research and science policy, taking into account the present position of the Dutch system along the time path.

The bureaucratic model, and the model of completely autonomous universities, can be regarded as the two outer poles of potential mechanisms for structuring the system. It will be clear that structuring the university system by means of a constant flow of government measures is not a very attractive perspective. By producing the HOAK document the government has attempted to make it quite clear that there is a wish to break away from this method of management and to give the universities more autonomy. The bureaucratic model does not therefore correspond with the aims of government. Although this model does provide for maximal political justification it also means that direct management of the university system by the government requires a constant flow of detailed and reliable information. Past experience has already shown that this precondition for central management of the university system cannot be met.

The option of completely autonomous universities must also be rejected. Contrary to the American system, the Dutch system is far too small to allow structuring issues to be solved through the introduction of a competitive model. We noted earlier that the fulfilment of supra-university tasks of coordination in a competitive model are not organized at level six. The most we see in this model is non-committal cooperative bodies of universities which reach no further than level five as far as their actual fulfilment of tasks. Because of their non-authoritative construction it is hardly likely that they would be able to accomplish level six tasks.

Nor does this decapitated model, in which there is no place for level six and the government is reduced to simply one of the actors in the university environment at level five, meet the government's present aims. It fails because of the fact that higher education and reseaerch remain to be both goal and instrument of government policy. The objectives of the government reflect the culture of the Dutch welfare state. Given the path-dependence of administrative systems the option of completely autonomous universities falls outside the realm of the real possibilities. This can only come into view after many interchanges have been crossed on the way towards increasing university autonomy. Even though after having travelled the HOAK path, continuing along this path is within the realms of possibility, it would still seem most unlikely.

Model three is the option of setting up an independent administrative body at level six which allocates the government higher education and research budget to the universities. Binding decision-making would also have to be possible within this body on such aspects as the distribution of tasks, concentration, discontinuation and and establishment of disciplines, centres of excellence, etc. The question is whether this UFC model would be able to meet the aims of government and what is the time dimension of its feasibility.

There are many answers to the former. If by 'increasing university autonomy' – the first government aim referred to – we have to think in terms of only a decentralizing movement from level seven to level five, then the answer is in the negative. If the government does not regard the strengthening of level five – as implied in the HOAK document – as a goal in itself, but rather as a means to relieve level seven of its managerial tasks and to manage the system as a whole at arm's length, then a decentralizing movement to level six does meet the aims of the government. For the universities, the creation of a momentous body at level six implies a loss of autonomy. If level six is to be able to fulfil its tasks adequately, decision-making at levels five and below must be loyal to it. To ensure this, level six must have sufficient strategic information about control mechanisms and sanction mechanisms. On the other hand, level six will also need to adopt a policy of management at arm's length and not wish to sit in the chair of university governors. To avoid – as is now the case at level seven – a substantial 'counter-bureaucracy' emerging at level six the level six body must not be too large and must be able to perform its tasks with a minimum of staff. In this model, level five can continue to play a role in the development of strategic initiatives, whereas decision-making concerned with the implementation of policy at level six is directorial. The question is whether one should mourn the relative loss of autonomy at level five that this implies. The recent past – especially within the framework of the retrenchment operations, TVC and SKG – has shown that level five has frustrated the allocation objectives of the higher levels through compensative behaviour.

With regard to the second government aim – the government maintains responsibility for higher education and research policy – again there are many answers to the question whether the UFC model can meet this aim. An independent administrative body at level six changes the nature of the government's responsibility. The minister cannot be called to account for the decisions taken by an independent administrative body in the same way as he could be for his own decisions, or those of his civil servants (compare the relationship between the Minister of Finance and the Nederlandsche Bank – the national monetary authority –, as established in the Bank Act). The ministerial responsibility for the university system is shifted from the direct curriculum level to the meta-level of being responsible for appointing and dismissing members of the level six board of representatives. Parliament will thus also have to be prepared to adopt a policy of management at arm's length. The introduction of a level six body will therefore need to be embedded in a process of gradual cultural change in which politics and science manage to keep their distance. Politicians will have to learn to refrain from intervening in specific parts of the research system. The ministry could be trimmed down as a number of tasks would be performed by a level six body. In short, if a body at level six is to be viable it is essential to strive for a policy of management at arm's length with regard to the research system and that the present inclination of level seven to act as interveners makes way for a culture of self-restraint.

Our somewhat tentative conclusion is that the model of strong institutionalization of level six can, basically, be conciliated with the aims of government. One major advantage of a level six body is that a wide range of influences surrounding the university system can be brought into effect thanks to its broad and mixed composition, whereas if the universities are directly dependent on the government the relevant environment of the education and research system is coloured and reduced because of the perception of politics and bureaucracy. A body that functions as a buffer at level six gives an additional guarantee that the research system will not become politicized.

Although – basically – conciliable with the aims of government, we feel that model three cannot be achieved as yet in the Dutch setting. Contrary to the situation in Great Britain, we have no rich tradition of university management in the Netherlands. We are presently suffering from the fact that in the Dutch research system managerial tasks are still performed at the various levels as a sort of 'fatigue duty'. Good university managers must progress in spite of considerable opposition. It will be clear that a place is only set aside for a weighty level six body if it can be staffed for the greater part by prominent figures in the scientific world who have built up a reputation in their (original) discipline and are widely experienced as managers in the university system and/or other research organizations.

Whereas the UGC option is probably too far away, the fourth option in which a level six body is not designated with the task of allocating to universities the overall national budget for higher education and research but only the allocation of that part of the budget intended for strategic developments (the profiling of universities), we feel could be achieved in principle. First of all we could think in terms of the government's plans to stimulate research schools and centres of excellence. The level six body would determine for which universities (working in collaboration) such institutes should be set up in certain disciplines. Such decisions on concentration for the purpose of profiling universities prevents fragmentation throughout all the various locations of a discipline (macro-efficiency). If level seven were to busy itself with this then government will be faced with substantial problems of defining, informing, balancing and coordinating. In that case, the procedures involved in initiating concentrated post graduate courses can be seen as a warning. These initiatives are dominated by direct contacts between level seven and (groups of) prominent researchers in a discipline. Intermediary levels only became involved in decision-making at a later stage. It would seem that a structuring of the system would be most welcome here. The creation of a level six body as an 'arena of negotiation' for the allocation of the budget for this task saves the government the expense of high information and transaction costs.

Within the framework of these tasks, leading to university profiling, the level six body could also be designated with the task of allocating sizeable budgets for equipment, such as data-expertise centres. At present, the Ministry of Education and Science makes all the decisions in this area after being advised by the NWO bodies.

Whereas we do not feel that the UFC option could be realized as yet – given that experience in the field of university management is still lagging behind along the specified time path – this fourth option can be regarded especially as an opportunity to gain experience in decision-making on strategic issues at a high level in the research system. The realization of model four could bring the UFC model as an option closer by. The next question that needs answering is how this level six body should be designed in the case of model four. Should it be in the form of a completely new body, or is it possible that one of the existing boards in the research system (VSNU, NWO, RAWB, ARHO) could take on the level six task?

If we pass the existing boards in review it will be obvious that the level six task cannot be designated to the VSNU. The decision-making structure of the VSNU is not selection-oriented but gives rise to proportionate allocation.

If we were to designate NWO with this level six task we would in effect be increasing the scope of the tasks of this organization up to level six. In any event, this would imply that the present task of NWO, as the organization that manages the indirect funding of scientific research, would need to be verified anew in view of this new task. It is, however, difficult to see how NWO could simultaneously perform the bottom-up role – providing a shelter for researchers who make disciplinary quality judgments in national networks of disciplinary foundations and study groups – and the top-down role of a national organization which is positioned above universities. Should the choice be made for this option, in which NWO performs the level six task, the present hybrid structure of NWO would definitely have to be transformed into a top-down structure (see Chapter 6).

A second major objection to NWO in the level six role is that NWO is a research organization, whereas the level six task relates to decisions concerning both research *and* teaching. A third objection to NWO in the level six role – which is the easiest to overcome – is that the NWO board would appear to offer an insufficiently wide administrative basis to be able to perform the level six task totally independently. The NWO board, as the top of an administrative organization at level five, comprises only four members, three of whom are part-timers.

Of the existing boards the RAWB is the most eligible, in terms of both size and composition, to perform the level six task in model four. However, the RAWB is a pure advisory body and designating an advisory body with a budget allocation task could frustrate the independency of its advice. These considerations equally apply to the ARHO, plus the fact that the area covered by the ARHO is more limited than that of the RAWB. In our structure there is a strict division between the budget allocation tasks and strategic advisory tasks, and in this sense the proposed level six body is more on the lines of the British UFC than the UGC.

In view of these considerations it would appear that there are major objections against all the existing boards being designated with the important tasks of structuring the system. It is because of this that we would argue in favour of setting up a new body at level six to deal with the strategic issues of structuring the university system, including the allocation of the relevant part of the budget. This council should preferably be staffed by a wide body of research managers who have no direct links (or no longer) with university institutions. The Minister of Education and Science should be the person responsible for the 'hiring and firing' of the members of this body and he should also establish that part of the Education and Science budget available for this purpose. Management at arm's length implies that the parliament can call him to account on these tasks but not on decisions concerning allocation taken by the level six body. This calls for a process to be set in motion (or continued) of cultural change in respect of the protocol between the government and the scientific world. The establishment of a level six body will need to find its momentum within such a process.

5.4 Conclusions in the light of the model

In this section we summarize the conclusions drawn in this chapter. Conclusions one to eight relate to the implications of the HOAK document in the present system. Conclusion nine reflects section 2: what could the – as yet – uncolonized world look like? If we wished to progress towards a system of completely autonomous universities, or to be more modest: what system-transgressing measures can we think of on our way towards the next stopping place after the HOAK halt? In contrast to conclusion nine, conclusion ten describes the colonized world which leans towards a dual university management system. Conclusion eleven reflects section 3. In that section we argued that the HOAK, in its aim towards increasing the autonomy of universities, has devoted insufficient attention to the subsequent problems of supra-university coordination. In this final conclusion we also formulate a proposal for the adequate institutionalization of level six of the research system.

1. The administrative relationship between the government and universities can be described as a mixture of *autonomy* and *co-management*. The proposals made in the HOAK document aim primarily at giving government co-management a somewhat different character: more repressive (checking quality afterwards); and less preventive (issuing regulations beforehand). This is a less rigid form of co-management and thus offers more latitude for university autonomy.

2. The greater degree of latitude for university autonomy offered by the HOAK document has no affect on higher education remaining to be both the instrument and concern of those government actions for which the Minister of Education and Science – within the present culture of education as a task of the welfare state – must continue to account

for to parliament. None of the relevant actors – i.e. the minister, parliament, civil servants, university governors, students – in the present situation are in favour of a different university system (in which there is a greater level of, or complete, autonomy for universities). All actors are, however, in favour of increasing the level of university autonomy as proposed in the HOAK document.

3. The HOAK document does not however give a description of the ultimate goal. The aim of the document is to bring about a U-turn in a trend which has lasted many years. If the small steps of the HOAK are realized satisfactorily the dialogue between government and the universities can progress to the next phase of university autonomy. This keeps open the perspective of a further increase in university autonomy. However, certain aspects require first of all that the universities are willing to really use the competences they already have (e.g. in the field of personnel policy). Once this point has been reached the next interchange will come into view, e.g. an own university personnel policy and terms of employment policy (see also point 7).

4. Concrete proposals ensuing from (giving consideration to) the HOAK philosophy can be realized to a substantial extent within the present university system. They will not result in radical changes in the system. The relevant proposals will be specified in more detail for teaching (conclusion five), research (conclusion six) and management (funding, organization, planning, personnel policy, etc.; conclusion seven).

5. With regard to *teaching*, the following measures aiming at more autonomy can be realized within the present university system:
   - abolishment of the nationally established attainment targets of disciplines (the so-called University Statute);
   - resulting in a more differentiated and flexible curriculum;
   - a modular study structure and a national system of credits on which to base the financial settlement between universities;
   - sectoral funding and the evaluation of curricula.

6. With regard to *research*, the following measures aiming at more autonomy can be realized within the present university system:
   - a remodelling of the system of conditional funding so that it becomes primarily a management tool at faculty level;
   - sectoral funding and evaluation of research.

7. The following measures aiming at more autonomy can be realized within the present university system for *management* (funding, organization, planning, personnel policy, etc.):
   - funding measures (including specific stimulation measures) to be linked to the HOOP planning procedure;
   - the possibility for universities to have external advisory bodies (think tanks);
   - the government refrains from setting regulations relating to the university structure. This is appropriate for a government that bases its management on output standards.

8. The following, in itself a measure that restricts university autonomy, can be regarded as a basically new element in the present university system:
   - the establishment of an inspection board for university education.

9. If, as an exercise in heuristics, we try to imagine a different university system with far greater, maybe even complete, autonomy, one can conceive the following system-transgressing measures (the point here is the problems that have to be cleared up to make such a system feasible):
   - universities are given the free choice to determine their own package of courses, research and services;
   - they therefore carry the responsibility themselves for any eventual downfalls in respect of finances and curriculum (cf. also Rinnooy Kan et al., 1987);
   - each university determines the price of its own products;
   - in consideration of their competitive position, universities have their products checked on a regular basis, both in-house and externally; government regulations to ensure that this is done are unnecessary (the market mechanisme sees to this);
   - a strict system of output-funding is introduced;
   - as a variant to the new funding system, it is conceivable for the government to stop direct university funding and introduce a system of subsidies for the potential consumers of university products. This could be in the form of issuing vouchers which the customer could then exchange at universities (Van Gendt, 1980; Florax and Van Vught, 1987);
   - the Minister of Education and Science (and other ministers) is accountable to parliament for the allocation of vouchers; the minister can no longer be called to account for the deeds of the universities; the Higher Education and Research Plan, plus the subsequent planning procedures, is not carried through;
   - the universities can choose their own form of administration and their own governors; this can lead to a stronger (more hierarchical) administrative structure and a change in the competences and status of the current councils;
   - the universities can pursue their own, more flexible personnel policy; civil service regulations no longer apply to university staff.

10. The chance that the above heuristic exercise will actually be realized in the Netherlands is out of the question. However, a few tentative steps have been taken in this direction through the HOAK. With regard to the *undergraduate* courses and the corresponding research it would appear that the universities will obtain slightly more autonomy without there being any real mention of the system being violated. On the other hand, certain system-transgressing elements (from the heuristic exercise under point 9) will be realized in a moderated form in *postgraduate* courses. This is evident from the establishment of research scools, centres of excellence, special research institutes, specific additional training courses co-financed by trade and industry, etc. There is more latitude for management in this senior education sector; the WUB structures will have less grip in this area. Although the WUB will be maintained the relative size of its domain will gradually shrink because of new administrative developments organized outside its system.

    As a result of these developments it would seem that here in the Netherlands we tend to lean towards a *dual* university system.

11. One main question which is not answered in the HOAK document is how, in a different method of administration in the higher education system, is decision-making organized with regard to concentration, distribution of tasks, cooperation, coordination, discontinuation, setting limitations on the intake of students with regard to subjects and sectors, etc. The HOAK concept should be worked out in full in this respect. The price and market

mechanism, according to the heuristic exercise, would seem neither suitable nor feasible to achieve this kind of regulation. Both present and past illustrate that the universities, in joint consultation, are also unable to bring these tasks to a good end. Nor is regulation resulting from constant government measures an attractive alternative. Therefore, the establishment of a strong and independent board at level six of the system is strongly recommended for the purpose of performing these tasks. We have presented two modalities with regard to designating the task of allocating the budget between the universities. We have not progressed far enough along the time path as yet for the most far-reaching one – allocation of the budget placed completely in the hands of a level six body on the lines of the British UFC. The option that provides level six, within the framework of its overall coordinating supra-university task, with the power of decision in respect of that part of the budget intended for strategic developments would seem to be viable.

6 Case study 3: From ZWO to NWO

A new mission and structure of the national science council

6.0 Summary

The research system comprises two organizational patterns: the physical pattern and the subject-specific pattern. The physical pattern was the subject matter of the previous case study in which we discussed the relations between universities, strategic national bodies and the government. This case study deals with the relations within the subject-specific organizational pattern: the networks of researchers in a certain field and their coordinating bodies. In the Netherlands this has been structured in the so-called indirect funding organization: the Netherlands Organization for Scientific Research (NWO; formerly ZWO). NWO consists of a large number of disciplinary foundations and below these, the study groups. The promulgation of the Act governing the NWO introduced a new administrative layer between the NWO Board and the foundations, the so-called councils. In this chapter we take a look at the relations between the various levels of this up-to-date, indirect funding organization from the (de)centralization perspective of our multi-level model.

We conclude that the introduction of this new administrative layer, the councils, leads to over-organization and is thus unnecessary – unless another administrative layer is discontinued: that of the coordinating board, or that of the foundations. We have also made a suggestion for reshaping the organization of those research programmes which cross disciplinary and establishment boundaries (the so-called priority programmes).

6.1 Introduction: the centres and circles in the research system structure

The lion's share of university scientific research and teaching is funded by the state. The government (level seven) and the basic level of the 'professionals' (level two) and their support (level one) are linked through a dual organizational pattern. The one organizational line being that of the *centres* (physical); the other, that of the *circles* (networks).

The physical organizational pattern is the most obvious one. This pattern of organization was taken as the basis in the previous chapter where the various aspects are geared towards the consequences of increasing the level of university autonomy.

The physical organization of the research system is roughly as follows: university researchers and their support are categorized in accordance with legally established structures under teaching and research units (level three). Teaching and research units are part of faculties (level four) which in turn form part of a university (level five). Supra-university bodies operate at the level above that of the universities (level six). In the practical situation in the Netherlands, although the tasks of these supra-university bodies are mainly advisory, principle bodies with directorial competences can also be located at level six (compare the argument contained in the previous chapter for a much stronger institutionalization of this level in the Netherlands). At the top of the system we find the governmental bodies (level seven) as the regulator and financier (direct funding).

Running alongside the physical organizational pattern we have the subject-specific pattern: the networks of researchers in a specific subject and their coordinating bodies. This second organizational pattern is of immense importance with regard to quality assurance. Researchers are called upon to account for their work, to be completely honest and open by presenting a panel of peers with a specific explanation of their research plans. This, then, is the *forum function* in research – whether or not in a systematized, quantified or other objectified form – which is performed in the network organizational pattern. This second pattern is generally more dispersed than the first. There is evidence of both overlapping areas and lacunas.

The existence of this second pattern of national competition and peer review is of major importance for those bodies in the physical organizational pattern. It provides the universities with the opportunity to obtain an indication as to the quality of its faculties in comparison with those of other universities. It provides the faculties with an indication of the quality of research groups and individual researchers. Given that the production of university scientific research is funded through the budgeting mechanism, and there is no market verification procedure involved, it is essential that university governors and faculty administrators can request and obtain independent expertise and thus enable them to put up a fight when claims are made by the professionals at the levels immediately below theirs.

Circles, in this context, are the circles of colleagues in disciplines and subdisciplines. In the Netherlands, this network is for the greater part incorporated in NWO, referred to as the indirect funding organization or national science council. It does not hold a monopolistic position as a network organization. In addition to NWO there are numerous other associations of researchers in certain fields which play a non-institutionalized role in researcher networks (Nederlandse Vereniging voor Openbare Financiën (Netherlands Association for Public Finance), Koninklijke Vereniging voor de Staatshuishoudkunde (Royal Netherlands Economic Association), etc., etc.).

The organizational structure of NWO is as follows. University researchers in a certain subdiscipline are organized in study groups (level three). Study groups in a certain discipline are coordinated by a foundation (level four). These foundations come under the Netherlands

Organization for Scientific Research (level five). Since the NWO Act came into effect we now have six councils which are positioned between this coordinating body and the foundations.

On relevant matters the NWO Board consults with other bodies at level five (e.g. universities, VSNU, TNO) and with national advisory and consultative councils at level six (RAWB, KNAW, sectoral research councils). Also at the top of this organizational line we see the government as the provider of funds (indirect funding).

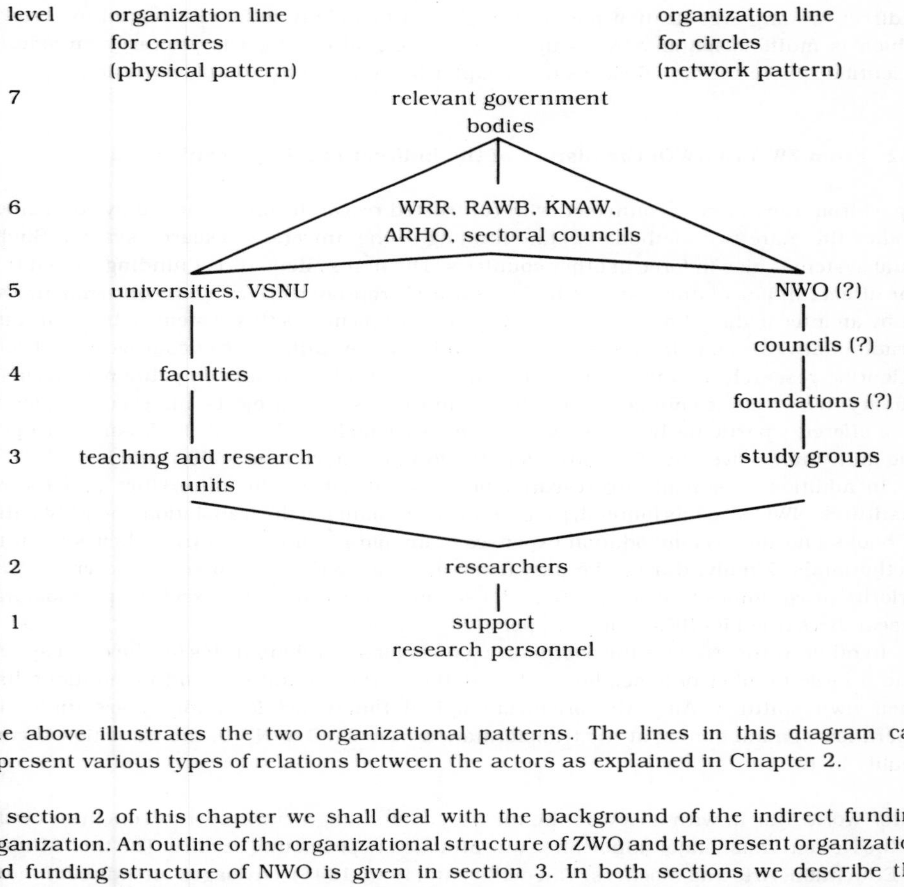

The above illustrates the two organizational patterns. The lines in this diagram can represent various types of relations between the actors as explained in Chapter 2.

In section 2 of this chapter we shall deal with the background of the indirect funding organization. An outline of the organizational structure of ZWO and the present organization and funding structure of NWO is given in section 3. In both sections we describe the backgrounds and history of the restructuring procedure from ZWO to NWO. This restructuring implies an up-dating of the mission and organizational structure of the indirect funding organization. One of the consequences of this being the establishment of the new administrative layer of councils. This is the reason for the question marks in the diagram after the NWO Board at level five, the foundations at level four and this new intermediate layer between the two. However, the transition from ZWO (Board and Council at level five; foundations at level four, study groups at level three) to NWO caused administrative and organizational friction within the multi-level system, to which the legislator had either given insufficient attention or had failed to adhere to an unambiguous concept consistently throughout the process of legislation. We also reveal the specific problems of transforming a bottom-up organization into a more top-down oriented organization.

In section 4 we discuss the consequences of this in terms of the seven-level model. At two levels (five and four) it would appear that at present three administrative layers are being pushed out. In section 4 we also present three options which could offer a solution to these problems: the dismantling of one of the NWO administrative layers (two options), or the upgrading of the range of tasks of the organization to level six in the column.

An organizational aspect which is linked to this is looked at in section 5: the role the indirect funding organization might or might not be able to fulfil with regard to research which is multidisciplinary by nature and/or the goal of which is primarily outside the scientific sphere. Section 6 closes this chapter by presenting several conclusions.

6.2 From ZWO to NWO: the history of the indirect funding organization

Apart from the finances connected with contracted research commissioned by government bodies there are two methods of state funding of the university research system. Such a dual system is also in force in other countries. The first system, direct funding, is just that: the direct funding of universities (the funds are appropriated either by the government itself or by an intermediary body). The second system supplements this system of direct funding. Traditionally, the main task of the indirect funding organization is to encourage unrestricted scientific research at universities through a system of national competition in terms of quality. Whereas the emphasis is on the funding of research projects, material facilities are also offered – particularly in the exact sciences – which are beyond the financial scope of the individual university. The latter is in the form of the various NWO institutes.

In addition to subsidizing research projects carried out in universities and its own institutes, NWO also has (limited) programmes for financing the translation and publication of books and the accommodation expenses of foreign researchers during their stay in the Netherlands. Finally, during the past few years the NWO has also set up several central priority programmes (see section 5) and a separate programme for excellent postdoctorate researchers (the PIONIER group support).

In other words, NWO is the coordinating body for several institutes (in the exact sphere) and a large number of (disciplinary) foundations. These institutes and foundations have their own statutes. After the organization had functioned for many years under the operation of a bill aiming at the transformation from ZWO to NWO, the transition became reality in 1988.

After World War II, with a view to the recovery and strengthening of the economic position of the Netherlands, major importance was attached to promoting science. The then Minister of Education, Arts and Sciences, Van der Leeuw (1945-1946), envisaged an indirect funding organization which could act as a powerful stimulus for university research. He also envisaged a wide sphere of action: extending to the humanities and social sciences as well as the natural sciences. Nevertheless, mathematics and the exact sciences held a prominent position in ZWO from the very start. Foundations for mathematics (SMC), physics (FOM) and astronomy (RZM) were even established before the ZWO Act came into force in 1950 and have since then been incorporated into the organization. It was these foundations which brought the institutes into the ZWO organization and this largely explains the still dominant position held by the exact sciences (see subsection 6.3.3 for exact figures), and physics in particular. In retrospect, ZWO has always aimed at giving support to the other disciplines as well. A large number of new foundations in the area of the humanities and social sciences have been established, especially during the last decade. A complete list of foundations and study groups covering all disciplines has now reached completion.

Since the foundation of ZWO in 1950, the attitudes towards the function and significance of scientific research have changed enormously. Science, society and government have become more interwoven. Nowadays applied scientific research is often carried out in universities and para-university institutes. Society has expressed the need for innovations, for instance in the field of medicine, engineering sciences and the natural sciences. Linked with this need is the wish – voiced more and more over the past decade – for scientific organizations to become more involved in the initiation and stimulation of research in new, as yet insufficiently opened disciplines which are of major significance to science and/or society.

As a result of these trends we have seen an enormous change in the ZWO *environment* over the years. This change resulted in the following problems concerning the functioning of ZWO:

- ZWO spent too much time waiting for applications from 'the field' and made too little use of new forms of support such as stimulation programmes, priority areas, periodic conferences for researchers and their foreign counterparts, etc.; all forms of support quite common in other countries;
- ZWO lacked a juridical basis to support and stimulate applied scientific research. This caused the ZWO to become isolated from other research institutes in the field of the exact sciences;
- as a result of the organizational separation of the administrative bodies from the ZWO main organization and the support departments on the one side, and the various foundations on the other, the organizational structure became quite inflexible;
- the procedures of evaluating applications for research project funding were complex and time-consuming.

It was partly against the background of the above problems that the minister set out three important lines of policy which also included financial plans with regard to the ZWO in the Beleidsnota Universitair Onderzoek (Policy Document on University Research; Ministry of Education and Science, 1979). These lines of policy were:

1. ZWO must increase its support to those disciplines which up to then had received only little (i.e. the social sciences and the humanities);
2. ZWO should give greater encouragement and introduce initiatives in those priority areas where new scientific or social trends showed this to be desirable;
3. and finally, the law should be amended so that in future applied scientific research could also be funded through the indirect funding system.

In order to equip ZWO for this shift and expansion of its tasks the budget for supporting university research (therefore excluding the ZWO institutes) should be doubled from 100 million to 200 million (guilders 1979). These funds should be transferred from the direct funding system to the indirect funding organization.

In connection with the expansion of ZWO tasks provided for in the BUOZ document a preliminary draft bill was drawn up in which ZWO was renamed NWO: the Netherlands Organization for Scientific Research. In 1985 this was presented to parliament as a bill and subsequently enacted in 1988. Compared to the ZWO organization the NWO Act gave greater emphasis to the structure of the intermediate level, the councils.

The role of these councils should make shifts between allied disciplines more dynamic and initiate action in the overlapping areas of allied disciplines.

In anticipation of the proposed amendment of the act, the Foundation for Engineering Sciences (Stichting voor de Technische Wetenschappen: STW) was established in 1981. Partly through the deployment of funds from the Ministry of Economic Affairs budget, STW pursued an indirect funding policy for technical scientific research with its own assessment procedures and criteria (scientific quality and utilization). The BUOZ document was also a stimulus for ZWO to promote the establishment of foundations in the field of the humanities and social sciences. Several main priority programmes were also developed with the aim of stimulating certain (multidisciplinary) areas of research (this is dealt with in more detail in section 5). The BUOZ perspective also motivated the setting up of the Huygens Programme in 1984, the aim of which was to create a special facility for (a small number of) excellent young postdoctorate researchers in a period when Dutch universities had little opportunity to do this. In 1989 the NWO Board transformed this Huygens Programme into a far wider programme for the provision of individual-orientated group support (the Pionier Programme).

Another major development in the long period before the promulgation of the NWO Act (which lasted from the presentation of the BUOZ document in 1979 up to 1988) was that the conditional funding scheme had meanwhile been introduced into the direct funding system. The government anticipated that this would bring about improved planning and increase quality. Because of the national coordination and assessment procedures – resulting from the conditional funding scheme – the indirect funding organization lost its distinct identity.

Partly due to the government's worsened budgetary circumstances, the counterpressure exerted by the universities, and the introduction of the conditional funding scheme, the passage dealing with funding in the BUOZ document was only implemented to an extremely small degree. It was only during the first year of its implementation (1981) that a substantial sum was transferred from the direct funding system to the indirect funding organization, even though this sum was not 10 million but 6.3 million guilders. Halfway through the period 1980-1990 the implementation of this policy was discontinued definitively.

Conclusion: On the one hand, the NWO organization attempts to retain ZWO tasks – which were mainly characterized by a bottom-up structure (establishing networks, peer review) – while on the other, to live up to its new status of an organization that steers and takes initiatives with regard to the research system. This double goal (or better still: a goal which has not yet been given its definitive form) leads to organizational friction. These problems are dealt with in the remainder of this chapter.

6.3 The organizational and financial structure of ZWO/NWO

6.3.1 Organizational structure of ZWO

The highest body of ZWO was the Council for Pure Scientific Research. This council consisted of a few dozen members, mainly professors, who were appointed on the recommendations of the universities.

The Council could be regarded as the parliament of ZWO. It assembled four times a year. A board was formed from the members with a chairman and vice-chairman. Furthermore the board included a representative of the Ministry of Education and Science who, by law, possessed the power of suspensive veto. This board met on a monthly basis; the executive committee once a fortnight. The director and two assistant directors took care of day-to-day management; one of the assistant directors being charged with matters concerning the humanities and social sciences, and the other with administrative aspects (personnel, finances). The director also functioned as the secretary to the ZWO Council. The directors were supported by a number of management staff. Central departments for personnel affairs and financial affairs were also set up.

The ZWO Board held regular consultations with the chairmen of the five standing advisory committees for the main disciplines, i.e. the exact sciences, medicine, biology, the humanities and social and behavioural sciences. The ZWO Act established that the appropriation of funds by the ZWO was only allowed after having requested and received the scientific judgment of a standing advisory committee. Since 1982 these standing advisory committees functioned as administrative bodies. In anticipation of ZWO's new legal status these advisory committees were upgraded to ZWO councils. As administrative bodies, the tasks of these ZWO councils were based on those of the ZWO Board and authorized to the ZWO councils by that board.

The foundations, about 25 at present, are found at level four. These foundations have quite a high level of autonomy: they determine which research projects will be subsidized and see to the management of those projects. The foundations have their own administrative bodies: a board and generally a foundation council (consisting of representatives of the foundation's study groups). They deal with their own administrative affairs; the higher ZWO bodies had never been authorized to do this. The statutes of the foundations did however have to be sanctioned by the ZWO Board. The frequency at which the different foundation boards meet varies: from three to ten times a year. All meetings are attended by an official of the ZWO council of a discipline in which the relevant foundation operates.

Study groups come under (most of) these foundations. Although this can range from three to twenty per foundation, the figure is generally between five and ten. Almost 200 study groups are overseen by the NWO foundations. These study groups have an important function within the framework of the main tasks of the indirect funding organization: that of improving quality and creativity and the national coordination of research (*network function*). Assessment of research plans is carried out primarily by the study groups. In addition to their other duties, these study groups also play a significant role in cultivating those subjects requiring special attention. Within the framework of their network function, study groups can also organize symposia, workshops, etc. Study group committees (boards) generally meet several times a year.

In actual fact these study groups form an open, accessible forum. There are no members, only participants. All qualified researchers operating in the sector in which a study group is active can become a participant. The number of participants per study group varies from a few dozen to several hundred.

Study groups are typical level three bodies: their duties are not financial or administrative but they advise the foundation boards on the acceptance of proposed research projects.

Up to the present these foundations and study groups function in NWO in the same way as they did within the scope of the ZWO Act. However, in 1991 the NWO Board will evaluate the working and continuation of the foundations.

6.3.2 Organizational structure of NWO

Although the growing number of foundations and study groups called for a greater degree of flexibility the organizational structure of ZWO showed a quite clear interpretation of levels five (council and board; strategic and coordinating tasks), four (foundations; tasks demarcated to a certain discipline) and three (study groups: assessment and coordination of developments at sub-discipline level).

The introduction of the NWO Act brought with it a number of major administrative changes which tended to complicate the relationships within the NWO organization from the point of view of the multi-level system. Especially the introduction of the new administrative layer of councils (this had been anticipated in the ZWO period in the form of ZWO advisory committees) implied that the tasks of the organization and the corresponding levels had to be re-conceptualized again. We feel that two trains of thought were followed when introducing the NWO Act and this led to organizational problems which have not yet been defined explicitly.

In section 4 of this chapter we shall deal in more detail with the organizational problems resulting from the introduction of the new administrative layer. In this context we will think through three possible options to bring the set of tasks and organizational structure at the different levels of the NWO organization (once again) into line, logically and with consistence. In this subsection we deal with the most significant administrative changes for the various levels in consequence of the introduction of the NWO Act. An organization chart depicting the structure of the NWO is to be found at the end of this chapter.

1. Contrary to ZWO, NWO does not include a Council. The Board of Governors is the highest governing body of NWO, its members being appointed by government. This is only a small board with a total of four members only. Unlike that of his ZWO predecessor the function of the NWO Board chairman is a full-time position. The other members spend one day a week on their tasks. Ministerial representation has been abolished. The relation between NWO and the Minister of Education and Science is established in the NWO Act as the exchange of planning-documents.

   Day-to-day management of the organization has not been affected in any way through the NWO Act. During the ZWO period the director also functioned as the secretary of the ZWO Council and ZWO Board; the director now fulfils the function of secretary of the NWO Board.

2. Since the transition from ZWO to NWO the councils have acquired the legal status of *councils*. The NWO Act also makes provision for foundations to be replaced by departments of these councils. This was even the explicit intention in an earlier version of the act but because of strong opposition on the part of the ZWO Board (in response to pressure from below, i.e. the foundations) the act established that the organization itself could determine whether or not to establish departments. Up to now, the NWO Board has only done this in two disciplines (both of which stated their preference for this form of organization). It was also established by law that these foundations that have institutes would in any event continue to exist as such.

   Contrary to the foundations, departments have no formal autonomy. Departmental committees are, in accordance with the NWO Act, appointed by the relevant council; foundations choose their own committee. Departmental committees perform their tasks on behalf of, and under the responsibility of the relevant council; foundation committees have autonomy in the performance of their tasks. In short, the status of departments differs essentially from that of the foundations.

   There are six councils in NWO, the members being appointed by the NWO Board on the recommendation of the council's current members. An appointment is set for a term of three years and members can be reappointed twice.

The councils interact with the NWO Board and the foundations in their specific area; this allows them to advise the board on matters of the foundations' budgets. They also integrate – within the financial scope indicated by the board – the foundations' budgets into a council budget. Council meetings are convened four to five times a year and additional meetings are sometimes held by the executive committee of a council.

6.3.3 Funding structure

The table below shows how the NWO budget is distributed between the various disciplines, including the NWO institutes (exclusive of investments in buildings and equipment and exclusive of the engineering sciences).

	1970 x Dfl. 1,000	%	1980 x Dfl. 1,000	%	1987 x Dfl. 1,000	%
The humanities	2,252	3.9	10,408	5.7	17,112	7.8
Social sciences	3,250	5.6	9,915	5.5	16,452	7.5
Exact sciences	44,140	76.3	132,618	73.1	152,582	69.1
Biology	4,513	7.8	12,663	7.0	14,286	6.5
Medical sciences	3,709	6.4	15,120	8.3	18,604	8.4
Not included	21	–	641	0.4	1,449	0.7
Total	57,885	100,0	181,365	100.0	220,485	100,0

Although the share has somewhat declined, the table still clearly illustrates the exact sciences orientation of NWO. This impression is strengthened if we also take into account the STW (Foundation for Engineering Sciences) budget (annual account 1987: 39 million guilders, of which 27 million was from the Education and Science budget and 6 million from Economic Affairs).

It must also be pointed out that various reasons limit the possibilities open to NWO for transferring sums from one discipline to another.

1. In the first place, the financial means for supporting university research is put into projects which as a rule take four years to complete. Shifting the budget from one year to another is therefore only possible in the so-called *financial margin* (that part of the annual budget of a foundation which remains after having taken into account the sums needed to cover the completion of projects started in previous years). However, this financial margin cannot be adjusted downwards to too great an extent from one year to another. This would have a negative effect on the research field which would then tend to turn against the indirect funding scheme. In turn, this would hit the network function fulfilled by the foundations and their study groups.

2. A second factor standing in the way of financial flexibility for NWO is related to the existence of NWO institutes. These receive almost half of the NWO finances (leaving aside investments). Institutes require a certain level of continuity, also in a financial sense.

3. Also, a major, formal restriction on the financial scope of ZWO resulted from the fact that the destination of a number of budgetary items was either earmarked by ministries or established in budgetary agreements with the minister (e.g. parts of priority programmes which had been set up in part through agreements made with the minister). This earmarking had been an eye-sore to ZWO for many years.

Although earmarking is not provided for in the NWO Act this does not affect the right of the Minister of Education and Science to approve the NWO budget.

6.4 Function and status of the councils

ZWO was very much a research organization. Indeed, that was both its strength and its weakness. In the performance of the organization's tasks emphasis was laid on the assessment of the quality of proposed research by peers in the relevant discipline. Study groups and foundations played the main role in this while the highest body – the ZWO Council – fulfilled the function of providing a meeting place for researchers. The introduction of the NWO Act placed a different emphasis on the goal of the organization: NWO also had to see to the innovation, initiation and planning of research. In terms of organization it was the intention to transform the bottom-up organization – which ZWO was – into an organization which could operate top-down: the 'federation of kingdoms' had to be transformed into a 'kingdom of federations'. The ZWO Council was disbanded and the NWO Board at level five was transformed into an efficient managerial body. The most significant organizational consequence of the NWO Act was, however, the introduction of the new administrative layer of councils.

In the original concept of the NWO Act the organization was consistently thought of as a top-down organization: the minister appoints the NWO Board, the NWO Board appoints the councils and the councils can appoint departmental committees; the foundations will be discontinued; nothing is said as regards the status of the study groups. Nevertheless, during the parliamentary discussions about the NWO Act the ZWO bodies strongly rejected the setting up of departments and wished to maintain the foundations. The ultimate result was a compromise: the act guarantees the status of the foundations that have institutes and it is up to the NWO itself to decide whether or not to replace the other foundations with departments. Both during and after the parliamentary discussions the minister left no doubt as to his preference for the original concept of the NWO as a top-down organization. The replacement of foundations by departments is not simply a matter of changing the name-plate. We are faced here with an organizational issue which is integral to the (de)centralization perspective, and which has not yet been fully defined. The question is whether there is a need within the research system for the NWO as a decentralized or as a dispersed organization. The organizational issue is therefore not only related to the question of whether a top-down construction is compatible with the sociology of science characteristics of research, it is also a derivative of the call for task and mission of an indirect funding organization in the research system as a whole.

The above illustrates that legislation processes too have 'garbage can' characteristics. Perspicuous concepts lose momentum, compromises are reached and points of friction are ingrained in advance. The NWO case shows this quite clearly. By, on the one hand, making it mandatory for the organization to establish the new administrative layer of councils, and on the other hand, by leaving open the option of departments or foundations, the legislator was inconsistent in his thinking through of the levels in the system, the distribution of their tasks and the interrelationships between the various levels. The consequence for the NWO organization is that it is now faced with a new administrative layer which is threatened with being crushed between the NWO Board at level five and the foundations at level four, and it would indeed seem that this new administrative layer has little real chance of development.

In the next three subsections we shall go more deeply into this organizational problem and the possible solutions. In 6.4.1 we present an overview of the various functions performed by the councils. In 6.4.2 we analyze the consequences of the introduction of this new administrative layer for the NWO as a (sub) system, giving particular attention to the behavioural aspects of how the councils function as a group. We conclude that the incontestable development is one which leans towards a series of frictions. Finally, in 6.4.3 we take a look at several possible options to solve this organizational problem. These solutions were considered from the angle of the multi-level system applied in this study: what the possibilities are for rebalancing the compatibility between the administrative layers and the tasks to be fulfilled in the research system given the real, or predictable, behaviour of the actors within that system.

6.4.1 Council functions

The councils have both an advisory and an administrative function. During the phase in which these councils were being established they were given a mandate for the administrative function from the ZWO Board. When the NWO Act came into force this administrative function was based on delegation.

Below is a list of the various advisory and administrative functions.

Advisory functions

1. Reviewing (and anticipating) the main lines of development in the council's area of research.

2. Pursuing a policy of steering and stimulating in the field of indirect funding through:
   - identification of backlogs in certain areas;
   - detection of new fields of research;
   - stimulation of a policy geared towards priority areas and group support;
   - identification of any new (central) priority programmes;
   - profiling and safeguarding the specific identity of the indirect funding organization.

3. Bearing the responsibility for multi- and interdisciplinary research (research which goes beyond the disciplinary research carried out in the foundations). Promoting new studies and research which goes beyond the boundaries of a certain discipline (research which has not (yet) been given a place within the foundations).

4. Becoming acquainted with 'national' study reports (evaluation committees, RAWB annual recommendations, etc.).

Administrative functions

5. Drawing up the annual budget for the relevant discipline and submitting proposals concerning the required financial sum. In this context:
   - analysis of the draft budgets of the foundations;
   - allocation and reallocation of finances to the foundations;

- encouraging a policy geared towards preventing an annual fluctuation in the 'financial margin' of the foundation's budgets. (Explanation: if a foundation can assign a relatively large number of projects in year t then the continuing costs imply that in the year t + 1 *ceteris paribus* relatively few projects can be assigned. Too great a difference between the number of projects assigned in one year and the next is considered unacceptable.)

6. Verifying the policy pursued by the foundations at a later date (i.e. the supervision of studies and checks on their quality) by means of:
   - analysis of the foundation's budgets;
   - marginal verification of the assignation policy pursued by the foundations.

7. Assessing and assigning those research applications that cannot be allocated to a foundation.

8. Superintending the policy pursued by the foundations with regard to output registration and output evaluation. This has both quantitative and qualitative aspects:
   - production (reports, publications, etc.);
   - judgment of quality (on a basis of the principles of a protocol).

9. Encouraging the foundations to pursue a policy geared towards the network function (cooperation between researchers).

The councils also hold internal discussion with the NWO Board, the boards of the foundations, committees for priority programmes, and maintain external contact (national, possible international) with national organizations, planning boards, advisory bodies, and so forth.

6.4.2 Status of the councils: system and behaviour

We shall now go more deeply into the organizational status of this new administrative layer and the associated behavioural aspects. The attitude of these councils depends, among other things, on the task assigned to them by the NWO of stimulating and initiating planned research which can overlap various disciplines. In terms of organization the model was based on the structure of the British research councils. In Great Britain there are five such national research councils, namely the Agricultural and Food Research Council (AFRC), the Natural Environment Research Council (NERC), the Science and Engineering Research Council (SERC), the Medical Research Council (MRC) and the Economic and Social Research Council (ESRC). Together, these councils are responsible for the indirect funding of research.

These research councils have not been brought under an umbrella organization. There is some degree of joint consultation in the Advisory Board of Research Councils; ABRC. Both this joint consultative body and the five councils operate at level five in the system.

The original intention of the NWO legislator was that, in analogy with the British research councils, the councils should have departments which would replace the ZWO foundations. In the parliamentary discussions on the NWO Act this shift towards centralization was rectified in part. Foundations that have institutes (particularly those in the sphere of the exact sciences) can in any event continue to exist; it is up to the NWO Board itself to decide whether to set up departments or to leave the foundations as they are.

If we now take a look at the resulting administrative status and scope of the councils it must be said that the result is an unfortunate hybrid. The councils find themselves between the hammer (NWO Board) and the anvil (the foundations). On the one hand the foundations have maintained their tasks and responsibilities towards the level below theirs, implying that the councils have little to do in connection with direct research management. On the other hand, the councils – contrary to the British research councils – are coordinated by a strong parent organization. It is even such that with the discontinuation of the ZWO Council, the slimming-down of the board, and the introduction of a full-time chairmanship, the strength of the level of the NWO Board, in comparison with its predecessor, has increased.

From the budgetary aspect we can also deduce that in actual fact the councils play a modest role. Lump sums are not placed at their disposal by the NWO Board for them to allocate as they feel appropriate within their disciplines, but they are required to submit a specified estimate (according to the foundations) every year.

What we now see is that the creation of this new administrative layer of councils will result in the *over-organization* (bureaucratization) of research funding from the indirect funding system unless another level is abolished: that of the foundations or the level of the NWO Board. The system explained in Chapter 2 shows that any administrative body must perform its own specific tasks otherwise there is little call for such a body within the system. If two hierarchically linked actors, A and B, operate on the same level there is always the danger of them trying to oust each other out: A starts to concern himself with the tasks of B, and B will consistently try to deal direct with the actor on the level immediately above. Because of the way in which NWO has been structured this danger threatens level four. The two bodies operating on this level – the councils and the foundations – will start to compete for each other's responsibilities. The fulfilment of the tasks of the one organization will obviously have to be at the expense of the tasks of the other organization. On the basis of this principle the sense of this new administrative layer of councils is questionable. These councils run the risk of doing no more than what the foundations did perfectly well before them. A second point is that the research field is more able to find itself in (disciplinary) foundations than in the far larger system of councils which, for researchers, represents an administrative artefact.

As we stated earlier, the reference point for the original version of the NWO Act was the British system of research councils: prominent councils and their departmental committees. Although this point of reference was watered down in the NWO Act we could ask ourselves whether such a development is not inherent in the structure of the NWO organization after all. To be able to answer this question it is essential that we first take a look at the actual functioning of the councils and the related aspects of behaviour.

Each council has a maximum of nine members and is organized such that all the relevant disciplines are represented. Although some of the members are former members of the foundation boards this is not the rule. The councils only meet a few times throughout the year and, contrary to the NWO Board, the members of these councils are not employed by NWO. All in all, these councils are boards which operate on a more ad hoc basis. Decision-making can be best described by using the 'garbage can' model: now and again choices have to be made at a time when we see a convergence between problems requiring a solution, solutions looking for problems and actors wanting to solve problems in order to acquire status.

In practice, the councils tend to lean strongly on their official bases. In their area they do not therefore operate as an Advisory Council on Government Policy (WRR). This results in the policy documents they produce often being characterized as the sifted aggregate of the policies of the foundations. There is no question of strong boards of representatives which develop their own views in their own area of research and which base their added value in the system on such visionary prowess.

The reason for this procedure can be explained by the theory of group behaviour. The members of these councils are constantly caught up in a prisoners' dilemma. Each member being constantly tempted to look after the interests of his discipline. This forces the others to do exactly the same, even if they would rather take a wider view and develop a supra-disciplinary perspective covering the entire area.

Such a prisoners' dilemma also emerges in a group which is too large to penalize undesirable behaviour (i.e. the protection of disciplinary interests) by way of social control. In this case certain aspects are given added weight given that the councils are designated with the task of allocating funds. This makes it even more difficult to adopt an altruistic attitude. In other words, there is no reason to assume that the councils might still emerge in a form similar to the British research councils.

Conclusion: in the present set-up the councils operate between the hammer (NWO Board) and the anvil (the foundations). The system has insufficient administrative latitude to allow councils to develop their own goal and identity. Addressing the NWO Board they present the sum total of the wishes of the foundations; addressing the foundations, they act as the serving-hatch for the (im)possibilities offered by the NWO Board. With regard to one another, the members of these councils are caught up in the prisoners' dilemma of looking after the interests of their own discipline.

The most obvious development with regard to the functioning of the councils is that they will become the telescopic limb of the NWO Board in the sense that they will tone-down the wishes of the foundations. The danger here lies in the fact that the foundations that 'want to do business' will then approach the NWO Board direct (compare Chapter 2, section 3 on 'skipping' levels in the system).

6.4.3 Modalities to resolve the organizational problems

In this final subsection we will outline three modalities to re-balance the various levels within the NWO organization and the tasks to be fulfilled in the research system so that each administrative layer can function at the proper level. The first option can be characterized as a revival of the ZWO organizational structure, the second corresponds with the British system of several research councils, and in the third modality the set of tasks for the NWO organization is upgraded to level six and given UGC/UFC-like features. When working out these three modalities for optimizing the working of the indirect funding organization we also take the 'if-then' approach. It will ultimately depend on the government's science policy whether there is a need for a decentralized indirect funding organization (option 1); several separately operating indirect funding organizations (option 2), or a single heavily equipped and centrally managed indirect funding organization (option 3). The choice between these options is a matter for science policy; we would only like to point out that it is of importance that such a choice is made otherwise the organizational structure will remain to be hybrid by nature.

The first option to solve the organizational problems of NWO is mainly related to re-establishing ZWO relations. The indirect funding organization remains a 'federation of kingdoms' even though slight adjustments can be made to the map for the purpose of efficiency. In this modality emphasis with regard to the fulfilment of tasks remains to be on the assessment of research proposals by peers. This has been the institutionalized forum function of indirect funding from time immemorial. Foundations and study groups play the main role here; the disciplines retain substantial significance. At supra-disciplinary level it is sufficient to have a light form of coordination performed by the NWO Board. To carry out this task the NWO Board could be given the support of a number of standing advisory councils for each main area (as was the case with ZWO). There is no need for an administrative layer between the NWO Board and the foundations, which perform their own administrative tasks independently. The present councils would therefore be discontinued.

Nevertheless, the efficiency of the existing network of foundations and study groups would need to be carefully looked at. At present it would sometimes seem as if too much segmentation has occurred. An investigation would need to be carried out to make sure that all the study groups are sufficiently large aggregates. To ensure that study groups transcend above the level of 'clubs' and that peer review activities do not become bogged down in a 'my dear friend' culture – in which no minus points are given – certain minimum requirements could be established as to the total number of participants in a study group. This could lead to those foundations which have ten or more study groups being brought down to a maximum of five or six.

With regard to efficiency at foundation level it will have to be looked into whether not too many foundations have been created which cover a too small field of research. Indirect funding could thus also reflect a development with regard to the direct funding organization. A certain upgrading of the organizational structure has been evident in recent years, for instance the discontinuation of subfaculties as a result of the University Education Act of 1986 (WWO'86). This has resulted, for example, in the present lack of separate (sub)faculties for social science or political science but a single faculty of both social and political science (which also includes the science of public administration). A second example is that direct funding does not include faculties for pedagogics. These, and other realities of direct funding could be directorial with regard to the compilation of the list of NWO foundations.

The second conceivable modality we would like to stage for the purpose of optimizing the indirect funding organization is based on the British system of research councils. In this option the councils operate at level five. The minister gives each council its own budget, which should imply a much more independent position. It also implies that council membership involves much more than simply occasional work; council membership should be either a full or part-time position.

There is no place in this model for the NWO Board as an independent administrative layer. In this model NWO is only conceivable as a weak coordinating body (a consultative body) of the five councils. Such a body functions at level five (compare the relation between the VSNU and the universities).

In this option the question is whether the critical mass (as regards budget and management capacity) of the Netherlands research system has sufficient weight to carry six directoral, heavily equipped research councils. It is here where we see the probable difference between the Dutch and the British system.

The third option is one in which the NWO becomes a central steering organization designated with heavy responsibilities up to and including level six in the research system. In the previous two options, in conformity with the present reality, NWO continues to be an organization which, in terms of the scope of its tasks, reaches up to level five; in this third option the NWO Board is no longer on the same level as the universities but is one level higher. In this modality, the division of tasks between the NWO administrative layers is as follows: the NWO Board at level six is engaged in dealing with the strategic missions of the universities, the councils at level five with the university research programmes, the departments at level four with the priorities and subsidization of research projects within disciplines, and the study groups at level three with the sub-disciplinary assessment of projects.

In this model the councils have quite a large amount of scope: they have lump sums at their disposal. As in the previous modality, more time and effort is required of the council members. The councils will have to be heavily staffed; it is quite conceivable that the members would be given an appointment (possibly part-time). The task of the councils is to initiate, encourage initiatives, draw up plans, etc., for all those research programmes which overlap various disciplines.

In this model the foundations have been discontinued and replaced by departments which, although they perform the same task as the councils it is for a smaller aggregate.

With regard to the functioning of the councils and departments this third option corresponds to a large extent with the original concept of the NWO Act. The main difference from that original concept – and also the previous modality in which NWO is at most a weak coordinating body of independently operating councils – is related to the task planned for the NWO Board. In this option the correspondence between NWO administrative layers and the tasks to be fulfilled within the research system is achieved by designating the NWO Board with important, strategic directorial competences. The top of the indirect funding organization is one level higher (level six) than that at which the universities operate (level five). The NWO Board is designated with the task of investigating the missions of direct funding bodies and allocating funds to the universities on the basis of their findings (e.g. for the selective founding of research schools).

This third modality was touched upon in the previous chapter. It is an option which is appropriate in a model of science policy where the steering stimuli come primarily from the indirect funding bodies; accordingly, steering stimuli through direct funding can be left out. For the NWO Board, and also the councils, the pursuit of such a UGC/UFC-like task implies that significant demands must be set as regards time, attention and representativeness of the board. The present NWO Board is, with its four members, in any case too small to be able to fulfil such a strategic task within the research system. Moreover, a problem is formed by the fact that the (present) NWO is only a research organization and this would tend to be restrictive if the indirect funding organization started to organize the strategic missions and profiles of universities in terms of both research and teaching.

6.5 The organization of multidisciplinary research programmes in the indirect funding system

In this section we look at the organizational problems of multidisciplinary research programmes within NWO. We first take a general look at the nature and position of multidisciplinary research. Giving shape to such research takes more administrative effort than the organization of disciplinary research. Since the publication of the BUOZ document government has attempted to give shape to the promotion of multidisciplinary research in two different ways through the various funding instruments. The consideration that university research should be geared more toward societal problems rather than keeping strictly within the academic disciplinary framework played a role in introduction of the conditional funding scheme in the direct funding. However, little came of this when actually implementing the scheme. Below we evaluate the reasons why the conditional funding scheme was apparently not the appropriate instrument to promote multidisciplinary research. As far as the indirect funding organization is concerned, the BUOZ document was the stimulus for the setting up of priority programmes which overlap various disciplines. A description of the organizational and funding structure of these programmes allows us to take a look at the behavioural aspects inherent in the structure of multidisciplinary research programmes. First of all we have the sociology of science behavioural aspects, which can explain why such programmes are difficult to get off the ground. Secondly, we see the behaviour that arises in connection with the funding and on-charging of finances if such programmes are superimposed on the existing NWO funding structure. We close this section with several conclusions. The main conclusion being that if NWO retains its specific character of being an organization structured according to disciplines, then it is not a very suitable organization to promote multidisciplinary research. A better alternative would be to give more arm's length to the sectoral research councils and planning boards which, given their organizational set-up, are geared towards the promotion of multidisciplinary research.

In Chapter 4 we noted that science, society and government have become more interwoven over the past few decades. Scientific research is increasingly being called upon to contribute towards resolving the problems facing society. These problems do not, however, present themselves arranged in disciplinary categories. The natural development in areas of science is the development of the cognitive object of the discipline. However, social problem areas can often be the empirical object of several disciplines and in order to gain scientific insight into such problem areas it is essential for teams of researchers from various disciplines to work together. Empirical object oriented, multidisciplinary scientific research therefore always requires an extra organizational step.

Up into the seventies the government's task with regard to scientific research was primarily one of providing funds. No steering elements were to be found in either the direct funding or the indirect funding organizations. In Chapter 4 a description is given of how the need for steering in research increased in the sixties and seventies. In terms of policy this was crystallized mainly in the BUOZ document. With regard to direct funding the BUOZ document laid the foundations for what several years later was to become the conditional funding scheme. Now that conditional funding has been with us for more than five years we are able to state that very little has changed as regards steering via direct funding (as some had feared and others had hoped).

Research programmes are now checked (marginally) on scientific grounds. The intended check on social significance failed to be realized. The main effect of the conditional funding scheme is that universities have now become more aware of their output, which has made research more perceptible and slightly more accessible for the universities' internal management. Nevertheless, the themes of research are generally so broadly defined, and the subsequent research projects – particularly those in disciplines operating on a small scale – are so heterogeneous that we can state that conditional funding is not an instrument in a policy geared towards setting priorities, giving direction, concentration, the distribution of tasks and the reallocation of university research. In short, it has not become an instrument at level seven or six of the research system; conditional funding is far too much a case of old ideas parading as new ones. A group of science sociologists, assigned by the Minister of Education and Science to evaluate the conditional funding scheme, concluded – as far back as 1984 – that the system "... resembles neither a paper tiger nor Big Brother but rather a 'virtuous citizen' who adjusts to the situation with a view to looking after his own interests" (Blume et al., 1984, pp. 74, 75).

The conclusion could be that there are still far too few steering elements in the direct funding system. Conditional funding has caused the existing disciplinary patterns to become segregated even further, rather than broken down. Programme evaluations are generally carried out by disciplinary committees headed by the KNAW. It is this structure which provides the impetus for programmes to be fed in under one discipline where possible. Given that there is no assessment as to social significance, scoring in the conditional funding scheme means, for researchers, scoring within the existing disciplinary frameworks.

With regard to indirect funding, the BUOZ document provided the stimulus for the NWO Act with its emphasis on initiation and innovation. Since then a far greater social orientation has been added to the mission of NWO. To be able to perform this new task, NWO developed the instrument of priority programmes: larger, multidisciplinary research programmes, in which the choice of theme is partly determined on a basis of non-scientific considerations. Characteristic of these priority programmes is that they are concerned with subjects which are given too little attention in the regular system and which are brought to the fore partly on social grounds. This was initiated in 1981 by ZWO and since then a number of priority programmes have been developed, each with its own background, structure and method of funding. They were realized partly through initiatives taken by foundations and partly under governmental pressure and encouragement to take up certain research themes. Initiatives should zero in on indications, plans and intentions of departments, sectoral research councils, RAWB, etc. Priority programmes are established by NWO in consultation with the minister. The central (at NWO coordination level) priority programmes listed below have meanwhile been developed:

a. biotechnology;
b. gerontology;
c. ethnic minorities;
d. information technology;
e. meteorology and physical oceanography;
f. surface science;
g. CO_2 research;
h. toxicology;
i. research into the emancipation of women;
j. demographic issues;
k. earth system disturbances;
l. Dutch culture in European context.

The total budget for all the various priority programmes is in the range of eight million guilders per year. It is the intention that priority programmes are given an average duration of about eight years to complete; the first three years serving as the initial period before the main theme is broken down into separate areas. Preparatory work leading up to the realization of a priority programme is carried out by committees of experts. The structure of these priority programmes differs: in some cases (e., g. and i.) the choice was made to form a special study group. The choice in the majority of cases, however, was for a (cross-sectional) committee operating at central NWO level. These committees have the task of assessing the projects submitted within the framework of the programme. This implies that these projects are assessed twice: they are also evaluated by the relevant foundations which assess the projects on aspects of the relevant discipline.

There are two distinct types of problem involved in shaping multidisciplinary priority programmes: one concerns the sociology of science (the disciplinary organization of research) and one concerns the financial side (the problems of coupled grants). Let us start with the sociology of science problem. NWO's central priority programmes are based on the concept that by nature these programmes should be at right angles to the programming established by the foundations. Such discipline-oriented boards with a bottom-up organization always give strong preference to the assessment of individual projects through judgment by peers. This organizational structure and culture is not the most appropriate one for developing large, multidisciplinary research programmes. The disciplinary structure of the NWO column is not only deceptive when launching multidisciplinary research programmes; a problem also arises in the foundations' and study groups' process of judging those research projects which are part of a priority programme. By nature, such projects are to be found at the edge of the relevant discipline, bordering on other disciplines. Past experience has shown that the further away the subject of a research project from the core of a (sub)discipline, the more problematic it is for that project in the assessment by study group and foundation. This makes it even more unattractive for researchers to enter into multidisciplinary territory given the fact that such research is slower in leading to recognition – a major driving force for researchers – because of the lack of identification with a specific discipline.

The financial problems of NWO priority programmes are connected with the present system of coupled grants. This system implies that organizational and budgetary stimuli are first given at central level and that only after some years do the programmes become embedded as much as possible in the regular, organizational structure of foundations and councils. It therefore follows that they should bear a substantial part of the funding of these programmes. The consequence of this is that the participation of foundations in central priority programmes is more often regarded as a punishment (a breach of their freedom to appropriate funds and procedures) than as a reward (additional funds for the discipline covered by the foundation).

If we look at the merits of the present system of central priority programmes we can draw a number of critical conclusions.

The introduction of central priority programmes has the intention of stimulating certain multi- or interdisciplinary areas of research, partly on a basis of considerations in the interests of society. Nevertheless, if we take a closer look at the priority programmes which have been developed to date it becomes apparent that the majority (a., d., to h.) are not really multi- or interdisciplinary, not even at the programme level. They are simply priority areas within the scope of one or two foundations. In order to avoid double procedures and coupled grants it would seem appropriate to recommend that these programmes be brought under the foundations in question.

But also those priority programmes which do relate to multiple subjects consist to a large extent of individual research projects which still fail to go beyond the boundaries of a single discipline. Also with regard to this type of priority programme the question is still whether the existence of standing, central committees, double procedures and coupled grants is justified. A simple stimulation scheme could suffice in such a system of priority programmes; a scheme whereby foundations could be promised an x% premium for research judged by the foundations as eligible for subsidization in the relevant area of research. It would thus be up to the foundations themselves to determine their level of activity in eliciting priority research projects. In this suggestion there is no need for permanent, central adjudication committees. The NWO Board itself can judge whether a research proposal is within a certain priority area. If necessary, the board can request the opinion of an independent expert.

The best possible way to do justice to true multidisciplinary research programmes would be to place both assessment and funding into the hands of separate frameworks: the cross-sectional committees. Priority programmes could then be completely separated from disciplinary research subsidization by foundations. At most, the relevant foundations could be asked for advice on the disciplinary aspects of the subject matter of applications. The advantage of the procedure suggested here is that it eliminates double assessment: such projects would no longer be included in the priority-setting of the foundations. Coupled grants are also out of the question (the projects would be subsidized in full out of the cross-sectional committee's central fund).

Such a procedure, in which NWO subsidizes parts of multidisciplinary research in a way which has become separated from the disciplinary lines of organization pursued by the foundations and study groups, ultimately gives rise to the question why the promotion of such research is part of the mission of NWO, and whether it would not be better to delegate this task to the sectoral research councils or other science policy planning committees. These considerations lead to the final conclusion that a discipline-structured organization is basically not very well-suited to perform the additional task of promoting multidisciplinary research.

6.6 Conclusions in the light of the model

We close this case study with eight conclusions. Conclusions 1 to 4 relate to the task and mission of the indirect funding organization, and to a certain extent its relationship with direct funding. Conclusions 5 to 8 concern the administrative tools of NWO: conclusion 5 relates to the organizational structure of the NWO organization, and conclusion 6 to the method of fund allocation both to and within NWO. Conclusion 7 is related to the structure of priority programmes and conclusion 8 to NWO personnel policy.

1. The most important task of indirect funding is the *forum function*; the nation-wide intercollegial assessment of the scientific quality of research projects and programmes (judgment by peers). The incorporation of the conditional funding scheme within the direct funding system did not reduce the university research system's need for the quality assessment function of the indirect funding organization.

2. The increased social and political need for the steering of research took shape in the BUOZ document which was published in the late seventies. This document made provision for the transformation from ZWO to NWO, an organization designated with the important tasks of stimulating and initiating research. For this purpose the budget for the indirect funding organization would be doubled over a period of ten years.

   Both the financial and organizational perspectives were only partially realized. Due to pressure from the universities, and other factors, the projected increase of the ZWO/NWO budget (at the expense of the direct funding of universities) planned in the BUOZ document was only partly carried through.

   The organizational transformation was embodied in the NWO bill and, although the discussion of the bill took many years, step by step a number of major pitfalls (in the form of organizational changes) were removed from it. The new administrative layer of the councils, established by the NWO Act, was not therefore based on a perspicuous concept but on two trains of thought.

3. This resulted in the introduction of the NWO Act causing friction given that it is unclear whether the emphasis in the mission of the organization should be on the top-down or the bottom-up elements.

4. In the Dutch research system it is the universities that govern direct funding, and the indirect funding organization acts as a supplement to that funding system. By tradition, the power of the indirect funding organization is that – taking into consideration university research on a national scale – it strengthens that which is good, stimulates new ideas, establishes links between research at various universities, and provides facilities which are beyond the financial scope of individual universities. It would therefore seem most appropriate for NWO to continue to stress both the network function and the forum function. The research system has no need for an indirect funding organization which would be set tasks that are already taken care of (to an increasing extent) within the direct funding system. NWO must stop "doing more of the same thing", but lay emphasis on tracking down gaps and initiating activities to do just that. The indirect funding organization can also give an extra stimulus to emerging developments in the early stage before they start to pursue their own independent course within the foundations of the direct funding system. Moreover, it is especially the indirect funding organization – which is after all geared towards innovation – which must provide opportunities for original and venturesome research, the success of which is uncertain. There is reason to assume that such research has less chance under the conditional funding scheme.

5. The core of the NWO column should therefore remain with the foundations and study groups as the crystallization points of national networks of researchers. In this configuration there would seem to be no independent place set aside for the new administrative layer of the councils. Assisted by public choice it can be predicted that there is only a small chance that the councils will develop into bodies that will generate greater knowledge than the foundations do at present. The conclusion must therefore be that the introduction of the administrative layer of the councils will lead to an over-organization of the indirect funding system. We have described various options to resolve the problems of organization; our preference is for NWO to develop in the direction of decentralization. This is in sharp contrast with the present NWO trend.

6. The NWO Act makes no provision for a system of earmarking those sums which are made available to NWO by the government. This can be qualified as a too drastic abstinence from regulation. It typically belongs to the tasks performed at level seven (the government) to indicate the extent to which it wishes to promote the main areas of science. Such action is common all over the world. In Great Britain, for instance, indirect funding is delegated by the minister to five separate research councils. In this context the research sector can be compared with other sectors of government policy, defence for example. In this sector, the financial apportionment to the navy, the army and the airforce is also established by the government and not left to the defence system itself. Something can therefore be said in favour of earmarking NWO subsidy for the six distinguished main areas of science, namely: the humanities, social sciences, the exact

sciences, geo- and biosphere sciences, medical sciences, and engineering sciences.

Such earmarking is the result of a legitimate political choice and deserves to be given preference above allocation to disciplines as the result of the balance of power which has grown over the years within the NWO organization.

7. The present organizational and budgetary structure of NWO priority programmes is a constant source of friction. The double assessment procedures by both a foundation and a programme committee is a complex and time-consuming procedure. It must therefore be recommended that the priority programmes should no longer be allowed to intervene with the existing (structure of) foundations. The system of coupled grants should also be discontinued. It is recommended to either discontinue the programme committees, to bring the priority programmes under the management of the foundations where possible, and, as an incentive, to introduce a simple system of premiums which are made known to the foundations in advance, or to place the assessment and funding of priority programmes completely in the hands of central programme committees as separate organizational frameworks within NWO and to refrain from involving the foundations in this work.

8. Finally, NWO should take a very careful look at the policy it pursues in the appointment of researchers. Several years ago the category of trainee research assistants (aio's) was introduced in the university world. Following in these footsteps, and also under pressure to do so, ZWO created an equivalent: the NWO research trainee (oio). The universities can take on relative large cohorts of trainee research assistants while, moreover, the procedure for this research apprenticeship is generally less difficult and much shorter.

   It may be concluded that the introduction of trainee research assistants, coupled with several other developments in the past few years (including the conditional funding scheme), has given rise to a continuing increase in planning, quality assessment, etc., in the direct funding system. With this in mind, the indirect funding organization will have to prevent itself from becoming a duplicate of the former.

   NWO will therefore need to try and find its own, unambiguous position. With regard to personnel policy, NWO – with its high demands of scientific quality and weighty assessment procedures – will have to aim for researchers with several years of experience, preferably postdoctorate researchers. The present Fellows programme that the minister has brought under the KNAW (which since its inception has never performed the task of subsidizing research) would in that model fit in perfectly with NWO. This would bring it into line with the NWO programme for individual-orientated group support (Pionier Programme).

Appendix

Organization chart NWO (1990)

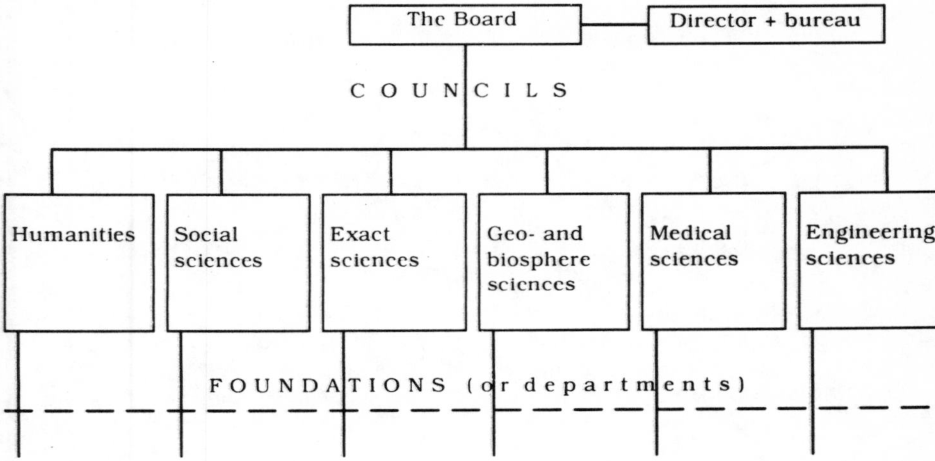

Under the council for the humanities come seven foundations: for history, linguistics, literature, theology, archeology, art history studies and philosophy.

Under the council for social sciences come six foundations: for psychology, social-environmental research, juridical studies, economics, sociology and pedagogics. There is also a department for political and administrative sciences.

The six foundations which come under the council for the exact sciences are for physics, mathematics, chemistry, astronomy, space research, and computer science.

There are four foundations which come under the council for biology, oceanography and earth sciences, namely: biology, biophysics, earth sciences and marine research. Also under this council are two independent study groups, one for meteorological research and one for CO_2 research.

Under the council for medical sciences come four departments: for cellular biology and cellular pathology, organic systems, hormonal regulation and neurology, and health sciences.

The council for engineering sciences is coupled with the foundation for engineering sciences.

Finally, under the NWO umbrella there is also a foundation for tropical research which, given the multidisciplinary character of this research, comes directly under the NWO Board and not under one of the councils.

PART III
CONCLUSIONS

7 Summary and conclusions

7.1 The theoretical framework

This book deals with a question of optimality: what interaction between institutions and behaviour leads to the best possible reconciliation of efficiency and effectiveness in the system of scientific research, especially that of university research. This system is seen from an economist's point of view: as a value conversion system. It consists of several levels of actors, each with their own specific tasks and responsibilities. To perform their tasks and responsibilities these actors are given a certain degree of freedom. Each actor is thus able to aspire to his own goals within certain boundaries.

In this study we have used a theoretical organizational model to establish which tasks and responsibilities are the most appropriate at which level. A theoretical element of behaviour is introduced in the 'ideal' allocation of tasks and responsibilities, the main point being to find those incentives which lead to promoting the maximization of the various actors' goals while at the same time counteracting any undesirable behaviour. The institutionalization of such incentives requires first of all that we have an understanding of the motives and driving forces behind the behaviour of actors in collectivities, hence the reason for the analytical framework of this study consisting of a symbiosis of organizational theory and behavioural theory. The theoretical organizational concept is a useful tool in that it allows us to *describe* the research system. However, in order to *explain* the workings of a system and the dynamics of that system we have a need for a behavioural theory. Because we are concerned with the conditions required for the system to generate optimal results (the economic aspect) and because in this case we have defined the boundaries of the system in such a way that we are dealing with the research system funded through the budgetary mechanism, the economic theory of public choice has been used as the behavioural theory.

In Chapter 1 we described how the theoretical organizational concept and the economic theory of group decision-making is used in this book. The relation between the two angles of approach was described as the 'warp' (the theoretical organizational concept as the principle for structuring the entire book) versus 'weft' (the economic behavioural theory which crops up from time to time).

The emphasis in this study is laid on the research system as a multi-level system with a stratified and dispersed decision-making structure; this characterizes our theoretical organizational concept. In this case we distinguish between seven different levels. On each level we see certain actors (individuals, organizations) that carry out specific tasks and responsibilities within the research system. The higher we climb in this multi-level system, the higher the level of aggregation and the greater the complexity of decision-making: from the execution of research projects and research programmes to planning, coordination and distribution of tasks, to coordinating the development of strategies, up to the translation of social norms and values into priorities for science policy. Based on a description of the tasks performed at the various levels and the corresponding actors, the multi-level model is shown (in Chapter 2) as follows:

level	*task*	*actor*
1	duties aimed at prescribed output	support research personnel
2	situational response	researcher
3	systematic provision	research group (teaching and research unit, NWO study group)
4	comprehensive provision	organization unit (faculty, institute, NWO foundation)
5	field coverage	coordinating organization (university, TNO, NWO)
6	conglomerate strategy	national advisory and consultative councils (WRR, KNAW, RAWB, ARHO, sectoral research councils)
7	articulation of social norms and values and the translation thereof into policies	minister(s), government and parliament

Levels one to three form the micro-structure of the research system: the 'shop-floor'; levels four and five the meso-structure: organizations and their main departments; levels six and seven form the macro-structure of political/non-political bodies responsible for giving direction to the research system at national level.

Many of the discussions about research policy and science policy are concerned with the question which actor should do what – and more importantly – what that actor should not do. Does the individual researcher have total academic freedom or do other organizations have a say in the choice of subject of his research? Should a faculty pursue research policy or leave it to the teaching and research unit? (this also applies to the relation between university and faculties). Should the allocation of tasks and the concentration of research capacity in a certain area be left to the universities, or should this be organized by the minister or possibly even a different body? Should the VSNU be allowed to make binding decisions or does the autonomy of organizations have highest priority?, etc., etc.

Given the large number of actors in the system, each with their own diverse goals, positions and competences, there is no single answer to these questions. However, it is quite clear that in order to answer them we must first of all know which levels can be distinguished in terms of a system hierarchy, and the whys and wherefores of these levels. In other words: what are their respective tasks and competences. Presenting the research system as a multi-level system is of both heuristic and practical value. The practical value has been tested in three case studies.

The heuristic value is to be found in the fact that light is shed on the origins of a number of bottlenecks and areas of friction in the implementation of policy. In practice, problems often emerge because certain levels have been inadequately institutionalized, giving rise to certain administrative outputs either not being realized at all or being realized at the wrong level. In the latter case decisions are made at a level which fails to correspond with the nature of that decision. If, for instance, certain decisions are made at too great a distance from the executive level, the result can be a higher degree of bureaucracy and an undermining of the competences of lower levels. On the other hand, if higher levels are inadequately equipped in terms of organization and instrumentation, and subsequently far too much is left to lower levels, strategic (directorial) decisions will not be accomplished.

In this book we have constantly stressed that the research system is not controlled from a single cockpit (at the highest level) through directives issued down to the lower levels. It is particularly characteristic of the research system that initiating, coordinating and performing research implies that the lower levels also carry heavy responsibilities. The organization of the research system is not therefore a centralistic rank and file system. The relations between the various levels can thus be established through various types of competences. Although there might be a direct line between levels it can also be the case that the task carried out by the level one step higher up is primarily one of coordinating, advising, monitoring, and so on. When referring to the research system as a hierarchical system we do not therefore mean the pure form of rank and file hierarchy. In order to make that difference quite clear we have used the term introduced by Simon: *holarchy*.

Research is a creative process. It is the search for the unknown. In this book that process of searching is modelled as a production process aiming at the production of certain results (achievements or outputs). However, this production process is a rather special one; it is a process which differs from the production process of motorcars or bicycles. In Chapter 3 we took a closer look at the primary processes involved in the research system: how are research results generated, measured and evaluated; and how are these processes controlled internally; what are the variables aimed at and by which actors?

In order to do full justice to the typical character of research and researchers the sociology of science was taken as the starting point for Chapter 3. Sociology of science teaches us that the behaviour of the producers of research is regulated by four quite specific norms and values: universalism, organized scepticism, communality and disinterestedness (in the sense of being objective and without bias). Together they form the constituent complex of the reward or exchange mechanism on which scientific production is based. This allows an interpretation in economic terminology and understanding. The characteristic features of economic goods have been set out for this purpose. These features can be used to make a dichotomy between market goods and public goods. Characteristic of a public good is that, contrary to that of the price and market mechanism, *exclusion* (of non-payers), *financing* of production and *information* (as regards the value placed on that good) is relatively difficult to arrange. Especially fundamental research – because of its sociology of science characteristics – generally has the economic characteristics of a public good. As already stated, one of the problems involved in the provision of such goods is that their efficiency and effectiveness cannot be assessed in the same way as market goods. The public sector therefore has its own mechanisms of accountability. By putting forward micro-economic theories in this context we explained which types of indicators can be conceived for measuring and controlling production processes in the public sector. These insights are subsequently applied to the scientific research produced in the public (in this case, university) sector. We explained how publication and citation indicators can be used to support qualitative assessment procedures (peer review) in scientific research. It is important to note that such 'sound' production information always requires expert interpretation. The choice for certain production indicators is based, among other things, on the specific characteristics of the relevant discipline, the field of research and the research group. In this context, background information is seldom to be found above level four in the system. This yields a significant conclusion in terms of the multi-level system. Output data can be a positive aid in the dialogue between level four (faculties, NWO foundations) and level three (study groups). At this level there is still a willingness and ability to interpret information. Information concerning the output of research groups is not however a suitable instrument in the hands of the higher levels in the system: levels five, six and seven. At these levels there is the risk that such information is looked at on its own merits and the 'automatic pilot' is switched on: the 'sound' figures then have to speak for themselves.

7.2 The practical situation: developments and recommendations relating to the different levels of the research system

The theoretical framework is checked against the practical situation in the second part of this study (Chapters 4 to 6). This was done in the form of three case studies. Chapter 4 looks at the most significant developments over the past 25 years in the science policy pursued by government and is therefore concerned with the macro-level. Chapters 5 and 6 deal with two case studies concerned with the various components and various decentralized levels of the (para) university research system. This analysis was aimed at investigating the consequences if tasks and competences were transferred to a lower (or higher) decision-making level in the system.

The case study discussed in Chapter 5 relates to the ministerial document 'Higher Education: Autonomy and Quality' (the so-called HOAK document; 1985). In this document the Ministry of Education and Science introduced a new policy concept of the relations between government and the universities, and subsequent to this, a new planning procedure (the Higher Education and Research Plan). In the HOAK document the government took a step back in order to give the universities more scope for policy-making. This policy philosophy was worked out in the case study in terms of the seven-level model. Particularly those consequences for the sixth level (of the distribution of tasks and coordinative strategy planning in the university system) were analyzed.

The indirect funding organization was dealt with in Chapter 6. After a lengthy history in 1988 the Netherlands Organization for Scientific Research (NWO) emerged from what was formerly ZWO. This transformation resulted in a new administrative layer being created at an intermediate level: the so-called councils. The tasks of the various layers of the indirect funding organization in its new form, and the relations between those layers, were analyzed in Chapter 6 from the (de)centralization perspective of the multi-level model.

Looking at the three case studies as a whole we will now summarize the main administrative and institutional developments in the top five levels of the system. These developments are described per level and checked against our organizational model: what, in the light of optimal efficiency and effectiveness of scientific research, are the most significant recommendations that can be made in connection with the position, tasks and responsibilities of the various system levels. We repeat that – in order to arrive at these statements – we followed a system of conditional criteria (described in Chapter 1) based on an if-then methodology. Given that no clear-cut, explicit and consistent goals have been defined in the research system – and therefore cannot be used for purposes of verification – we have taken the only logically applicable criteria for the research system of efficiency and effectiveness. It must also be pointed out that especially the concept of effectiveness is not a constant quantity but is influenced by changes in social opinions. This implies that if necessary we have to be more explicit in our explanation of the term 'effectiveness' by applying the if-then argument.

Level seven is the level of science policy. It is at this highest level that form is given to national science policy and the institutional structuring of the intermediate levels in the research system. The main actors at this level are the Minister of Education and Science, the Minister of Economic Affairs and, up to 1981, the Minister for Science Policy. The most important institutional developments for level seven over the past 25 years were discussed in the first case study – on science policy pursued in the Netherlands. In the sixties and seventies there was a strong belief in social reform and government policy was based on that belief. Science policy during this period was characterized by the pretension of a synoptic and coordinated entity.

In the eighties, the disappointing outcomes resulted in a deterioration of the belief in social reform. Another social and political flow of values emerged. For our verification framework this implies a change in the significance of effectiveness and thus also the optimality we are searching for. During this period we also saw a change in science policy: it became more fragmentary, selective and decentralized. The main conclusion to be drawn in respect of level seven is that the government's presence in the system became more modest. In the eighties the government withdrew to the gallery referred to as "management at arm's length". Level seven started to stress the importance that the lower levels (especially level five: universities, NWO, TNO) were able to take care of their own management. Hierarchical thinking made way for holarchic insights. The most important developments with regard to level seven are:

1. the separate ministership for science policy is abolished;

2. government's science policy strongly emphasizes innovation and the stimulation of technology in trade and industry. The relative status of the Minister of Economic Affairs is given more weight;

3. the need for specific planned stimuli in the research system increased enormously over the past few decades. Science policy was geared towards channelling that development along the proper responsibility-structure lines ensuing from the stratified model. Optimal institutionalization of that need for planned stimuli implied taking the wind out of the sails of direct dealings between level seven (in this case the various ministries) and levels four and lower, or declaring it forbidden ground. It is against this background that we see the quite clear intention in present science policy to give more weight to the relation between levels seven and five (for instance, the restructuring of the administrative protocol between the Minister of Education and Science and universities by means

of the HOOP procedure). To make this possible, government policy was geared primarily towards strengthening the institutions operating at level five: the restructuring of TNO, the transition from ZWO to NWO, and the HOAK document with its emphasis on university autonomy (see point 4.). Government wishes to do business with powerful organizations, the top echelons of which (at level five) interpret and pass on the arrangements and regulations to the lower levels;

4. subject to the explicit restriction that higher education and research continue to remain both the concern and instrument of government policy, the government wishes to create more latitude for university autonomy in its administrative relationship with the universities. The emphasis is shifted from a preventive check on university inputs and throughputs (regulations and rules concerning expenditure) to checking the quality of university output afterwards. In doing this, government assumes a meta-role: it does not check quality itself but makes sure that a quality assessment system is created; a system which is to be implemented by the association of universities (VSNU) and the University Education Inspectorate ;

5. the government also adopts a less paternalistic attitude towards the indirect funding organization. The ministerial representative – who had always had a place on the ZWO Board – has been withdrawn from the NWO Board.

If we try to assess the institutional developments at level seven in the light of efficiency and effectiveness, the transition from the synoptic science policy of the sixties and seventies to a fragmentary and selective policy in the eighties, can basically be regarded as realistic if we consider the meaning given to the term effectiveness in the eighties. With regard to the curriculum content component, science policy is presently aimed at selecting likely areas of research for the Netherlands. Such policy is more appropriate for the nature of scientific research which, by definition, is a complex of activities with uncertain outcomes which cannot be influenced by blueprints. Science policy is now geared more towards making strategic choices: in which areas do we strive towards acquiring a prominent position in the world; where is international cooperation called for in particular; in which areas are special social issues to be solved; which areas of research are the spearheads for trade and industry?, etc. A strategic science policy of this kind is appropriate for a small country in a relatively wide international setting.

The logical consequence of the loss of the pretension of a synoptic science policy was the loss of a separate ministership. This implies the risk of the 'law of the jungle' coming into force in the vacuum that has emerged at level seven. Since the eighties we have seen that the Ministry of Economic Affairs – riding on the waves of the revival in the market sector – as the clientele department for trade and industry with its research priorities and research programmes has had a definite influence on the science policy of government. The policy pursued by Economic Affairs is aimed at stimulating technology and innovation in the market sector. This has weakened the link between science policy and wider social issues. The danger of too great a bias towards the interests of trade and industry is that little attention and resources are given to long-term research given that the incentive is to stimulate research which is productive in the shorter term. The present relations of power at level seven can therefore lead to an unstable science policy. Government should give more consideration to the question concealed in the Chinese proverb "who feeds the pigs?"; in other words: is sufficient concern being given to research which is not in the direct interest of any specific group, or of which the stakeholders are a diffuse and unorganized group? A possible answer to this is that the government itself ensures a counterbalance by establishing organizations at level six which are able to formulate the research questions in these sectors and help to steer the relevant planning and organization. The sectoral research councils which have been established by government in the past reflect this approach.

Level six is described as the level of coordinative strategy development. This coordination is on a national scale and covers all the various segments of research organizations. In terms of size it is of a larger scale than, for example, the joint universities or the joint large technological institutes. Level six is immediately below the science policy level and immediately above the research system in the strict sense. It performs an interface function between these two complexes in terms of (1) effecting a conversion between the values and interests of level seven and those of the research system, (2) providing a platform at a high level in the system where government representatives, research organizations and interested groups in society can meet, and (3) acting as a buffer, i.e. somewhat protecting the research world from direct government involvement and vice versa.

The level of abstraction and degree of complexity of the tasks at level six imply that the institutionalization of this level of the system is relatively the least crystallized. In practice, various modalities have developed alongside one another:

a. The mildest form of institutionalization: a body of representatives which acts as the *consultative platform* for the organizations operating at level five. We can only speak of a level six organization if decision-making at this level is binding for the actors at the lower level. If this is not the case, and the autonomy of the level five organization is sacrosanct, all we have is an extension for level five. Because of this we have positioned the VSNU at level five in our model.
b. Actors at level six performing mainly *advisory tasks*. In this interpretation of level six we can think especially in terms of government's external advisory councils which fulfil a strategic function, such as the RAWB and the WRR.
c. One step further is taken in the modality of actors at level six who, *in addition to an initial advisory task*, are also able to use the *budgetary instrument as lubrication* (incentive instrument).
d. Finally, we can also envisage an interpretation whereby level six fulfils the important *task of budget allocation* (which would then not take place at level seven and/or five). Contrary to a number of other countries there is no such independent administrative body in the Netherlands in the area of science policy.

The strategic function of level six is of increasing importance. By nature the government tends to 'play safe'. Yet in a society which is becoming progressively more complex the degree of uncertainty also grows. This applies à fortiori in the selection of strategic areas for research. All the more important therefore is the function of external organizations at level six which, if necessary, are able to counterbalance the political issues of the day. From the government's viewpoint the institutionalization of (scientific) strategic expertise at level six implies less uncertainty, and consequently a saving in transaction and information costs.

The institutional interpretation of level six is of relative recent date. The majority of the boards we have at this level at present – RAWB, WRR, sectoral research councils (with the exception of the NRLO for agricultural research) – were all established within the past twenty years. Before that the dominant view towards science was that it should be allowed to take its own course. Government mainly pursued a favourable policy with regard to those organizations operating at level five. There was no need in that concept for level six organizations which concerned themselves with the development of coordinative strategy.

The institutional structuring of level six is an arduous process. Illustrative of this is the development of the system of sectoral research councils which was set in motion in the seventies, and subsequently came to a standstill in the seventies. It becomes apparent yet again that it takes the self-denial of departments to set up organizations outside the rank and file system, whose specific task it is to provoke and contradict the government, yet still take their statements to heart. This demands that government acquires more insight or foresight; that it is prepared to limit its own reach voluntarily. Assisted by the theory of public choice, in Chapter 1 we explained that this concept of '*self-restraint*' (Elster, 1979 and 1983; see also Van Gunsteren, 1987) need not automatically imply that an actor, the government in this case, acts against his own interests. Self-restraint can be explained in a rational behavioural paradigm: by imposing restraint on future competences and options one impedes one's own future irrational behaviour.

In the light of an effective functioning of the system Chapter 5 backs up the establishment of an independent administrative body at level six to allocate the state budget (in whole or in part) for higher education and research between the universities. The British University Funding Council, or its predecessor: the University Grants Committee, should serve as the model for such an agency; an organization in which binding decisions are taken on the distribution of tasks, concentration, the discontinuation and establishment of disciplines, centres of excellence, etc. The presence of a strong institution at level six with sufficient powers to take decisions and impose sanctions would basically render the above described strategic behaviour of universities and government – the consequence of non-binding decision-making – impossible. This implies that both institutes and government would sacrifice part of their autonomy and subject themselves to decision-making at level six. Such a structure is quite the opposite to those administrative structures which have been developed in public administration in the Netherlands to date.

Problems of scale, cost, labour market perspectives for students, etc., tend to turn the distribution of tasks, concentration, collaboration, coordination, establishing the main points of disciplines, into permanent problems in the university system of today, apart from the budgetary (economizing) aspects which at times gain the upper hand. These tasks should preferably be performed at level six. Non-obligatory university associations do not generally come higher than level five in fulfilling their tasks; they tend to act as an extension for the universities. Given their non-compulsory structure they cannot be considered capable of performing level six tasks adequately. Conversely, fulfilment of these tasks at level seven is an unnecessary form of centralization. It gives rise to high transaction and information costs, which are increased due to the fact that the mechanisms for self-management at university level are undermined. This implies the need for a powerful and directorial body at level six. Such a body should be independent and be allowed to make binding decisions; a body which we feel should also be given the power of the purse. This is an essential element for it to be able to act as manager in the university system. This weighty allocation of responsibilities to level six would obviously be at the expense of the budgetary and other responsibilities which at present are in the hands of organizations operating at levels seven and five. We feel that this is the best method of institutionalization for the university system and which offers the best guarantee against the constant threat of governmental involvement or academic autism. In this sense it is the logical complement to the HOAK proposals which fail to provide an answer to the question how the supra-university processes of coordination should be regulated if the universities obtain more autonomy. That such an institution can work is apparent from the situation in Great Britain (UFC/UGC) and Sweden.

This board could also be given the responsibility of setting up evaluation committees (to assess the quality of research in a discipline). Debate is presently under way as to whether evaluation committees should advise the minister or whether they should advise the joint universities (VSNU). It will be quite clear that the former is less desirable given that it would impede 'management at arm's length'. On the other hand, the VSNU is far too inadequately equipped to be able to enforce the recommendations of an evaluation committee in the event that some universities disagreed. An independent administrative body at level six would also solve this problem. We are well aware that this option cannot be achieved overnight, and that a certain time is needed. The stronger institutionalization of level six calls for the development of research management at all levels in the research system – starting with the lower faculty levels – during the initial stage.

Level five is the highest level in the research system in the strict sense. Operating at this level are those concerns which can coordinate a large number of organizational units and which also pursue a strategic policy with regard to those units. In anticipation of the needs of the surrounding environment, new units can be set up and obsolete units closed down. The scope of operation at level five is thus wide and not demarcated beforehand. The main examples of actors operating at level five in the scientific world are: TNO, which coordinates numerous institutes; the universities, which take care of a whole range of faculties; NWO, under which come a large number of disciplinary foundations and councils in the main areas of science. In this book TNO has not been included in the case studies; the universities were dealt with in Chapter 5 and the NWO organization in Chapter 6. The most significant conclusions we have drawn as regards level five are:

1. The eighties saw the start of a movement towards strengthening level five. This was mainly the result of planned government policy. There was an increasing awareness at level seven that an increase in the administrative power of level five bodies was crucial for science policy at arm's length. This strengthening of level five was expressed in the new TNO Act, the transformation from ZWO to NWO, and the emphasis on university autonomy, which has become *bon ton* since the HOAK document and the HOOP. The University Education Act of 1986 (WWO'86) also had an influence on the administrative powers of universities (see point 4).

2. The analysis made in Chapter 5 shows that the proposed changes to the system, which would increase the power of level five, are only modest despite the pretensions of the HOAK document. The proposals contained in the HOAK document aim primarily at giving government co-management a somewhat different character: more repressive (checking quality afterwards); and less preventive (issuing regulations beforehand). Moreover, government regulation is coupled to the procedures contained in the HOOP: this could lead to more orderly arrangements but not in itself to less regulation.
   Where the HOAK document has been successful in bringing about a higher degree of university autonomy it relates principally to the education structure. The universities in particular are given more opportunities to establish a more diverse and flexible curriculum.

3. Neither the HOAK nor the HOOP have affected the current strong regulation of policy on university personnel and terms of employment. Yet it is especially here that we see

an area where expansion of university autonomy would be extremely welcome from the viewpoint of reducing information and transaction costs. We could not agree more with the various recent proposals (Commissie Financieringsstructuur, 1985; Rinnooy Kan, et al., 1987; VSNU, 1988) calling for universities to be allowed to adopt their own policies with regard to terms of employment and composition of staff. The consequence of this could be that university personnel would be in the employ of the university instead of having civil servant status.

4. One important feature of level five bodies is that they concern themselves with strategic planning. In industry it is the concern management that takes decisions on 'new combinations', new products, new markets, new plants. In the university world strategic planning for new faculties, disciplines, etc., are reflected in university development plans. To be able to execute these plans the universities are dependent upon the government as the main provider of funds. Expanding university autonomy consists of encouraging the universities to become involved in planning; not in the sense that they can take autonomous decisions on new faculties and disciplines – they still need the government's permission for this.
   That consideration is still given to these aspects is apparent from the provocative ideas voiced by Rinnooy Kan et al., (1987) for an even more independently operating level five. Rinnooy Kan and co., argue for instance that universities should have the opportunity to borrow from the capital market to carry out their plans.
   For the time being we can rest assured that it will be a long time before such ideas stand any reasonable chance of success. This brings us to the cultural limitations of the Dutch higher education system. That culture was described in Chapter 5 as being egalitarian by nature, implying that elements taken from another system (the American system for instance), and the goals inherent in that system, cannot simply be brought into the Dutch university system without being modified. Pursuing a policy for higher education and a science policy in a country such as the Netherlands is regarded as the task of government, and this involves a certain degree of regulation with regard to the university system. In other words, level seven cannot allow itself to hand over all its instruments.

5. The WWO'86 resulted in the responsibilities of the Governing Body of a university being drawn up in outline, with an emphasis on establishing policy, while an exhaustive account was given of the responsibilities of university councils, with an emphasis on control and legitimization. This adjustment vis-à-vis the WUB implies that level five can operate more effectively. It also brings up the fundamental question of whether control and legitimization of management in an organization such as a university is best served by a directly elected council or, for instance, a federation of representatives of the various faculties. For example, it is quite remarkable that no comparable organization where the duties involve working with people (e.g. colleges of higher vocational education, hospitals) has the same form of management as universities. There is no other conclusion than that the WUB has gradually become an anomaly. It is equally remarkable to see that the administrative structure of postgraduate teaching and research (the creation of research schools and centres of excellence) sails around the framework of the WUB. It would therefore seem only appropriate to add an experimental article to the WWO which makes provision for the universities and faculties to gain experience in other forms of management. A selection can then be made at a later date from the forms of management thus acquired for the best alternative to replace the WUB.

6. As a result of government policy (the conditional funding scheme, etc.) there is an increasing level of steering, channelling and planning research within the direct funding system. It would therefore seem unnecessary, maybe even inadvisable, for NWO to perform these tasks. One major reason for the transformation from ZWO to NWO thus looses its value. There continues to be an unabated need for the original forum function of the indirect funding system: the nation-wide, intercollegial assessment of scientific quality. It is therefore advisable for NWO to return to the original task of indirect funding, but for all disciplines. This would do justice to both the forum function and the network function (offering national platforms for researchers in a certain area). The research system has no need for indirect funding organizations which are to undertake tasks already being fulfilled (to an increasing extent) in the direct funding system. In the past, both universities and ZWO pursued a passive research policy. Government's reaction in the seventies and eighties to encourage both universities and ZWO/NWO to adopt an active research policy seems to be a case of overshooting. These conclusions with regard to NWO apply à fortiori should our suggestion be carried out to establish a powerful body at level six of the research system which would carry responsibility for the constant processes of restructuring and profiling within the university system.

7. NWO must therefore not be allowed to become an organization which steers research to too great an extent. The core of the NWO column should therefore remain with the foundations and study groups. Section 6.4 gives an exhaustive argumentation as to why there is no independent place for the councils as an administrative layer in the system, but rather as advisory bodies for the NWO Board at most.

8. The NWO Act makes no provision for earmarking those government resources available to NWO. This can be qualified as a too drastic form of abstinence from regulation. It typically belongs to the level seven (government) task of indicating the extent to which it wishes to promote the main areas of science. It is therefore advisable to introduce a system of earmarking the NWO grant for the six foremost science areas, namely: the humanities, social sciences, the exact sciences, geo- and biosphere sciences, medical sciences, and engineering sciences. Such earmarking is the result of a legitimate political choice and deserves to be given preference above the allocation to disciplines as has grown over the years within the NWO organization as a result of historical processes.

9. The present organizational and budgetary structure of the priority programmes within NWO is a constant source of friction. The double assessment procedures by both a foundation and a programme committee is a complex and time-consuming procedure. It must therefore be recommended that the priority programmes should no longer be allowed to intervene with the existing (structure of) foundations. Also, the system of coupled grants should be discontinued. We recommended either to discontinue the central programme committees, to bring the priority programmes under the management of the foundations where possible, and, as an incentive, to introduce a simple system of premiums made known to the foundations in advance, or to place the assessment and funding of priority programmes completely in the hands of central committees as separate organizational frameworks within NWO, and to refrain from involving the foundations in this work.

10. Finally, NWO should take a very careful look at the policy it pursues in the appointment of researchers. Several years ago the category of trainee research assistant was

introduced in the university world. Following in these footsteps, and also under pressure to do so, ZWO also created an equivalent: the research trainee (oio). The universities can take on relative large cohorts of trainee research assistants while, moreover, the procedure for this research apprenticeship is generally less difficult and much shorter. We have already concluded that the introduction of trainee research assistants, coupled with several other developments in the past few years (including the conditional funding scheme), has given rise to a continual increase in planning, quality assessment, etc., in the direct funding system. The indirect funding system is threatened with becoming a duplicate of the direct funding system. NWO will therefore need to try and find its own, unambiguous position. With regard to personnel policy, NWO – with its high demands of scientific quality and weighty assessment procedures – will have to aim for researchers with several years of experience, preferably postdoctorate researchers. The present Fellows Programme which the minister has brought under the KNAW (otherwise performing no research funding tasks) would, in that model, fit in perfectly with NWO. This would thus bring it into line with the NWO programme for individual-orientated group support (Pionier Programme).

At *level 4* a specific set of tasks within a defined area is taken care of in a given territorial or organizational context (determined by level five). As a rule, the demarcation of territories in the research world is based on the areas of disciplines. The administrative output of level four consists of the management of larger organizational units such as a faculty or an NWO foundation. There is also a strategic dimension involved in the management task of level four: that there is no aversion to introducing new products and services (curriculum subjects, research specialisms) in his field, nor to the discontinuation of producing outputs which are no longer adequate. Market research is carried out at this level for the purpose of mapping out the potential needs of the target groups (students, consumer groups, scientific forum, etc.). Management at level four is responsible for integral decision-making on matters of planning and budgets, whereas the most important decisions concerning investments are taken at level five. The management task at level four also includes organization development: the (re)arrangement and coordination of groups at level three and the allocation of funds thereto.

As stated previously, in the research system it is especially the faculties and NWO foundations that operate at level four. As is also the case at level five we see a tendency towards strengthening the administrative effort at level four. The following points outline the main recent developments.

1. The enormous increase in the demand for education has resulted in an increase in the need for stronger management at level four over the past few decades. Chapter 1 described how the traditional professoriate universities were replaced by educational enterprises. In the eighties the introduction of the conditional funding scheme also gave rise to the need for a stronger administrative structure in these educational enterprises.

2. In general, this need for stronger management has only been met to date with some degree of hesitance. The WWO'86 boosted the responsibilities of the faculty board vis-à-vis the faculty council and thus increased the board's influence. Another effect of the WWO was that subfaculties were disbanded and once again integrated in the parent faculty.

   Another effort to increase the strength of management at level four was the trend to replace the 'deanship-as-drudgery' model with a professional deanship. Although this has been achieved in some faculties it is not a structural phenomenon. No incentives to make the pursuit of an administrative career have as yet been incorporated into the research system. Researchers are forced to interrupt their study in the discipline they have chosen, fall behind in their scientific career, are regarded as 'oddities' by others in the profession, and face an uncertain future as administrator. One can reach the following paradoxical conclusion: the faculty as an association of professors has disappeared but is often still run on the basis of the remnants of sentiments from days gone by of fellowship and a sense of duty. It is against this background that we argue two points (see also Van Buchem, 1987, pp. 144, 145):

a. that an experimental article be added to the WWO, making provision for universities to choose for a faculty management organization which gives them more scope should they so wish;
b. that incentives be incorporated into the system to ensure that the status of a dean is recognized as such, that the emoluments and authority are approporiate to that status, and that this position is comparable with that of the American dean. The position of dean must be regarded within a faculty as the culmination of a scientific and administrative career and not that the person in question has been put on the sidelines. The task of a professional dean must be extensive: this includes, in addition to his main responsibility for the faculty's curriculum and research, general coordination, financial management, personnel management and the development of faculty strategy.

3. The need to strengthen management at level four is met with reluctance and, on balance, inadequately. The ultimate consequence could be the position of faculties at level four being undermined. We noted in Chapter 5 that there was a trend towards a dual system: faculties still come under the WUB system while the best research programmes and curricula are singled out and brought under separately structured research institutes and research schools, etc. These institutes are geared to training trainee research assistants, specific follow-up courses and commissioned research. Some are co-financed by government or trade and industry. Such institutes do have a strong management and have been achieved from below: actors at level three have taken control of level four tasks.

   Rather than encourage this dual development any further we argued above (point 2.) that government should strengthen the administrative functioning of level four in the short term by adding an experimental article to the WWO. In the longer term this could lead to the WUB being adjusted and geared to that which is most appropriate for an organization such as a faculty.

4. In the indirect funding system (disciplinary) foundations operate at level four. Since the recent transition from ZWO to NWO the indirect funding organization has acquired an extra administrative layer in the form of six coordinating councils.

   The establishment of these councils was made in connection with the task designated to NWO of stimulating and initiating research programmes. However, the creation of this new administrative layer resulted in the funding of research – financed through the indirect funding system – being threatened with *over-organization*. The system explained in Chapter 2 shows that any administrative board should perform its own specific tasks, otherwise the research system has no need for the board in question. The original intention of the NWO bill was for the foundations at level four to be replaced with councils (and departments). After this centralizing move had been rejected in part during the parliamentary debate on the NWO Act (the foundations can continue to exist, subject to the approval of the NWO Board), a situation threatens to emerge whereby two organizations – councils and foundations – operating at level four will come into conflict about the other's responsibilities. The tasks of the one organization will be at the cost of those of the other. Proceeding from this starting point the aptness of the new administrative layer of the councils can be queried. This layer run the risk of duplicating the work already done satisfactorily by the foundations. Another aspect is that the research world identifies itself more readily in (disciplinary) foundations than in the much larger aggregate of councils. Hence our reason to argue for an amendment of the NWO Act on this point.

7.3 Final conclusion: the research system of the future

In this study the research system is described as a system consisting of seven different levels. These levels correspond with certain functions that have to be fulfilled within the system. The relationships between these levels differ from the typical rank and file hierarchy; they form a *holarchy*. In the previous section we presented several conclusions with regard to the main developments at the highest levels of the system. In this final section we will deal with the system as such.

By presenting the Dutch university system as a seven-level system, incorporating both research *activity* (levels one to five) and *science policy* (levels six and seven), we feel that we have created both an adequate description and a framework for analysis. We do not profess that the seven-level system will be an ageless system in the sense that all seven levels can be successful in all university systems. The seven-level system can be applied in a system where there is a certain scale of operation, i.e. a system which is not applicable at any time and place. In other words: the larger the scale of a university system, the greater the number of steering processes and the higher the number of different system functions. This can be illustrated by reviewing the history of the university system. The roots of our present-day university system can be traced back to Medieval Europe. The typical institutional union of teachers and students – presently known as universities – came into being at various locations during the twelfth and thirteenth century. The first European institute of higher education was the University of Bologna, founded in 1288. The first university in the Netherlands was the University of Leiden, founded in the year 1575. Soon after the inauguration of the University of Leiden various others cities were given their universities, some of which no longer exist. The majority of Dutch universities in existence today were founded as late as the twentieth century. If we take a look at the university system as it was prior to the sixties we see that that system consists of only five levels: government (as the provider of funds), universities, faculties (which for centuries only totalled four: theology, law, medicine and philosophy), professors and assistants. If we compare this system with the seven-level system we miss, in the research part, the level comprising of staff united in teaching and research units, and in the managerial part, level six, which advises on strategic matters in the research system at arm's length from government.

In Chapter 1 we gave an account of the effect of the increase in student intake on this static system. Since the sixties we have seen an enormous increase in the intake of students from various social backgrounds (see table in Chapter 1). This has resulted in the universities being transformed from sheltered, elite sanctuaries to large, democratized institutions. The university of today is part and parcel of the welfare state, which is characterized by widely spread wealth and relatively egalitarian relationships. This has resulted in the universities having definitively lost their insular position. At present they are expected to contribute towards resolving the problems of society, that they deliver graduates with the right qualifications, that they contribute towards increasing the innovation potential of industry, etc., etc. In an organizational context, the economics of scale of the university system led primarily to the five-level system described above, which had existed since the Middle Ages, being upgraded to the present seven-level system described in this book. A system level has emerged in both research activity and science policy: levels three and six respectively. With regard to research activity, there is an increasing number of personnel other than professors involved in teaching and research. The number of scientific staff has increased tremendously over the past few decades. In the WWO'60 scientific staff were officially given the opportunity to participate in faculty management. The next step was the introduction of the WUB in 1970, in which the phenomenon of 'teaching and research units' was introduced. This implied a formal shift in position from individual professors to collectivities in a certain discipline. The true development behind this is that economies of scale, working with valuable equipment such as laboratories and computer data bases, is progressively becoming the work of research groups within the wider framework of connected research programmes. The science disciplines were at the forefront of this development, a development which brought about a shift in the task of the professor from that of primarily a researcher/teacher (level two) to the manager of a research group (level three). Today, it is more often a question of research groups rather than individual researchers who are regarded as representing the basic expected work level. We explained in Chapter 3 that it can be useful to measure research performance when speaking in terms of the performance of larger aggregates (research groups, faculties); conversely, the value of top 30's and top 40's based on individual achievements is really only one of entertainment.

An additional level has also gradually emerged at the top of the system. On the one hand, the increase in size, and on the other, the increase in the demands and expectations required of the university system by its surroundings (society) has resulted in government adopting an increasingly more active role. Government no longer acts as the passive provider of funds but since the sixties has also gradually pursued a steering policy with regard to higher education and science. This means that the government itself has started to develop instruments to enable it to assume a more directorial role as regards the university system. However, the precarious and uncertain nature of research activity gave rise to an increasing government demand for more advice on strategic matters, for bodies which could interpret social research needs into political research needs on the one hand, and promising areas of research on the other. The administrative need, and latitude, for the level we have called level six has arisen over the years between the research system in the restricted sense and the government.

In this respect, the most important bodies set up by government were the advisory councils: the WRR, the RAWB and the sectoral research councils. Advisory councils such as these – which have a strategic function – are generally composed of external experts who fulfil the relevant function as private persons and not in their professional capacity. This lifts these bodies above level five. The strategic function of level-six bodies is to be found in the fact that they are able to provoke and, if necessary, contradict government – which by nature tends to become fossilized in instruments of control (rules, planning, hierarchy) in order to force predictability of policy, and on the other hand, these bodies take a disinterested stand vis-à-vis the research system in the restricted sense.

If we review the development of the research system it may be concluded that the main aspect is that the seven-level system has started to function more as an *entity*. Up to the sixties both government and science were probably best described as two adjacent columns. In true Von Humboldt tradition, members of the scientific world have attached a great deal of importance to academic freedom. The historical background to this being that science has had to liberate itself from church and state by way of a process of emancipation. Science should be disinterested in the sense that it should be objective, free from bias. The accumulation of knowledge became a goal in itself without the question being asked of which accumulation of knowledge was beneficial. In that concept reference was made to knowledge unavailable as yet, without a link being made to social trends. However, together with the emergence of the welfare state society, government policy and science have become progressively more interwoven. The buck did not stop at the portals of the Alma Mater. Scientific activity has become part and parcel of the welfare state.

Finally, if we were to predict how the multi-level system will develop over the next twenty five years it would seem that the system will expand to become an eight-level system given that an extra policy-making level will be superimposed onto the present system. This eighth level in the making is the European Community, which is undertaking more and more in the area of technology and science policy without national governments having given this area of policy out of their hands (completely). Should this be the case, the European Community at level seven would take the place of national policy-makers. Nonetheless, this could turn out to be a period of transition; it is quite possible for the European policy level to have completely replaced national policy levels over a few decades.

The description of the research system as a seven-level system should not be understood as a blueprint. We have already explained how the system changes as a result of the increase in research activity and the activation of the system's environment (demands made by society and government). It is important however that the system shows sufficient dynamism at all times, that it is adaptable but still sufficiently selective with regard to trends and issues of the day. Inherent in research activity is the aspect of uncertainty; the unknown. This should also be translated into the organizational institutions of research activity which have to be able to deal with uncertain factors. It is essential that the system has the capacity to learn through, in the event of new developments, first incorporating variety (redundancy) so that choices can be based on experience (cf. Landau, 1969; Van Gunsteren, 1976). This also applies in those situations where previously made arrangements have become obsolete or rules are apparently ineffective. This argues against allowing institutional arrangements and structures to solidify, but to make sure that changes are made to the system. One of the changes argued here is to smooth the path for the introduction of a powerful body at level six which would perform a number of strategic tasks with regard to the university system. However, even before the establishment of such a body we may assume that after it has been in operation for ten to twenty years, other institutions will be required if the system is to retain its dynamism.

Appendix: Criticism and discussion

The author was awarded his doctorate at the Faculty of Economics of the Erasmus University Rotterdam in 1989. This book is based on his original Dutch-language dissertation, which aroused both interest and response from scientific researchers and policy-makers. The object of this appendix[1] is to summarize the most significant points of discussion put forward in this book.

Most of the reactions to this dissertation were concerned with the model of organization-levels as described in Chapter 2 and used in the case studies. We detected two main themes in these reactions: a. the explanation of the seven levels of the multi-level model (which organization belongs at which level?), and b. the significance of the number of levels and their functions with regard to the degree of decentralization of decision-making on scientific research. The first theme is more empirical/normative by nature; the second is more theoretical. Although these two themes are interrelated they are discussed here in more detail separately.

Which organization at which level?

Chapter 2 sets out the basic principle for the system model. This principle is based on the various functions performed within the complex of research production, research policy and science policy. We have set out seven functions in an ascending level of abstraction and aggregation. These functions are incorporated in the description of a multi-level system, in which the different levels are linked according to a system hierarchy (not necessarily a rank and file hierarchy). Various actors are to be found at the various levels, some having executive tasks, some with advisory tasks, while others perform a combination of tasks (various tasks performed by a single actor is not generally advisable). In Chapter 2 (and elsewhere in this book) we stress that the model is by no means an executive model. Naturally, there are many actors who are linked by rank and file at the various levels, yet this model accommodates other relationships too.

Substance was given to the model by indicating the level at which the Dutch bodies function by describing the tasks they perform. A crucial point in the discussion is the demarcation line between levels five and six. In our model level five (covering a wide, previously undefined area) is the top level of research activity; the top of the meso-level. In the Netherlands the main actors presently functioning at this level are NWO, TNO and the universities. The function of level six is to develop national strategy, above those at top meso-level. It is a macro-level which contributes towards science policy. In the Netherlands there are only a few important (advisory) bodies that operate at this level: RAWB, WRR, etc. (these give advice to level seven and level five and obviously do not address all the levels in the system). Although there is no executive body at level six acting as the national agency for science policy, such an agency is certainly conceivable (vide the British University Funding Council – the successor to the University Grants Committee – or if the Directorate-General for Science Policy in the Netherlands – the present ministerial support at level seven – became decentralized). A proposal was worked out in Chapter 5 for strengthening the Dutch system's level six by establishing a body which would see to the allocation of the budget in the research system on the lines of the UFC.

Particularly those who are responsible for establishing policy at the Ministry of Education and Science hold different views on the interpretation of the levels of this model. They regard level six as the executive level with which government holds strategic dialogue. The relation between science policy and the research system is therefore focused on the relation between levels six and seven. In this concept there are a number of executive bodies at level six that fulfil a wide, strategic coordinative role, such as a Dutch UFC, but also the NWO Board and the TNO Board of Directors. This diverges from our presentation of the model in so far that we see the boards of NWO and TNO as the top levels of coordinating organizations which cover a wide area in the performance of their set tasks and missions in the research system, and which we have placed alongside the universities at level five. The difference in insight between our presentation of the model and the alternative interpretation sketched above lies in the fact that in the alternative view the model consists solely of actors with executive tasks. Although advisory bodies can also function on several levels they are not linked vertically. This concept is illustrated below.

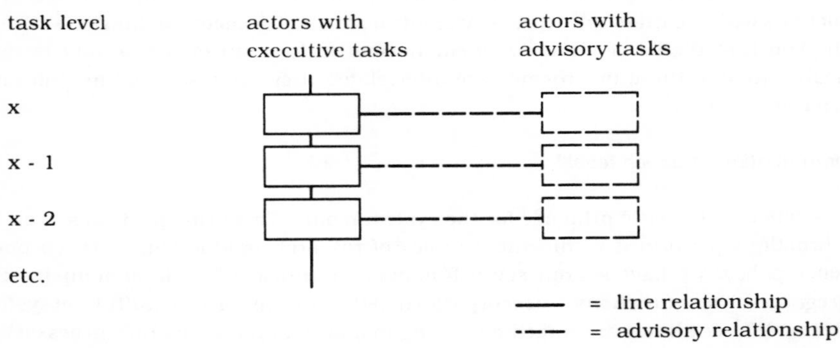

It must be pointed out that where, for example, at level x the advisory body only advises the executive body at that level, yet the subject matter of that advice might not relate to that level only but can also relate to levels x to x - n (like, for instance, the RAWB advises the minister on the desirability of a separate teaching and research organization for faculties).

Focusing on the organizational problems of NWO – one of the case studies discussed – this alternative view implies that the government deals with the NWO Board at level six, and that the NWO councils operate one level below – level five. For the other levels, this alternative corresponds with our description of the model: the NWO foundations operate at level four, and the study groups that come under the foundations at level three. We see the individual researchers at level two and assistants of researchers at level one.

The alternative interpretation of the multi-level model is based on a – completely legitimate – difference of opinion as to the required level of research steering in the system. Ministry of Education and Science policy-makers see NWO primarily as a top-down steering organization which is designated with important tasks for the structuring of scientific research. We have described NWO – in the tradition of its predecessor ZWO – as a research organization which in the first place offers an orderly framework for peer review of the quality of research. It is also where the ideas for research and cooperation in research are conceived on the shop-floor so to speak before they work their way up through the gradually widening disciplinary echelons of the organization. Such a research organization does not work with powerful, centrally organized governing bodies, and by nature, has only a low hierarchical structure in its upper echelons. These consist of a few administrative layers which, in our concept, need reach no further than level five.

That it is possible to arrive at several concepts as to the actual position of NWO within the research system is because government was inconsistent in its reasoning when drawing up legislation for the transition from ZWO to NWO. In the case study on NWO it was explained how the legislation in question ultimately resulted in a compromise between NWO as a central organization for steering research, and NWO as a network of researchers. Given that NWO has only been in existence since 1988 it is as yet uncertain which orientation will gain the upper hand; it is an organization which is still developing and can take a turn in either direction. In the case study on NWO we therefore worked out three different options for the possible organizational development of NWO in the terms of our model. In the third option we suggested the possibility that NWO could develop into the national research management board which, in that capacity, should be located not alongside but at the level above the universities. According to the system adhered to throughout this book NWO (idem TNO) would operate at level six if the important tasks of structuring and developing strategy for the university system were placed in the hands of the NWO top, varying from budgetary allocation responsibilities to holding the authority to instruct the universities at level five to achieve a clustering of faculties where economies of scale make this necessary.

The option advocated in this book is to place such tasks in the hands of a Dutch UFC (and to keep NWO at level five).

In our model TNO also operates, alongside the large technological institutes (GTI's), at level five. Should a coordinating body be established above TNO and the GTI's, and thus govern the entire non-university, public-oriented research – on the lines of the Dutch UFC for universities – that actor would operate at level six. Conceptually, the same would occur if the GTI's were incorporated in TNO. The main point being that level six bodies take up a monopoly position in their field (they then find themselves at a national, macro-level; we still only have one national government) while at level five, at the top of the meso-level, the mission does not implicate a monopoly position. Therefore, in our model TNO reaches no higher than level five either.

The essence of the difference of opinion referred to above with regard to the interpretation of levels six and five can be brought down to the question of how much top-down steering of research is considered appropriate in the system; or in other words: how much science policy is required? This is a question of political will and cannot be answered by scientific researchers without having made an assessment. The independent analyst can only – as is the case in this book – take an 'if-then' approach to show that *if* society and politicians at level seven feel that a relatively large amount of top-down steering of research is essential, *then* there must be powerful coordinating organizations (at level six) with which the government can deal direct. The executive line is thus predominant. However, *if* level seven is of the opinion that government's task in scientific research is primarily one of stimulating, *then* more lightweight organizational structures will suffice. The coordinating bodies of research organizations then reach level five and the bodies operating at level six have, in this set-up, the task (amongst others) of fulfilling an advisory role between the political system and the research system in the strict sense, thus safeguarding the research system to a certain extent from direct government interference. Anyone can fill in his own ideological preference for the policy to be pursued by government.

Organizational structure and decentralization

The second main theme we are concerned with in this appendix is not so much characterized by being normative but has a more theoretical orientation. It relates to the effect of the number of organizational layers on the choices made in scientific research.

In an article entitled "The architecture of economic systems: hierarchies and polyarchies" in the American Economic Review (September 1986, pp. 716-727) Sah and Stiglitz make a connection between organizational structures and mistakes that can be made by actors.

The basic principle of Sah and Stiglitz's contribution (see also Douma, 1988) is that limited rationality and lack of information lead to actors making mistakes. Decision-makers sometimes fail to recognize good projects (in this case research projects or programmes) as good projects and inferior projects as inferior projects. Mistakes are therefore unavoidable: some good projects will wrongly be rejected (*Type-I error*) and some inferior projects will be wrongly approved (*Type-II error*).

In an organization which is made up of several actors the decision-making procedure can be organized in various ways. Which decision-making structure gives the best results? There are at least three conceivable options:

an entrepreneur:
an actor that makes decisions independently;

a hierarchy:
an organization comprising two decision-makers; projects having received the approval of the first decision-maker are also assessed by the second decision-maker. The second decision-maker makes his assessment independently[2]. Only if the second decision-maker also reaches a favourable judgment is the project given the go-ahead;

a polyarchy:
an organization comprising two decision-makers. Projects approved by the first decision-maker are carried out. The second decision-maker only assesses those projects rejected by the first decision-maker. If the second decision-maker reaches a favourable decision the project goes ahead.

With the assistance of a simple model, Sah and Stiglitz prove that:

a. A hierarchy makes more Type-I errors than an entrepreneur. An entrepreneur makes more Type-I errors than a polyarchy.
b. A polyarchy makes more Type II errors than an entrepreneur. An entrepreneur makes more Type-II errors than a hierarchy.
c. Suppose that the risk of making a Type-I error is equal to the risk of making a Type-II error for each individual decision-maker. In such a situation a polyarchy would produce better results than an entrepreneur and an entrepreneur better results than a hierarchy only if the consequences of making Type-I errors are more serious than the consequences of Type-II errors.

Management literature points out that good innovation projects often, quite wrongly, fail to receive the go-ahead in a large bureaucratic organization. Furthermore, in a hierarchy a single 'no' in a whole series of 'yeses' is sufficient for a project to be rejected. This leads to the recommendation of centralizing decision-making as far away as possible to divisions or operating companies. With a view to the above this is the sensible thing to do if the consequences of Type-I errors are more serious than Type-II errors, but not if the consequences of Type-II errors are more serious than those of Type-I.

Sah and Stiglitz point out the general problem that Type-I errors and Type-II errors must be weighed against each other, and that the structure of an organization must be in line with the weight attributed to the two sorts of errors. We feel that where scientific research is concerned Type-I errors must be considered as being of a far more serious nature than Type-II errors. After all, research is the search for the unknown. In Chapter 3 we set out the special features of the scientific research production process. This is a production process which involves a high level of risk: research must be allowed to fail. The contribution of Sah and Stiglitz shows that the more hierarchic the organization structure, the greater the chance that particularly low-risk projects will be carried out. This calls for the organizational structure of the system in which the production of scientific research is generated to be kept as flat as possible.

In assessing Sah and Stiglitz's contribution it should be pointed out that it relates to the functioning of an organization (rank and file hierarchy). Their concept is therefore most applicable for levels one to five of the system as set out in this book. All of these levels are possible within a single organization. However, levels six and seven go beyond that scale. These highest levels in the system express an inter-organizational network of independent bodies which are linked hierarchically but it is not a hierarchy based on a rank and file order.

Within the framework of research policy organization (levels one to five) - without alluding to Sah and Stiglitz's frame of reference - their reasoning is still followed in this book. This is very clear in the NWO case study where we explained that the establishment of the new administrative layer of councils would be an undesirable form of centralization.

Why then do we suggest strengthening level six by setting up a Dutch UFC at that level? This proposed reinforcement implies a curtailment of the responsibilities of level seven on the one hand, and the same for level five on the other. With regard to the former this is a question of partial decentralization, in this case given shape by setting aside tasks for the level six body which are currently performed by national government. Unlike the Minister of Education and Science/Science policy at level seven, such an agency need not justify itself in the political processs. It need not give the guarantees required in a political process of accountability and thus is in a more independent position to take scientifically strategic decisions which involve risk.

On the other hand, strengthening level six also implies that level five will become slightly weaker: limits will be set on the decisions that can be taken. It first sight it would seem that this is a movement towards centralization, yet if we consider the fact that if we did give level five enormous freedom the consequence would be – we fear – that level seven would affect regularity given that the terms required for a market-type of university system would not have been met. This is founded on the presupposition that a powerful body at level six is more able to counteract any potential imperialistic tendencies of the government than the associated universities at level five in their dispersed position.

Notes

1 I am most grateful to Prof.Dr. H. Schreuder (University of Limburg, Maastricht, the Netherlands) and Prof.Dr. D.J. Wolfson (Scientific Council for Government Policy, The Hague, the Netherlands) for their comments on a previous version.

2 Note the idiosyncratic definition Sah and Stiglitz give of the term hierarchy: the independence of the hierarchically higher decision-maker implies that he neither knows nor considers the reasoning of the first decision-maker.

Bibliography

Adviesraad voor het Hoger Onderwijs (Advisory Council for Higher Education), 1988, *Advies inzake de versterking van de bestuursorganisatie van universiteiten en hogescholen* (Recommendations for strengthening the administrative organization of universities and colleges of higher vocational education), The Hague, the Netherlands (ARHO)

Arrow, K.J., 1962, Economic welfare and the allocation of resources for invention, in *The rate and direction of inventive activity*, Princeton, USA (Princeton University Press), pp. 609-625, reprinted in K.J. Arrow, 1970, *Essays in the theory of risk-bearing*, Amsterdam, the Netherlands, (North-Holland), pp. 144-163

Blankart, C.B., 1980, Bureaucratic problems in public choice: why do public goods still remain public?, in K.W. Roskamp (ed.), 1980, *Public choice and public finance*, Paris, France (Cujas), pp. 155-167

Blume, S.S., 1986, *The development of Dutch science policy in international perspective, 1965-1985* (A report to the Advisory Council for Science Policy, The Hague, the Netherlands (Staatsdrukkerij/uitgeverij)

Blume, S.S., Spaapen, J.B., and Prins, A.A.M., 1984, *De externe beoordelingsprocedure 1984; Big Brother of Papieren Tijger* (External assessment procedure 1984; Big Brother or Paper Tiger), Amsterdam, the Netherlands (University of Amsterdam, Department of Science Dynamics)

Bradford, D.F., Malt, R.A., and Oates, W.E., 1969, The rising cost of local public services: some evidence and reflections, *National Tax Journal*, pp. 185-202

Buchanan, J.M., and Tullock, G., 1962, *The calculus of consent* (Logical foundations of constitutional democracy), Ann Arbor, USA (The University of Michigan Press)

Buchem, M.T.E. van, 1987, Versterking van de bestuurskracht: de bestuurders of het bestel? (Strengthening administrative power: the administrators or the system?), in P.B. Boorsma, C. de Hart and F.A. van Vught (eds.), *Versterking bestuur universiteiten en hogescholen: beperkingen en mogelijkheden* (Strengthening the boards of universities and colleges of higher vocational education: limitations and possibilities), The Hague, the Netherlands, (VUGA) pp. 133-147

Buiter, W.H., 1987, *The right combination of demand and supply policies: the case for a two-handed approach*, NBER working paper No. 2333, Cambridge, Mass., USA (NBER)

Clotfelder, C.T., 1977, Public services, private substitutes, and the demand for protection against crime, *American Economic Review*, pp. 867-877

Cohen, M.D., March, J.G., and Olsen, J.P., 1972, A garbage can model of organisational choice, *Administrative Science Quarterly*, pp. 1-25

Cole, J.R., and Cole, S., 1973, *Social stratification in science*, Chicago/London, USA/ England (The University of Chicago Press)

Commissie Financieringsstructuur Onderzoek en Ontwikkeling (Committee on Financing Structures for Research and Development), 1985, *Rekenschap van creativiteit* ; English language edition: *Accounting for creativity*, 1988, The Hague, the Netherlands (Staats-drukkerij/uitgeverij)

Demsetz, H., 1969, Information and efficiency: another viewpoint, *The Journal of Law and Economics*, pp. 1-22

Doel, J. van den, 1979, *Democracy and welfare economics*, Cambridge, England (Cambridge University Press)

Douma, S.W., 1988, Innoveren, organiseren en concurreren (Innovating, organizing and competing), *Maandblad voor Accountancy en Bedrijfseconomie*, pp. 227-242

Easton, D., 1965, *A systems analysis of political life*, New York, USA (Wiley)

Elster, J., 1979, *Ulyssus and the Sirenes*, Cambridge, England (Cambridge University Press)

Elster, J., 1983, *Sour grapes*, Cambridge, England (Cambridge University Press)

Florax, R.J.G.M., and Vught, F.A. van, 1987, Planmatige sturing of natuurlijke selectie? Een beschouwing over de nieuwe besturingsfilosofie van de beleidsnota 'Hoger onderwijs: autonomie en kwaliteit' (Planned steering or natural selection? Reflections on the new management philosophy in the policy document 'Higher education: autonomy and quality'), in: R.J. Bijleveld and F.A. van Vught (eds.), *Sturing van hoger onderwijs; de veranderde rol van de overheid* (Steering higher education; the changed role of government), The Hague, the Netherlands (VUGA), pp. 11-38

Furubotn, E.G., and Pejovich, S. (eds.), 1974, *The economics of property rights*, Cambridge, Mass., USA (Ballinger Publishing Company)

Garfield, E., 1979, *Citation indexing; its theory and application in science, technology, and humanities*, New York, USA (Wiley)

Gaston, J., 1978, *The reward system in British and American science*, New York, USA (Wiley)

Gendt, M.C.E. van, 1980, *The voucher concept and the publicness of basis education*, Meppel, the Netherlands (dissertation, University of Amsterdam)

Groenewegen, J., 1987, Ondernemende universiteit (Entrepreneurial university), *ESB*, pp. 1146-1148

Grondsma, T., 1987, *Spelbenadering en contractie* (Game approach and contraction), seventh report in the series of publications of the project group on Decision-making about retrenchment in the public sector, Rotterdam, the Netherlands (Erasmus University)

Gunsteren, H.R. van, 1976, *The quest for control*, London, England (Wiley)

Gunsteren, H.R. van, 1987, Jon Elster. Rationele-keuzetheorie, speltheorie en marxisme (Rational choice theory, game theory and Marxism), in J.W. de Beus and F. Vuijsje (eds.), *Politieke economie* (Political economy), Utrecht, the Netherlands (Spectrum), pp. 174-192

Hagstrom, W.O., 1965, *The scientific community*, New York/London (Basic Books)

Hirschleifer, J., 1985, The expanding domain of economics, *American Economic Review*, pp. 51-68

Hotelling, H., 1938, The general welfare in relation to problems of taxation and of railway and utility rates, *Econometrica*, pp. 242-269, reprinted in K.J. Arrow and T. Scitovsky (eds.), 1969, *Readings in welfare economics*, London, England (Allen & Unwin)

Jaques, E., 1976, *A general theory of bureaucracy*, London, England (Heinemann)

Kar, H.M. van de, 1987, Subsidies en begrotingsbeheer (Subsidies and budget administration), in P.R. Heij and P.H.J. Vrancken (eds.), *Subsidie in revisie* (Subsidy under review), The Hague, the Netherlands (VUGA), pp. 77-97

Katz, D., and Kahn, E., 1978, *Social psychology of organizations*, second edition, New York, USA (Wiley)

Kaufman, H., 1974, *Administrative feedback*, Washington D.C., USA (Brookings Institution)

Lancaster, K., 1971, *Consumer demand: a new approach*, New York, USA (Columbia University Press)

Landau, M., 1969, Redundancy, rationality, and the problem of duplication and overlap, *Public Administration Review*, pp. 346-358

Liebowitz, S.J., and Palmer, J.P., 1984, Assessing the relative impacts of economic journals, *Journal of Economic Literature*, pp. 77-88

Lindblom, Ch.E., 1959, The science of muddling through, *Public Administration Review*, pp. 79-88

Lipsey, R.G., and Lancaster, K., 1956, The general theory of the second best, *Review of Economic Studies*, pp. 11-32, reprinted in M.J. Farrell (ed.), 1973, *Readings in welfare economics*, London, England (Macmillan), pp. 144-165

Merton, R.K., 1973, *The sociology of science*, Chicago, USA (University of Chicago Press)

Mesarovic, M.D., Macho, D., and Takahara, Y., 1970, *Theory of hierarchical multilevel systems*, New York, USA (Academic Press)

Miller, J.G., 1960, Information input, overload and psychopathology, *American Journal of Psychology*, pp. 695-704

Minister for Science Policy, 1974, *Nota Wetenschapsbeleid* (Science policy document), Dutch Parliament, session 1974-1975, 13 221

Ministry of Education and Science, 1979a, *Beleidsnota universitair onderzoek* (Policy document on university research), Dutch Parliament, session 1979-1980, 15 825

Ministry of Education and science, 1979b, *Innovatie. Het overheidsbeleid inzake technologische vernieuwing in de Nederlandse samenleving* (Innovation. Government policy on technological innovation in Dutch society), Dutch Parliament, session 1979-1980, 15 855

Ministry of Education and Science, 1981, *Kernnota inzake beleidsvoornemens betreffende het universitair wetenschappelijk personeel* (BUWP-nota) (Key-document on policy plans concerning university academic staff), The Hague, the Netherlands (Staatsdrukkerij/ uitgeverij)

Ministry of Education and Science, 1983, *Beleidsnota gedrags- en maatschappijwetenschappen* (Policy document on behavioural and social sciences), Dutch Parliament, session 1983-1984, 18 161

Ministry of Education and Science, 1985, *Hoger onderwijs; autonomie en kwaliteit* (HOAK-nota) (Higher education, autonomy and quality), Dutch Parliament, session 1985-1986, 19 253

Ministry of Education and Science, 1987, *Schets betreffende de toekomst van het hoger onderwijs en wetenschappelijk onderzoek* (Picture of the future of higher education and scientific research), Dutch Parliament, session 1986-1987, 19914

Ministry of Education and Science, 1987a, *(Ontwerp) Hoger onderwijs en onderzoek plan* (HOOP) ((Draft) Higher education and research plan), The Hague, the Netherlands (Staatsdrukkerij/uitgeverij)

Ministry of Education and Science, 1988, *(Concept-ontwerp) Wet op het hoger onderwijs en wetenschappelijk onderzoek* (Draft) Bill on higher education and scientific research), The Hague, the Netherlands (Staatsdrukkerij/uitgeverij)

Ministry of Education and Science, 1988a, *Beleidsnotitie internationalisering van onderwijs en onderzoek* (Policy memorandum Internationalization of education and research), The Hague, the Netherlands (Staatsdrukkerij/uitgeverij)

Ministry of Education and Science, 1988b, *Naar een wetenschapsbeleid voor de jaren negentig* (Towards a science policy for the nineties), The Hague, the Netherlands (Staatsdrukkerij/uitgeverij)

Moed, H.F., Burger, W.J.M., Frankfort, J.G., and Raan, A.F.J. van, 1983, *On the measurement of research performance: the use of bibliometric indicators*, Leiden, the Netherlands (Leiden University)

Moed, H.F., 1989, *The use of bibliometric indicators for the assessment of research performance in the natural and life sciences. Aspects of data collection, reliability, validity and applicability* (dissertation), Leiden, the Netherlands (DSWO Press)

Moore, F.T., 1967, Incentive contacts, in: S. Enke (ed.), *Defense management*, Englewood Cliffs (Prentice Hall), pp. 213-231

Mueller, D.C., 1979, *Public choice*, Cambridge, England (Cambridge University Press)

Newman, W.H., 1975, *Constructive control*, Englewood Cliffs (Prentice Hall)

Niskanen, W.A., 1971, *Bureaucracy and representative government*, Chicago, USA (Adine Atherton)

Olson, M., 1965, *The logic of collective action* (Public goods and the theory of groups), Cambridge, Mass., USA (Harvard University Press)

Oort, C.J., 1958, *Decreasing cost as a problem of welfare economics* (dissertation), Amsterdam, the Netherlands (Drukkerij Holland)

Organisation for Economic Cooperation and Development (OECD), 1980, *Het meten van wetenschappelijke en technische activiteiten. Voorgestelde standaardprocedures voor het meten van wetenschappelijke en technische activiteiten* (Measuring scientific and technological activities. Proposed standard procedures for measuring scientific and technological activities) ('Frascati Manual'), The Hague, the Netherlands (Staatsdrukkerij/uitgeverij)

Organisation for Economic Cooperation and Development (OECD), 1986, *Reviews of national science and technology priorities; The Netherlands*, Paris, France (OECD directorate for science, technology and industry)

Pratt, J., 1987, *Contraction in higher education: the Netherlands and Britain*, tenth report in the series of publications of the project group on Decision-making about retrenchment in the public sector, Rotterdam, the Netherlands (Erasmus University)

Raad van Advies voor het Wetenschapsbeleid (Advisory Council for Science Policy), 1971, *Voorlopige nota over de organisatie en financiering van het wetenschappelijke onderzoek aan universiteiten en hogescholen* (Provisional document on the organization and funding of scientific research performed in universities and colleges of technology), The Hague, the Netherlands (Staatsdrukkerij/uitgeverij)

Rinnooy Kan, A.H.G., et al., 1987, *Naar een ondernemende universiteit* (Towards an entrepreneurial university), Utrecht/Antwerp, the Netherlands/Belgium (Veen)

Ritzen, J.M.M., 1988, *Why fund university research? An exploration of the rationale for government intervention in university research* (working paper)

Rossum, W. van, 1979, *The organisation and financing of (para)university research in Western-Europe: a comparative view*, The Hague, the Netherlands (ZWO)

Rowbottom, R.W., and Billis, D., 1977, The stratification of work and organizational design, *Human Relations*, pp. 53-76

Rowbottom, R.W., and Billis, D., 1987, *Organisational design. The work-levels approach*, Aldershot, England (Gower)

Sah, R.K., and J.E. Stiglitz, 1986, The architecture of economic systems: hierarchies and polyarchies, *American Economic Review*, pp. 716-727

Secretary of State for Education and Science, 1987, *Higher education; meeting the challenge* (white paper), London, England (HMSO)

Sen, A.K., 1985, *Commodities and capabilities* (Professor Dr. P. Hennipman lectures in economics), Amsterdam, the Netherlands (North-Holland)

Shattock, M., 1987, The last days of the University Grants Committee, *Minerva*, pp. 471-485

Simon, H.A., 1976, From substantive to procedural rationality, in S. Latsis (ed.), *Method and appraisal in economics*, Cambridge, England (Cambridge University Press), reprinted in F. Hahn and M. Hollis (eds.), *Philosophy and economic theory*, 1979, Oxford, England (Oxford University Press), pp. 65-86

Simon., H.A. and Ando, A., 1961, Aggregation of variables in dynamic systems, *Econometrica*, pp. 111-138

Small, H., and Sweeney, E., 1985, Clustering the Science Citation Index using co-citations: I. A comparison of methods, *Scientometrics*, pp. 393-409

Sociaal en Cultureel Planbureau (Social and Cultural Planning Office) / Centraal Planbureau (Central Planning Office), 1986, *Kosten van kwartaire diensten 1970-1983. Een statistische verkenning van kostenstructuur en voorzieningengebruik* (The cost of public services 1970-1983. A statistical investigation of cost structure and use of facilities) (Project personnel facilities public sector bulletin No. 6), The Hague, the Netherlands (Staatsdrukkerij/uitgeverij)

Spangenberg, J.F.A., 1989, *Economies of atmosphere. The joint impact of scale, scope and atmosphere on scientific performance in clinical medicine and economics*, Assen, the Netherlands (Van Gorcum)

Stevers, Th.A., 1967, Een economische analyse van het democratisch proces (An economic analysis of the democratic process), *Maandschrift Economie*, pp. 37-70

Tinbergen, J., 1984, On collective and part-collective goods, *De Economist*, pp. 171-182

Vereniging van Samenwerkende Nederlandse Universiteiten (Association of Universities in the Netherlands), 1988, *Van regelrecht naar doelgericht. Arbeidsvoorwaardenbeleid Nederlandse universiteiten* (From rules orientation to goals orientation. Terms of personnel policy for Dutch universities), Utrecht, the Netherlands (VSNU)

Vught, F.A. van, 1987, *Plan- en marktcoördinatie in het hoger onderwijs* (Planning and market coordination in higher education) (oration), Enschede, the Netherlands (University of Twente)

Wolfson, D.J., 1981, Continuïteitsvoorwaarden voor de verzorgingsstaat (Conditions of continuity for the welfare state), in: Vereniging voor de Staatshuishoudkunde (Association for economy), *Overlevingskansen van de verzorgingsstaat* (Chances of survival for the welfare state). Preliminary reports 1981, Leiden/Antwerp, the Netherlands/Belgium (Stenfert Kroese), pp. 1-37, reprinted in G.M.J. Veldkamp (ed.), 1983, *Ombuigingen in de sociale zekerheid, een paradox voor de economie in de jaren tachtig* (Reorganization of social security, a paradox for the economy in the eighties), Deventer, the Netherlands (Kluwer), pp. 99-143

Wolfson, D.J., 1988, *Publieke sector en economische orde* (Public sector and economic order), Groningen, the Netherlands (Wolters/Noordhoff)

Wolfson, D.J., 1988a, Het beheer: Mijnheer Van Dalen wacht op antwoord (Management: Mr. Van Dalen is awaiting reply), in: *Krijgt onderwijs de ruimte. Risico's en omgevingsfactoren bij toekomstig onderwijsbeleid* (Will education be given space. The risks and relevant factors in future education policy), The Hague, the Netherlands (Staatsdrukkerij/uitgeverij), pp. 18-27

ZWO, 1979, *Beleidsnota ZWO 1979: plaats en perspectief* (ZWO Policy document 1979: place and perspective), The Hague, the Netherlands (ZWO)

List of abbreviations

ABRC	Advisory Board of Research Councils (UK)
A&HI	Arts and Humanities Index
AIO	Trainee research assistant
AR	Universities Council
ARHO	Advisory Council for Higher Education
AWT	Advisory Council for Science and Technology
BRITE	Basic Research in Industrial Technologies for Europe
BUOZ	Policy document on university research
BUWP	Key-document on policy plans concerning university academic staff
CBS	Central Statistical Office
CFSOO	Committee on Financing Structures for Research and Development
CPB	Central Planning Office
DGHW	Directorate General for Higher Education and Scientific Research (Ministry of Education and Science)
DGWB	Director General for Science Policy (Ministry of Education and Science)
ECN	Energy Research Centre Netherlands
ESPRIT	European Strategy Program for Research and Development
ESRC	Economic and Social Research Council (UK)
EUREKA	European Research and Coordination Agency
EZ	Ministry of Economic Affairs

GTI's	Large technological institutes
HAR	High Universities Council
HBO	Higher Vocational Education
HOAK	Policy document on higher education: autonomy and quality
HOOP	Higher Education and Research Plan
INSTIR	Innovation Incentives Scheme
IOP	Innovation-oriented Research Programmes
ISI	Institute of Scientific Information (USA)
JCS	Journal citation score
KNAW	Royal Netherlands Academy of Arts and Sciences
LGM	Laboratory for Soil Mechanics
L&V	Ministry of Agriculture, Nature and Fishery
MARIN	Maritime Research Institute Netherlands
MRC	Medical Research Council (UK)
NERC	Natural Environment Research Council (UK)
NRL	National Laboratory for Aviation and Space Research
NRLO	National Council for Agricultural Research
NWO	Netherlands Organization for Scientific Research
OECD	Organisation for Economic Cooperation and Development
OIO	research trainee (NWO)
O&W	Ministry of Education and Science
PCFC	Polytechnics and Colleges Funding Council (UK)
PRO	Programming Council for Environmental Planning Research
RACE	Research and Advanced Communications in Europe
RAWB	Advisory Council for Science Policy
RAWOO	Advisory Council on Development-related Research
REO	Energy Research Council
RGO	Health Research Council
RMNO	Research Council for Environment and Nature
SCI	Science Citation Index
SCP	Social and Cultural Planning Office
SERC	Science and Engineering Research Council (UK)
SKG	Selective shrinkage and growth
SSCI	Social Science Citation Index
STW	Foundation for Engineering Sciences
TNO	Netherlands Organization for Applied Scientific Research
TVC	Distribution and concentration of tasks

UFC	University Funding Council (UK)
UGC	University Grants Committee (UK)
VF	Conditional funding scheme
VRA-OGO	Research Council for the Urban Environment
VROM	Ministry of Housing, Regional Planning and Environment
VSNU	Association of Universities in the Netherlands
WHW	(Draft) Bill on Higher Education and Scientific Research
WL	Hydrodynamic Laboratory
WRR	Scientific Council for Government Policy
WUB	University Administration Reform Act
WWO	University Education Act
ZWO	Netherlands Organization for the Advancement of Scientific Research

General index

Index of authors